Mira Matikkala is Academy of Finland Research Fellow in the Department of History, University of Helsinki. She holds a PhD from Cambridge University.

LIBRARY OF VICTORIAN STUDIES

Series ISBN: 978 1 84885 247 1

See www.ibtauris.com/LVS for a full list of titles

EMPIRE AND IMPERIAL AMBITION

Liberty, Englishness and Anti-Imperialism
in Late-Victorian Britain

MIRA MATIKKALA

I.B. TAURIS

LONDON · NEW YORK

Published in 2011 by I.B.Tauris & Co Ltd
6 Salem Road, London W2 4BU
175 Fifth Avenue, New York NY 10010
www.ibtauris.com

Distributed in the United States and Canada
Exclusively by Palgrave Macmillan
175 Fifth Avenue, New York NY 10010

Library of Victorian Studies 4

ISBN 978 1 84885 609 7

A full CIP record for this book is available from the British Library
A full CIP record for this book is available from the Library of Congress

Library of Congress catalog card: available

Printed and bound in Great Britain by CPI Antony Rowe, Chippenham, Wiltshire
Camera-ready copy edited and supplied by the author

MIX
Paper from
responsible sources
FSC   FSC® C013604
www.fsc.org

'EXPANSION'

I'm not a 'Little Englander' – a 'patriot' am I,
Endowed with all that's good and great – which no one can deny;
I'm proud of all my ancestors, and love my native land,
And in her great and sacred Cause I'm longing to 'expand.'

A frog of old, we have been told, for Glory felt a thirst,
And, trying well his skin to swell, expanded till he burst.
A Jingo true, no doubt, will view the moral of that story,
And say with pride, 'See how he died, expanded in his glory.'
Then let us all expand, my boys, by Glory fed and nursed;
Expand, expand, in every land, expand until we burst!

January 1899
Poem by Sir Wilfrid Lawson, Bart., MP
Drawing by F. Carruthers Gould[1]

---

[1] Sir Wilfrid Lawson and F. Carruthers Gould, *Cartoons in Rhyme and Line* (London, 1905), p. 59.

CONTENTS

ABBREVIATIONS

BL	British Library (London)
BLPES	British Library of Political and Economic Science (London)
CR	*Contemporary Review*
FM	Fitzwilliam Museum (Cambridge)
FR	*Fortnightly Review*
NAI	National Archives of India (New Delhi)
NC	*Nineteenth Century*
NR	*National Review*
OHBE	*The Oxford History of the British Empire*
OIOC	Oriental and India Office Collections (British Library, London)
PR	*The Positivist Review*
SHL	Senate House Library (University of London)

INTRODUCTION: MULTIPLE FACES OF AN IMPERIAL CULTURE

Imperialism, anti-imperialism and national identity

This study examines the modes of thought that were described as anti-imperialist in the late-Victorian era. It argues that the common ground between the various critics was that they all declared to represent 'true Englishness' in contrast to what they regarded as a 'distorted' imperial identity. Thus, there were two versions of 'Englishness' or 'patriotism' at the time: one that was centred around Britain's imperial world role, and another that advocated a more domestic-centred point of view and was often labelled an 'anti-imperialist' or, disparagingly, a 'Little-England' approach. Linda Colley has shown how the British identity was closely connected with the idea of a *British* empire – as opposed to an *English* empire.[1] According to this view, Britishness was connected to the imperial idea, even to the extent that the empire was to many the most essential thing in Britishness.[2] Although any simple equation between imperialism/anti-imperialism and Britishness/Englishness cannot be drawn, anti-imperialists usually preferred the term Englishness. They emphasised the long line from 1688: liberty, constitutional rights, and parliamentary development – there was no place for an authoritarian empire in this view.[3]

Wilfrid Scawen Blunt, perhaps the most famous late-Victorian anti-imperialist, expressed this vision clearly when discussing a prospect of a radical party with his friend:

> In my opinion ... there were only two policies on which Party lines could run – one Imperialism, which meant a bid for the Empire of the world, a gambling venture which entailed the sacrifice of everything else we had of value at home, liberty, freedom from corruption & financial prosperity – the other, anti-imperialism, which meant letting the world alone, & the Colonies to work out their own destinies without our interference & the same for Ireland.[4]

The present study largely develops the main point raised by Miles Taylor in an article nearly twenty years ago.[5] Instead of seeing imperialism merely as British control over other peoples, he examined the repercussions of imperialism on the structure of power in the metropole. He argued that it was this 'Caesarist' notion of imperialism which was most common at the time and provoked critique from a wide range of political opinion. The main concern was always 'how dominion over distant territories affected English character and English institutions'.[6] Taylor pointed out that the main concern in the anti-imperialist debate throughout the nineteenth century was not the process of British expansion overseas as such, but the status of liberalism at home: when liberalism seemed to be weakening domestically, the radical critique of the empire revived, as happened in the age of Palmerston in the 1850s and Disraeli in the 1870s.

This study is mainly a contribution to British intellectual and political history. In addition to analysing the intellectual and political arguments, it also vivifies the picture of late-Victorian moral and cultural attitudes. This era is too often seen as characterised by monolithic imperial culture, when there actually was a rich cultural environment, consisting not only of imperialism but also of various anti-imperialisms with various agendas.

British attitudes towards the empire were not simple and straightforward. The campaign against the slave trade and the parliamentary debates on the East India Company's governance of India from the late eighteenth century onwards brought a strong humanitarian critical element forward. However, in the latter part of the nineteenth century humanitarian motives were more often used in advocating imperial expansion than opposing it.[7] Only by annexing African territories to the British empire could the slave trade be stopped, and the 'barbarous and cruel native customs' eliminated, the expansionists argued.[8] Missionary influence in particular could be so strong that it was able to draw major attention to imperial issues in Britain, thus turning the domestic culture more in favour of expansion.[9] The Aborigines Protection Society, established in 1837 and active throughout the century, was never against or for imperialism as such. It concentrated on the treatment of natives and was 'against oppression' in any form.[10] The annexation of Transvaal was approved in 1877, since it was thought to bring positive consequences for the natives; the 'disgraceful and disastrous Zulu War of 1879', on the other hand, was vigorously protested against, as well as 'the making of Rhodesia', because of the British South Africa Company's harsh treatment of native inhabitants.[11]

E. H. H. Green has well described that 'many in late Victorian and Edwardian Britain appear to have been for the empire in the same way that many were against sin, that is, they supported a general proposition rather than a particular faith'.[12] The feeling could be strong but vague: whenever more rigorous definitions were expressed, whether in regard to constitutional or economic issues, a diversity of opinions emerged.

It has also been suggested that the British were not actively interested in the empire. Henry Pelling and Richard Price have argued that the working class did not care about the empire.[13] Bernard Porter has gone even further, arguing that – apart from the upper and upper-middle classes who actually ruled the empire or the middle-class settlers – the British were ignorant about and uninterested in their huge empire.[14] Above all, Porter shows that British opinion on the empire was far from monolithic. Even in the case of the upper-class rulers Porter points out that their interest in the empire was not necessarily strictly imperialistic: they were already used to 'ruling' other classes in Britain and to them 'governing

Indians was simply an extension' of this.[15] However, the 1870s and 1880s onwards the ruling class began to need the support from the rest of British society in its imperial enterprise. The competition over colonies became more severe which increased state expenditure, at the time when the trade depression further accelerated the fears and the electorate was expanded to include more working-class people. The result was an extensive propaganda campaign towards the end of the century.[16] While some scholars regard this immense propaganda as evidence of the popularity of the empire,[17] Porter convincingly points out that it rather indicates the opposite: 'the magnitude of the empire's new crisis' as well as 'the unsatisfactory state', from the imperialists' point of view, 'of British public opinion towards the empire up until then'.[18]

Nevertheless, despite the ambivalent and indifferent attitudes towards the empire, very few Britons opposed the spread of 'western civilisation' in the world. This kind of 'cultural imperialism' was usually opposed only by those who thought that 'other races' were inherently incapable of progress. Educating them in western ways was then regarded as waste of time and energy; and in many cases, especially in India, many British officials wanted to preserve the native society as it was without western cultural influences – if no progress along the western lines was to be expected, British rule would be permanent. In contrast to this, the concept of humanitarian and civilising imperialism implied the eventual end of empire, for the whole ideology was based on the notion that some day the dependencies would all be like England.[19] Anti-imperialists, on their part, often considered that Asians and Africans deserved the 'blessings of western civilisation' as much as the British did, though they still condemned the policy of forcing it upon them. These complexities are confusing even to Porter, who states that 'if this is counted as imperialism, then there was no *anti*-imperialism in Britain at this period at all';[20] however, he continues that 'this was as anti-imperialist as anyone in Britain got at the time'[21] – i.e. opposing imperialism *as they saw it*. While many accepted this 'cultural imperialism' (in today's terms) they still were 'highly critical of Britain's version of imperialism, and could even be deeply ashamed of it'.[22]

The fact is that in the late nineteenth century Britons did not think in terms of 'cultural imperialism' as the term is used today. That the British were culturally more progressed went without saying to most, even in relation to other European cultures, and although it was an important underpinning in the imperial effort, labelling them all 'imperialists' because of that would not be a fruitful approach. Clear distinctions were made at the time between imperialists and anti-imperialists, and these distinctions were not based on their views on other cultures, but on how they defined Englishness and saw Britain's role in the world. Of course, the sole fact that anti-imperialists were against imperialism because it was 'un-English' implies a sense of cultural superiority: Englishness, as they saw it, represented everything that was good, whereas any 'bad' policies were simply 'un-English'.[23]

The main concern in late-nineteenth-century anti-imperialism was thus different from that of the following century, when the emphasis was on the relationship between the coloniser and the colonised. However, signs of change were there, especially in the debate on British India. To William Digby, in particular, the main point of criticism was not the English character or reputation or even British imperial expenditure, but the fact that, in his view, India was 'drained' of its resources and condemned to increasing poverty because of British mis-rule. Nevertheless, in these cases too the effectiveness of the message usually seemed to demand an appeal to English virtues, and the two approaches became mixed. A good example is Digby's close friend, Indian nationalist and Liberal MP Dadabhai Naoroji, who continuously emphasised Indian poverty as a consequence of both the 'drain' and the 'un-Britishness' of British rule in India.[24] Thus, in the late-Victorian era the traditional and modern anti-imperialist approaches existed side by side: one stressing that Englishness should be protected from imperialism, the other that the dependencies needed protection from British imperialism.

Late-Victorian anti-imperialism has been touched upon in many biographies and studies on anti-imperialists.[25] There still is, never-theless, a major gap in the story, for two reasons. First, these people were often primarily well known for something else than their anti-imperialism, as is especially the case with the philosopher Herbert

Spencer; while there are plenty of studies on Spencer, they all have focused on other, more famous aspects of his thought. Second, and more important, while the anti-imperialisms of John Morley, J. A. Hobson, or W. S. Blunt, among others, have been studied before, it remains unclear how these criticisms related to each other. The present study thus explores a much wider scope of British anti-imperialism, with a larger spectrum of its varieties and complexities.

The same 'fragmentariness' applies to other previous studies as well. There are several articles and monographs on specific campaigns, especially on the Boer War, but nothing with a more all-inclusive or comparative approach. A. J. P. Taylor's *The Trouble Makers* and A. P. Thornton's *The Imperial Idea and Its Enemies* go to the other extreme, both being very general studies with wide time periods.[26] Bernard Porter's *Critics of Empire* is the major exception. Although limiting his study to Africa, Porter has managed to explore a wide spectrum of critical opinion in the somewhat later period than the present study, from the Jameson Raid to the First World War. These radicals protested against 'the worship of power and force' and 'the glorification of war', as well as the 'perverted patriotism, composed of national conceit'.[27] The things that stirred the opposition were not primarily the 'injustices' that happened overseas: it was above all 'the popular temper which made them possible and applauded them', i.e. the *domestic* manifestations of imperialism.[28] Hence, Porter stated it already in 1968: 'The anti-imperialism was there, but it was directed more against jingoism at home than imperialism in Africa.'[29] While the present study thus elaborates Porter's statement, it argues more overtly that the certain notion of 'Englishness' was at the centre of the whole debate; moreover, since Porter did not develop the idea beyond some passing references to it, it is most likely that this rhetoric was more powerful in the period of this study (1878–1901) than it was in that of Porter's (1895–1914).

Paul Ward has employed the concept of 'oppositional Englishness' when discussing the patriotism of the British left in this period.[30] To him 'Englishness' represents 'traditional, loyal and hegemonic views', whereas 'oppositional Englishness' is used 'where alternative assumptions ... were taken up', especially in view of 'a democratic version of

national identity'. These definitions leave too much scope for imagin-
ation and are not put in any use in this book. Moreover, it is question-
able which of the competing versions of Englishness can be described
as the dominating one historically: the constitution-centred view
stretched back 200 years and could be said to be the stronger one
now in the twenty-first century, while the empire-centred view was
more powerful at the time, in the late nineteenth century. John W.
Auld has also noted that during the Boer War the Liberal imperialists 'were opposed on the other side of the party by an *anti-imperialist*
section which represented a *continuing* tradition in liberalism'. Besides
being the older trend between the two Liberal currents, Auld argued
that it was also the more enduring one, being 'more indicative of
twentieth-century radical thought concerning imperialism than did
Liberal Imperialist nostrums'.[31]

The constitutional view of Englishness was without doubt the dominating one at least until 1880, as Jonathan Parry has argued. He has
pointed out how the reign of Napoleon III in France indirectly contributed to the Liberal dominance in Britain from the 1850s until 1874.[32]
Britain's constitutional arrangements were contrasted with those
of Napoleonic France, and Britain's stability and economic success
were attributed to these. The Liberals developed a patriotic language
declaring first and foremost 'the importance of defending the British
Constitution against continental threats to it'.[33] Indeed, the campaign
against French 'imperialism' was seen as a patriotic struggle 'for the
soul of England'.[34] After Napoleon's defeat in 1870 the Liberals needed
another adversary, which they found in Disraeli. The result was that in
the 1880 election there was a clash between two visions of patriotism:
the Liberal constitutional conception of Englishness on the one hand,
and Disraeli's new empire-centred conception of Englishness on the
other.[35] The Liberal victory demonstrated the continuing supremacy of
the mid-Victorian view, but from then on the constitutional definition
of national identity was ever more under attack. The late-Victorian era
saw a prolonged competition between the two views of Englishness:
whether the prevalent theme was 'the glory of English constitution' or
'the glory of the empire' was continuously debated, anti-imperialists
and imperialists representing the extremes on both sides.

A division between 'mid-Victorian separatism' and 'late-Victorian imperialism' was rather popular among historians in the first half of the twentieth century.[36] In contrast to the increasing imperialism towards the end of the nineteenth century, the 1850s and '60s were regarded as an era of 'separatism' because of the 'Little-Englanders'' strong support for the self-government of the white colonies, especially Canada. However, this rather simplistic division has been challenged in historical research for several decades.[37] According to the older view the foundation of the Royal Colonial Institute in 1868 and the Imperial Federation League in the 1880s, for example, illustrated the revitalised interest in the empire, which was taken to signify a turn from 'separatism' to 'imperialism'. It is, however, important to note that all this enthusiasm was always about the settler colonies, whereas the 'empire proper' was not touched upon. India was treated, as one MP said it should be, as 'an embarrassment and a snare, a gorgeous richly baited trap'.[38] In this case as well it was the same liberal constitution-centred view of Englishness that generated interest in the settler colonies, which were spreading 'the energy and enterprise of the English character'. The essential point was that they were to follow English rather than continental 'imperial' constitutional practices, which fuelled the demands for colonial self-government. Thus, because of its emphasis on freedom, this enthusiasm about the settler empire can be perceived as the *opposite* of imperialism, as Parry has pointed out.[39]

The new empire-centred patriotism brought a change in the British monarchy as well. In earlier decades – and in accordance with the more traditional view of Englishness – the Queen was referred to only in the imperial context as an ultimate safeguard of the liberties of her subject peoples, most notably in the case of post-mutiny India in 1858. In the later nineteenth century, however, the Crown's role as an imperial symbol became more pronounced: 'royal' became 'imperial' and 'kingdom' the 'empire'.[40] It was in the context of the Royal Titles Bill, declaring the Queen Empress of India, that the debate on British – or actually 'Disraelian' – imperialism emerged in the late 1870s.[41] Even British rule in India was criticised to the extent that John Morley, who was writing his biography of Richard Cobden at the time, stated that there were more people then than in Cobden's days 'who cannot see any advantage either to the natives or their foreign masters of this vast possession'.[42] In regard to the Royal Titles Bill, John Bright wrote in his diary that the House was 'insincere and voting what it is secretly against'.[43]

The main controversy in the debate of the late 1870s was, therefore, between constitutionalism and imperialism. Disraeli, like Napoleon III before him, was seen to be after personal fame and military glory for his own sake, which fitted ill with 'the constitutional and moral values that defined an English patriot'; the crucial thing was, as Parry has put it, that 'Disraeli did not understand that an *English* attitude to her global responsibilities was the reverse of "imperialist"'.[44] Disraeli's 'personal rule' was criticised for ignoring the House of Commons when sending Indian troops to Malta, twisting the English constitutional tradition with the imperial Royal Titles Bill and wooing a jingo mob – all this 'imperialism' or 'sham-caesarism' was seen in stark contrast to the English traditions of 'rational public debate and a respect for freedom'.[45] Furthermore, the new departure in British policies – focusing on 'foreign' India rather than the settler colonies – was largely attributed to the fact that Disraeli as a Jew was 'oriental'; he had 'Asian blood' and was thus *un*-English or even *anti*-English.[46]

The two aspects of Englishness were well represented by Edward Dicey, editor of the *Observer*, and William Gladstone: when Dicey argued that Britain owed its power and greatness to its being an imperial nation,[47] Gladstone replied that 'the central strength of England lies in England'.[48] Robert Lowe argued the anti-imperialist case even more strongly. He defined imperialism as 'the assertion of absolute force over others' and 'the apotheosis of violence'.[49] He considered it a line of policy that 'a single despot' might willingly pursue, but surely not the 'some thirty-five millions of people' who were 'called England', especially if they knew all the costs involved.[50] In his view it was not particularly wise to regulate the policy according to the interests of the empire rather than those of the kingdom, especially when the 'whole strength lies in the kingdom, and our weakness mainly in the empire'.[51] Lowe was especially displeased with British rule in India and stressed that 'the conquest of India was not the work of the English Government but of a mercantile company': 'At the time when it passed into the hands of the Crown ... we had a wolf by the ears which it was as difficult to let go as to hold. We could not go back, we could not stand still. We had no choice but to advance.'[52] He contrasted the principles which had helped Britain to grow and prosper – 'industry and freedom at home, and peace, fair dealing, and moderation abroad' – with 'the stupid worship of mere size and bulk'. He stressed that the choice was not 'between a great and a little, but between an honest and happy and a disgraced unhappy England'.[53] Lowe's attack on imperialism can be seen as logical development on the line he had taken when opposing the Reform Bill in 1866. The 'jingoism' of the 1870s was to him a concrete manifestation of the 'bellicose propensities of democratic man' he had warned about a decade earlier.[54]

Towards the end of the century the imperial discourse became much stronger and even the mildest criticism was easily dismissed as 'unpatriotic'.[55] Many anti-imperialists regarded this as serious confusion of thought. They stressed that far from being *un*patriotic, their approach actually represented 'true' patriotism in contrast to imperialism.[56] One of them, 'Free Briton', argued that it was Joseph Chamberlain who was 'against England': 'The conduct of our Government, through the Colonial Office, towards these people [Boers] has for some years past been unjust, dishonourable, weak, and un-English, altogether unworthy of the great country whose flag we have loved as the symbol of right and freedom all over the world.' To 'Free Briton' it seemed absurd that the opponents of Chamberlain's policy were called 'pro-Boers', since they criticised the policy exactly because they were so 'keenly British'. No matter what one thought of the Boers, to 'Free Briton' it seemed clear that 'fraud, deceit, and corruption, extensively practised in order to rouse our nation to war against them, are hurtful to ourselves', not to mention 'the sacrifice of thousands of lives, the ruin of the health of many thousands of Englishmen, the devastation of homes, the loss of £100,000,000 of British savings, the control of the Press by financial rings, the encouragement of savagery and discouragement of social progress'.[57] The conclusion was that 'Mr. Chamberlain is against England. He is the real enemy; because, through his bad work, we have lost in honour, lost in justice, lost in freedom, and lost in that humanity which, above all, should be the distinguishing quality of power. These elements of strength have made the England that we love.'[58]

To some extent the late-Victorian anti-imperialists can be seen as 'public moralists': they thought that imperialists did not live up to the traditional English ideals, which amounted to significant 'failings of character'.[59] Victorian moralists put great emphasis on altruism in the context of 'right' character.[60] The opposition to imperialism was, in this sense, part of larger antipathy towards 'selfishness' in general. As one old-school anti-imperialist, Lord Hobhouse, put it: ' "My country, right or wrong" is a cry which one has heard called of late years a patriotic one. It is just as patriotic as "Myself, right or wrong".'[61] Altruism was seen 'as the heart of all moral virtue' especially by positivists,[62] who also formed the most committed anti-imperialist group in late-nineteenth-century Britain. One has to remember, however, that humanitarian concerns, especially if religion was involved, could be equally imperialistic, as mentioned earlier: in contrast to 'selfish' motives, imperialist efforts became publicised as an utterly altruistic 'white man's burden'. On the occasions of great imperial debates the opinions of intellectual moralists were therefore divided.

Conceptual and methodological clarifications

G. M. Young once wrote that 'the real, central theme of History is not what happened, but what people felt about it when it was happening'.[63] This definition applies well to the present approach, which is to examine imperialism and anti-imperialism first and foremost in the contemporary ideological context. Thus, central to the concept of imperialism has to be how it was perceived *at the time*.[64]

J. Lawson Walton, a Liberal MP, formulated the moderate imperialist stance in 1899 in the following terms: 'Why are we Imperialists? As well ask the owner of an estate why he is a landlord. We have inherited empire and intend to do our duty by the many peoples included within it. ... We are, and shall be, Imperialists because we cannot help it.'[65] Walton's definition was common among the imperialists, who by the turn of the century equalled their ideology with duty and vague empire-pride. Anti-imperialists, however, defined the situation differently, by drawing a definitive distinction between 'imperialism' and 'the British empire' – which, indeed, many imperialists did as well until well into the 1890s. To the critics, anti-imperialism did *not* mean anti-empire. Robert Lowe, for instance, formulated the common critical position by stating that the empire as such had positively expanded 'proper English values' in the form of the settler colonies in America and Australia and connecting imperialism only with foreign dependencies like India.[66] In many cases anti-imperialism even meant opposing imperialism exactly because it was considered harmful to the British empire. In this sense, then, the question was simply what kind of 'union' the British empire should be and what principles and policies it should pursue: as long as it represented 'true' Englishness and not imperialism anti-imperialists were quiet. The critics thus accepted the word 'empire' as a figure of speech, referring to a geographical English-speaking entity and not representing any 'real' empire signifying imperial rule.

The greatest enthusiasm for the empire was expressed towards the settler colonies, which at the same time were not considered to be 'empire proper'; indeed, they were not even usually thought of in terms of 'imperialism'. In this sense the interest which the Imperial Federation League generated in the 1880s was not necessarily imperialistic as such: it might as well be interpreted as an attempt to turn the attention away from the 'irksome' imperial issues, like Egypt, the Sudan, or India, back to the settler colonies. It was an attempt to remind what the British empire first and foremost was really about. In this picture the empire was the result of a 'natural expansion of England' – *colonisation* was the term used – whereas India and Africa, and the *imperialism* they represented, were distracting factors. Miles Taylor has expressed the same idea when noting that the Imperial Federation League, as 'a revival of the positive version of empire, based on the transplantation of Englishmen overseas', could be seen as 'indirect opposition to Gladstone's occupation of Egypt' in 1882.[67] It would therefore be quite mistaken to equate the sense of affinity with 'white settler colonies' straightforwardly with Britons being 'imperialistic'.[68] While the late-century Liberal imperialists, in particular, comprehended imperialism in these terms (as 'empire patriotism'), there were plenty of those who saw imperialism in more traditional terms, connecting it with authoritarianism and militarism; the whole definition of 'imperialism' was thus in this sense continuously contested.

Whereas the empire signified emigration and kinship to most, imperialism was connected to militarism. Francis Hirst, an anti-imperialist and young Oxford academic, defined imperialists as people 'who favoured expansion all over the world and did not shrink from the wars that might so easily come from a clash of rival imperialisms'.[69] The philosopher Herbert Spencer's disgust at imperialism sprang out of his conviction that the rise of militarism led to the 're-barbarisation' of the nation, threatening vital liberal, intellectual, and industrious virtues.[70] Even to the historian J. R. Seeley imperialism signified military dictatorship.[71] In short, empire with imperialism was strictly against traditional and 'true' Englishness. Frederic Harrison, a positivist and front-row anti-imperialist, put it like this:

> The events of 1857 [the Indian mutiny] forced all of us to consider the whole question of the Empire. From that day I became an anti-imperialist, as I am still, in the sense that our vast heterogeneous scattered bundle of dominions is not a normal and permanent development of English nationality, and in many ways retards and demoralises our true national life.[72]

Defending the empire from imperialism and all the vices connected to it formed a general current in a wide spectrum of criticism. Major Evans Bell, when campaigning for an Indian prince against British imperial administration, claimed 'to represent the interests of the Empire in opposition to Mr. H. M. Durand, who champions the interests of a family, a class, and a profession'.[73] John M. Robertson declared in 1901 that fanatical imperialists in South Africa were in fact 'wrecking the empire' with their methods of farm-burning, looting, unjust imprisonments, folly and tyranny: the result of imperialism was martial law and military society.[74] 'Free Briton', too, wrote how Chamberlain's actions had led to 'the degradation of the moral tone and health of the British Empire', leaving it without honour, justice, freedom and humanity.[75]

Sir William Harcourt – a rather ambiguous critic and frontbench Liberal who, like John Morley, first supported Gladstone's Egyptian policy but soon turned against it – defined the imperialism which he opposed as 'extensionism'. Harcourt strongly emphasised that opposing this kind of imperialism did not amount to opposing the empire: if imperialism meant simply 'pursuing a policy which is the wisest and best for that great Empire to which we belong, of course we are all Imperialists in that sense', he stated. But the problem was the *right policy* of imperialism. He was all for 'the consolidation of the vast dominions', 'the development of their resources, the lightening of their burdens, the fostering of their natural growth', and 'the relief of distress' within the empire. But the other 'and exactly opposite view of imperial policy', he argued, was 'to postpone and subordinate all these objects to vanity, to the acquisition of fresh populations, the adoption of additional burdens', which was the 'extensionists' theory'. Harcourt compared these 'extensionists' to 'inflationists' in currency, since they thought that 'the more paper you issue the more wealth you create and the more prosperity you will have'. Instead of this kind of 'inflated Imperialism' – 'expansion, at any rate, at whatever cost, and by what-ever means' – Harcourt considered it 'a greater and a wiser policy to cultivate an Empire than to boom an Empire'. This would have meant an empire of social reform instead of an empire 'committed to land speculators' and 'mining syndicates', who determined 'the limits of the Empire and the methods of its administration'.[76]

Contemporaries were quite confused about these issues and often used the concepts imperialism, anti-imperialism, or the British empire inconsistently. This applied to imperialists and anti-imperialists alike as well as to those who did not really take either side. Regardless of the concepts used, however, a clear distinction was made between Britain's 'natural' relations with its settler colonies and 'problematic' relations with Asia and Africa. For instance, H. M. Hyndman, the social-democratic anti-imperialist, had no difficulties in combining his consistent oppos-ition to British 'ruinous' policies in India and South Africa with staunch support for the federation of the self-governing colonies.[77]

Three young anti-imperialists and Oxford academics, Francis W. Hirst, Gilbert Murray, and John L. Hammond, were among the few who recognised these confusions. They regretted 'the common use of that word [empire] as ambiguous and unfortunate'. They stressed that 'empire' meant 'the rule of one nation over other nations':

> We hold empire over India, over the Soudan; we do not hold empire over Canada or Australia. Free Canada and free Australia are grander evidences of England's greatness and solider elements in her strength than all those tropical provinces which she has won as a conqueror and holds as a foreign despot.
>
> The word 'empire' has blurred this great distinction. More, it has infected ordinary English thought about the colonies with associations drawn from the regions that are ruled despotically and held by the sword. Even so laudable a movement as that for the federation of all the free English commonwealths began by calling itself 'Imperial', and ended by pinning its whole faith to militarism and protection and certain large financial enterprises!
>
> The greatness of Greater Britain lies not in these things, and is not compatible with these things. Our conceptions of it must be utterly freed from the false atmosphere that has now clogged and blinded them.[78]

Hence, anti-imperialism rarely meant opposition to the British empire as such, especially in regard to the settler colonies. W. S. Blunt was no exception in this sense, although he declared to be against the whole imperial enterprise. When Britain met significant resistance from Russia, France, and Germany in its efforts to expand in China at the end of the century, Blunt wrote that he was 'rejoiced at it & the prospect there seems at last to be of the British Empire breaking up'. Nevertheless, when he continued to explain why he wished this, it becomes clear that he did not count the settler colonies among this negative vision of the British empire: he looked forward to the end of empire because Britain 'had done too much harm in the world & though the other nations also would do harm they could not do it so effectively as we do' – adding most importantly: 'also because the Empire is after all a mere cockney affair invented hardly 20 years ago & which was ruining our position as Kingdom at home'.[79]

The anti-imperialist declaration of two positivists, Henry Crompton and Richard Congreve, came perhaps closest to include the settler colonies in their negative vision of empire, although even they did not do it in so many words. They wrote that 'rejection and reversal of the Imperial policy, together with all ideas and schemes of empire, is the essential political condition of future progress':

> Not only is conquest in every form, whether by annexation or protectorate, to be deprecated, but the fundamental idea of *Imperialism, namely, one centralised administration for vast and widely scattered countries*, is mistaken in theory, in practice impossible to be realised, and productive of mischief and misery where it is attempted.[80]

They even went far enough to point out that the Liberal attacks against Disraeli's foreign policy at the time, in 1879, were not real attacks upon imperialism, 'but only upon particular forms and aspects of it which are thought objectionable'.[81] They were appalled that even Henry Fawcett, of whom they had expected more, advocated 'the necessary continuity of statesmanship, maintaining that the Liberal party if they came into power would not be bound to retire within the limits of our former frontier'. This, 'in plain words', was 'Imperialism, the cause of our wars and crimes'.[82] Nowhere had Gladstone and his supporters showed 'that abhorrence of our crimes and wars upon lower races, which is an essential feature of the anti-imperialists'.[83]

It is also interesting to compare how anti-imperialism was seen in the United States at the same time.[84] The main theme was very similar to the one in Britain: imperialism 'represented a flagrant violation of the fundamental principles upon which the government of the United States was based'. The American anti-imperialists opposed imperialism because, in their view, the role of the United States was to stand as 'the champion of liberty, democracy, equality, and self-government throughout the world', whereas 'imperialism, by its very nature, was a denial of the universal validity of these tenets'.[85] The most interesting connection is that they were greatly influenced by the British example, from Adam Smith and Richard Cobden to contemporary anti-imperialists like John Morley.[86] The interaction was close on the imperialist side as well: as it is well-known, Rudyard Kipling wrote his famous poem urging the Americans 'to take up the white man's burden' in regard to the Philippines in 1899.[87]

Like the British, American anti-imperialists did not oppose 'cultural imperialism' as it is understood today. They 'did not challenge the more subtle, though more prevalent and important, ways in which the United States sought to impose its values and institutions on the Third World', and they were all for American trade expansion. It has been stated that it was this combination which led to the curious American policy of 'imperial anti-imperialism', referring to the huge American economic and cultural influence around the world – to 'one of the greatest empires in history' – almost without any formal empire at all.[88]

It is easy to assume that there was no anti-imperialism in this period because there was no significant anti-imperialist movement in Britain. This, however, was mainly due to the diversity of the whole 'ideology': besides their anti-imperialism, the various critics had often little in common. This was the case even inside the Liberal party, for the intellectual John Morley despised 'undisciplined radicals' like Harcourt and especially Henry Labouchere despite their shared anti-imperialism.[89] Furthermore, H. M. Hyndman, who approached the issue from a Marxist point of view, was, due to his socialism, quite extensively rejected by every other anti-imperialist. On the other hand, to a certain extent anti-imperialism was able to unite people who otherwise had little in common, especially when the debate became violent during the Boer War. It seems that at some point or another they all were in contact with each other, some more and some less closely. In this sense there was an anti-imperialist network in Britain, although it was not official or formal in any kind. The uniting spirit was expressed even by Hyndman in 1899:

> I feel proud, no matter how much I may differ from them on other matters, to be abused in common with such 'Little Englanders' as Herbert Spencer, Russell Wallace, Frederic Harrison, John Morley, and Edward Beesly, as well as my old and intimate

friends Frederick Greenwood and George Meredith. I had far
rather be damned with these than saved with those others.[90]

This book does not intentionally focus on any certain individuals or groups. However, the fact that it concentrates on the public
debate puts more emphasis on active publicists. This leaves out persons like William Morris, who was an anti-imperialist but did not
take any public part in the debate. As a consequence of this approach
the most prominent and active anti-imperialists – or, active critical
publicists – who emerge in this study are the poet and ex-diplomat
Wilfrid Scawen Blunt; the philosopher Herbert Spencer; the propa-
gandist for India, William Digby; Liberal MPs John Morley, Henry
Labouchere, and Sir Wilfrid Lawson – who in Blunt's opinion was 'the
most honest man in Parliament'[91] – and a Liberal Unionist Leonard
Courtney. The list also includes all positivists, especially Frederic
Harrison, Edward Beesly, and Richard Congreve as well as a large
group of 'New Liberals', in particular William Clarke. These anti-
imperialists formed a scattered but continuous force which contributed to the public sphere in many ways.

The main forums for great structural questions like those of imperialism and the British empire were pamphleteering and periodical
reviews. The reviews provided an important platform for more detailed
exposition of views and debate than the newspapers and were characterised both by high quality and high price. The thoroughly prepared
articles were written by influential and leading individuals, who, in contrast to the anonymous journalism of the daily press, signed them. All
major reviews – *Nineteenth Century*, *Fortnightly Review*, and *Contemporary
Review* – published quite regularly articles criticising British imperial
policies, even if not often advocating any anti-imperialism as such.

Contemporary pamphlets, books, and articles thus provide the
major source material for this study, and citations from them are used
extensively to illustrate the important rhetoric of 'Englishness'. A
large number of manuscripts have also been consulted and are used
whenever relevant, but the major emphasis is on the public debate.
In articles, pamphlets, and books the thoughts were more thoroughly
developed and expressed than in private correspondence or diaries,

which, on the other hand, often shed light on the 'background stage'. Parliamentary papers are used to some extent, but not systematically. Many critics seemed to think that whereas MPs *represented* public opinion, journalists and publicists *formed* public opinion. Two frontbench anti-imperialist intellectuals, Herbert Spencer and Frederic Harrison, refused to stand for parliament. Both considered it more important to influence events and opinions through writings and pressure groups, since these methods aimed directly at improving the character of the population.[92] William Clarke, too, pointed out that 'the intellectual man does not like the House; he does not approve of its short views, of its carelessness of general principles, of its indifference to logic and to ideas'; and that the House showed 'an instinctive distrust for men who do not live merely for the moment'.[93] Even John Morley is more often depicted as 'a literary man' than as an MP.

The first part of the book examines the two main economic approaches. One, dating as far back as Adam Smith, maintained that the empire caused enormous costs to Britain without corresponding benefits; the other, more modern approach, stressed the view that the empire 'drained' resources from the dependencies, thus causing extreme poverty in them. Since the debates on trade, economy, expansion, and war were closely linked, the various pacifist and anti-expansionist movements of the period will also be discussed in this connection.

The second part then expands the intellectual debate on Englishness and patriotism and compares the 'old' and 'new' Liberal anti-imperialist approaches. 'Old' Liberalism – represented by John Morley and Herbert Spencer, for instance – advocated non-intervention both in international and domestic politics, whereas the 'new' Liberal generation – William Clarke, J. A. Hobson, J. M. Robertson, and others – advocated non-intervention in international relations but interventionism in domestic politics.

The last (third part) explores anti-imperialism in practical politics. It expands the debate on the nature of the British empire and examines the relations between British anti-imperialists and Indian and Egyptian nationalists. It also highlights the limitations and inconsistencies in their anti-imperialism, paying special attention to the debate on India.

PART I

THE DEBATE ON ECONOMY AND IMPERIAL EXPANSION

CHAPTER 1

THE COSTS AND GAINS OF
THE EMPIRE

Anti-imperialists regarded the empire as a burden to British tax-payers. The economic criticism can be traced back to Adam Smith, who argued in the *Wealth of Nations* in 1776 that colonies caused severe strains on British economy, distorted the allocation of funds at home, and dangerously increased threats of war.[1] Smith and his followers put their faith in the development of free trade, which would increase prosperity throughout the world through a mutually beneficial international division of labour, thus naturally excluding monopolies and empires.[2] The belief in the international harmony of free trade led many to think that every penny spent on imperial campaigns was a penny lost. Moreover, the free-trade principle of non-intervention led to strong opposition against militarism and imperial expansion in any form. Richard Cobden and John Bright are the best-known mid-Victorian protagonists of this view,[3] and John Morley, in particular, is a good representative of this 'old Liberal' school at the end of the century.[4] William Gladstone, too – before his reluctant imperialism of the 1880s – denounced the policy of imperial expansion in these terms several times in his famous Midlothian speeches in 1879.[5]

Nevertheless, late-Victorians, in the 1880s and 1890s, found themselves in a situation where continuing adhesion to free trade led to further imperial expansion. A larger empire seemed to provide the best way for trade expansion at the time when Europe and the United States turned to protectionism.[6] By the early 1880s even the Cobden Club was inclined to support British military expansion overseas,[7] and by the 1890s the policy of free trade was closely linked to the idea of a strong British empire.[8]

Antipathies towards military expenditure and imperial expansion remained largely prominent, but there was a new sense of inevitability in the whole imperial enterprise. Sir David Wedderburn, a Liberal MP, stated that Britain had become involved 'in a course of action contrary alike to our notions of justice and of expediency', and it was 'indeed certain that a large proportion of our conquests and annexations would never have been made, if the British nation, or even the British Government, had been fairly consulted in the matter'.[9] Sir George Campbell, another Liberal MP who had made a long career as an administrator in India, expressed the regrettable inevitability even more clearly in 1887:

> I think there is no people whose lot one feels more inclined to envy than the Swiss. It is not only that they are comfortable and content in their own democratic way, but with no great wealth, moderate taxation, and a small revenue, more seems to be done for the people than elsewhere. In respect of roads and railways, they are behind none; nor in hospitals and other public institutions. In an efficient system of public education they are far ahead of us, and in most modern improvements ... they seem ... to be ahead of almost any other people – certainly very far indeed ahead of us.[10]
>
> We are not so fortunate. ... in spite of our enormous wealth and great revenue, so much seems to be absorbed by debts, and naval and military armaments, and wars, and operations, and complications of all kinds, that we are almost niggardly in expenditure for the benefit of our own people at home – compared to the Swiss, for instance. ... In truth, our Empire is attended with many cares and anxieties, alarms and troubles, and a heavy expenditure. Yet we cannot shake off these responsibilities if we would. Citizens of a great Empire we are and must be.[11]

It is largely agreed that British imperialism was mainly driven by economic and financial causes rather than strategic considerations, although both were important.[12] Lance E. Davis and Robert A. Huttenback, among others, have examined in detail the economics of the empire, the flows of capital, imperial expenditure and investment, as well as the groups who paid the costs and those who gained the financial benefits.[13] They have argued that imperial Britain was the most heavily taxed nation in the world[14] and that the tax burden fell extensively to the middle class while the profits of empire went to the upper class.[15] Their conclusion was, therefore, that being part of the empire was economically profitable to individual investors and the colonies, but not to Britain.[16] They calculated that during the period of 1860–1912 British military expenditure was 'about two-and-a-half times as great as that borne by the citizens of a typical developed country and almost twice that of the French and Germans', while the British colonies and dependencies faced only a quarter of the expenditure which their developed or underdeveloped equivalents did.[17] In addition, Britain had to spend large amounts of money for the 'non-defence component' such as general infrastructure in support of British businesses overseas, telegraphs, or subsidised interest rates.[18]

On the other hand, Paul Kennedy has given his support to the traditional imperialist theory, stating that if those costs had not been met there would almost certainly have been other costs to pay.[19] Moreover, as Avner Offer has illustrated, any balance sheet of empire depends crucially on the imaginary alternative or counter-factual which is chosen for comparison.[20] Nevertheless, despite these reservations the fact remains that, as Patrick O'Brien notes, 'modern research in economic history now lends rather strong empirical support to Cobdenite views of Britain's imperial commitments from 1846 to 1914';[21] i.e. to the views which the late-Victorian anti-imperialists shared.

The anti-imperialist arguments of the time are best examined focusing on three key issues: first, the debate on Egypt, the Suez Canal shares, and the interests of the bondholders; second, the debate on British expansion in Central Africa; and third, the question of how the anti-imperialists met the argument that imperial expansion was a necessary presupposition for trade expansion.

Egypt gained enormous debts during the rule of the Khedive Ismail in the 1860s and 1870s. British interest in Egypt increased simultaneously, when European powers financed the Khedive's modernising projects with loans upon loans and, in addition, Britain purchased the Egyptian government's shares in the Suez Canal in 1875. Worsening financial chaos led to bankruptcy in 1876 and to the deposition of Ismail in 1879. The new Khedive Tawfiq began his rule under the Anglo–French Dual Control which represented the principal creditors. New strict financial rules and restlessness in the Egyptian army led to revolts in 1881; many regarded these as ordinary military revolts, but others, especially their leader, Urabi (contemporaries in Britain transliterated his name as 'Arabi'), claimed them to represent a genuine nationalist movement. Britain and France published a Joint Note on 8 January 1882 aiming to end the restlessness by interfering more fiercely into Egyptian matters. The result was, however, the opposite, stirring the revolt further, as did the sending of British naval forces to Egypt in May. After severe riots in Alexandria in June, Britain finally bombarded the city. France having withdrawn from the military operations, Britain was left to occupy the country unilaterally after its victory in Tel-el-Kebir on 13 September 1882.

The occupation of Egypt was defended by referring to the 'anarchy' and the uttermost importance of the safety of the Suez Canal as a route to India. The critics were amazed to realise, as Annie Besant summed it up, that Gladstone was now supporting the kind of 'policy of aggression on weak countries, under the pretence of safe-guarding British interests ... and for the supposed protection of India' on which the nation had 'pronounced a distinct vote of censure' only two years earlier. Besant claimed that Gladstone had won the election exactly because he had proclaimed to represent the policy 'of peace, of righteousness, and of respect for the rights of others'.[22] John Bright was equally disappointed: he bitterly announced that, including the Egyptian expedition, he could calculate as many as seventeen wars as 'the price we pay for that great, historical, marvellous dependency of the British Indian Empire'.[23] In Bright's view there was no doubt that 'the Canal was never in the smallest danger': 'The excuse of self-defence is ludicrous and wicked', he wrote to his old friend Goldwin Smith, complaining:

> This year we shall raise in taxes about 56,000,000 sterling, to pay for wars past or preparations, it may be, for wars to come. In India 20,000,000 more are raised from the Indian population to keep it in subjection to our supremacy. These are tremendous figures, and the great Empire some day will be in difficulty, and the people of these small Islands may grow weary of the burden they now sustain.[24]

Most likely, the Suez Canal was not in risk in 1882 and, as Cain and Hopkins have pointed out, the state of anarchy in Egypt on the eve of the British occupation has been exaggerated.[25] The reasons for the occupation had more to do with economy and finance than mere strategic concerns, as many, indeed, suspected at the time. 'Why is it a special concern of ours whether Egypt is well governed or ill governed?' asked John Morley in his editorial for the *Fortnightly Review*. The first answer was that there was 'a considerable quantity of British capital in Egypt'; Morley continued, 'as a matter of future policy' the British people 'should be told that if they choose to risk their lives or their property in unsettled countries, they do so at their own risk and peril'[26] – it was not the place for the British government to go and safeguard their investments, as many thought was happening.

'Money, Sir, Money', wrote Frederic Harrison in the *Pall Mall Gazette*, was the key to the question. Anything that jeopardised the safe capital returns for the investors was being called 'insurrection', 'disorder' or 'terrorism', while 'anything that secures their dividends a few years longer is "civilization"', he declared.[27] Harrison stated that all the 'idle talk' about 'international duties, about the Canal, and the interest of England in her Indian Empire' was 'wide of the true facts', since no one had threatened the Canal which was 'more than 100 miles from Alexandria'. Even though it was in British interests to safeguard the Canal, it did not follow that the rulers of Egypt were to be 'mere puppets' who the British could 'unmake' when they did not 'feel quite satisfied' that they were 'looking after' their money.[28]

Sir George Campbell, although not an anti-imperialist like Harrison, put it even straighter: 'Practically we only hold our present position there on condition of paying the interest of the debt, which we cannot do without great sacrifices on our part. While the revenue goes to pay the bondholders, we defend Egypt, and the British taxpayer pays for that defence.'[29]

Alexander Johnstone Wilson, a journalist who specialised on issues of finance and commerce, claimed that ever since the purchase of the Suez Canal shares the British government had 'at first shamefacedly, and then openly, taken the Egyptian bondholders under protection'. Furthermore, the bondholders had 'contrived ... to get Ismail Pasha into their debt' in the first place, since they should have known that the Khedive had no right to 'pledge the credit of his country'. The Egyptian people in whose name the money had been borrowed 'got absolutely no benefit from the loans at any time', Wilson argued.[30] In his opinion the Liberal government should have recognised this from the start and pursued the only 'honourable policy, worthy of the name England claims to bear' and 'cut the country adrift from this Egyptian coil the moment it came into office': 'It was no part of the duty of an English Government to act as debt collector to a gang of extortioners.'[31] Wilson pleaded that it was not too late for a new departure – but soon the English constituencies would begin to cry 'Are these the men who promised to lead us in ways of peace, retrenchment, and reform?'[32]

A. G. Hopkins has argued that the bondholder thesis was advanced 'by a clutch of writers grouped around Wilfrid Scawen Blunt',[33] which does seem to be somewhat exaggerated. Although Blunt was the fig-urehead of the Egyptian campaign in Britain, he always was first and foremost the defender of Egyptian nationalism and Muslim culture. He did advocate the bondholder thesis as well, but it was never the main issue for him and did not originate from him. In contrast to Blunt, Frederic Harrison, in particular, was an economic critic first and defender of Egyptian nationalism second. Blunt's main thesis was to argue continuously that Britain's role in Egypt was harmful to *Egypt* – hence the nationalist movement – whereas the main advocates of the bondholder thesis wanted to emphasise the harmful effects for *Britain* in particular. About the fact that the bonds were the real reason for the occupation, Blunt was, however, never in any doubt. Over ten years after the beginning of the occupation he campaigned for British withdrawal as hard as ever, arguing that the Egyptians did not want them and Britain did not need 'Egypt proper' but only a piece of land around the Suez Canal; the occupation was continued only on bondholders' account, he maintained.[34]

In practice the bondholder theory can be rather convincingly applied to Henry Labouchere. At first Labouchere was a strong supporter of the Egyptian expedition, stressing the strategic importance of the Suez Canal and denying entirely that it was a bondholders' war.[35] At this time he had, however, his fortune in Egyptian bonds, which he sold between October 1882 and February 1884, gaining a very good interest for his money.[36] By the time he began selling his bonds Labouchere had turned his coat completely and become the foremost advocate of the bondholder theory in parliament, insisting that the importance of the Canal was greatly exaggerated in the bondholders' interests. From then on he contended that the whole Egyptian business was in fact injurious to the prosperity of Britain and the safety of the British empire, all in the mere benefit of the bondholders.[37] Similarly, it might also be worth noting that Gladstone himself had 37 per cent of his investments in Egyptian stock in 1882, which he sold some two years later when prices had considerably recovered.[38]

Right from the start both political parties declared the occupation to be temporary. Indeed, some potential critics, like John Morley and Leonard Courtney, ended up supporting, albeit reluctantly, Gladstone's Egyptian policy only for this reason.[39]

After the first decade many began to question these pledges and demand the decision of either a formal annexation or withdrawal. After fourteen years of 'temporary occupation', asked one, 'Has the time not come when we may ask ourselves, without being exposed to the imputation of being "Little Englanders", whether we are going to make any serious attempt to relieve ourselves from the burden of Egypt?' After all, 'no patriotic Englishman' could desire the 'fettered and impotent condition' where the British were 'bound by pledges which we have neither the hardihood to violate nor the courage to fulfil'.[40] Nevertheless, Britain stayed in Egypt without formal annexation.

Already before the occupation of Egypt some had criticised British presence in South Africa and advocated its independence; in their view, like in the case of the Suez Canal, Britain only needed 'a naval port at the Cape', not the whole South Africa.[41] Labouchere went in 1883 far enough to state that even a naval base was 'conditional upon retention of India'.[42] When British presence in Egypt continued and even led to further difficulties in the Sudan and Central Africa, the criticism was also bound to continue. George Baden-Powell, without any meaning to criticise, made the situation even worse by testifying that the British public did not 'at all realise the great total of the minor sums from time to time paid away in South Africa by the home tax-payer. The various native wars alone have cost very many millions, and as I write, at the least £100,000 of English taxes is still being paid each month to assert English supremacy in Bechuanaland.'[43]

South Africa was, of course, to stir hot debate by the late 1890s, but between the occupation of Egypt in 1882 and the Jameson Raid in 1895 the main attention was focused on the confusing 'scramble' in Central Africa. Interestingly, British expansion there was opposed by various people, not only by overall anti-imperialists like in the case of Egypt; in fact, critics like Frederic Harrison and Blunt hardly participated in this debate at all. Even the well-informed Sir George Campbell – member of parliament and the India Council – confessed in 1887 that the territories attached to British African settlements were 'very ill-defined, and do not seem to be very populous and important. We seem to be continually adding to them small strips of sea-coast, or small protectorates over chiefs on rivers', with the result that Britain's position in Central Africa was 'difficult to understand'.[44]

Furthermore, Sir John Pope Hennessy, a former colonial governor who was in strong disfavour at the Colonial Office, argued that Africa had no value to England whatsoever: it all was a big prestige game against Germany and France.[45] Sir Henry Hamilton Johnston, another colonial administrator with experiences from Central Africa, was ready to contradict Hennessy's view, stating that tropical Africa was 'of value to the British nation' and 'even a necessity to the expanding enterprise of the empire'. He even argued that new Central African dominions would provide not only 'fresh markets for British manufactures' but also 'new homes for our surplus population'.[46] Hennessy further contradicted these views and, rather surprisingly, was supported by Edward Dicey.[47] Dicey thought that 'the acquisition of vast territorial rights in Central Africa' would not 'prove beneficial to the interests of Great Britain' and Britain was therefore 'competing for stakes not worth the winning'. Although a staunch imperialist, Dicey stressed that he could only advocate *profitable* expansion of the empire.[48]

Similarly, the severest criticism in relation to British dealings in Uganda in 1892–3 came not from the anti-imperialists but from Sir Charles Dilke and Sir William Harcourt, who was the chancellor of the exchequer in Gladstone's Cabinet. Uganda, which was strategically situated between Egypt and the Cape, had attracted both French Catholic and English Protestant missionaries which ended up quarrelling with each other as well as with the native Muslims. The Ugandan territory was then approached by the British East Africa Company, under Captain Lugard, and a German expedition, both offering 'protection' to the Christians. The British East Africa Company was, however, in severe financial difficulties and was soon compelled to withdraw. Salisbury's government had not been willing to back the Company or take over the responsibility in Uganda. The Company had then delayed the evacuation after the change of government, adding pressure on the public as well as the parliament.

Harcourt was extremely hostile to the idea of Britain paying off the Company's Ugandan expedition. 'I will die a thousand deaths rather than have anything to do with it', he declared to John Morley.[49] To the prime minister he wrote:

> The Company have ordered evacuation because 'the occupation is so costly' and because the 'territory yields no funds', *ergo* the British Government are to undertake it! ... *Cui bono?* Is it *trade?* There is no traffic. Is it *religion?* The Catholics and Protestants (as they call themselves) are occupied in nothing but cutting each other's throats, with their bishops at their head. Is it *slavery?* There is no evidence that there is any slave trade question in this region. ...
>
> I see nothing but endless expense, trouble and disaster in prospect if we allow ourselves to *drift* into any sort of responsibility

for this business, and devoutly hope we shall have nothing to do
with it. The Company have made this terrible mess, and they
must bear the responsibility.[50]

When the matter was discussed in parliament Dilke testified that
the only information he had received about it was in favour of annexation.[51] Emphasising that he was not 'one of those who object under
all circumstances to the extension of the responsibilities of this country' he, nevertheless, was compelled to object the British occupation
of Uganda.[52] In his opinion the imperialist fervour had gone out of
proportion and this was, to some extent, a counter-reaction to anti-
imperialist criticism:

> There are many people who seem to think that the best way
> to protest against the views of those who desire to contract the
> responsibilities of the Empire is to advocate their extension on
> every side, and we are subject, in consequence, to waves of unrea-
> soning feeling, to hot fits, which are followed by cold fits from
> time to time.[53]

Dilke was against British entanglement in Central Africa because
he thought it was not profitable to Britain in any respects and British
responsibilities were already greater than the provisions for safety. Most
of all, he warned that there was 'great danger that the public spirit and
patriotism of the nation may be exhausted by the drains made upon
it in wrong quarters'.[54] Harcourt also emphasised that Britain already
had 'as much Empire as the nation can carry'. 'What seems to me to be
at issue is a whole policy. Are we to attempt to create another India in
Africa?' he wrote to the foreign secretary, Lord Rosebery:

> It is said, 'We have India and Canada and Australia, why not
> Africa?' That is like a landowner who, having secured many
> great estates which he can with difficulty manage, thinks it an
> argument for buying more and mortgaging those which he has
> for the purchases. That can only end in bankruptcy. I am amused
> at the people who call themselves Imperialists.[55]

Uganda was retained, mainly as a result of strong missionary campaigning. First it was decided that it should not lead to extensive public expenditure, but a few years later Britain built a railway in Uganda after all, with a cost of millions of pounds to the British taxpayer.[56]

British occupation of Uganda through the actions of the British East Africa Company reminded many of the similar story with the East India Company before. Dilke, for instance, pointed out that the British should ask themselves 'how far it is safe for the country to allow itself to be committed by chartered companies to Imperial action'.[57] The advocates of the chartered companies insisted that they did valuable work advancing civilisation and ending slave trade more efficiently than any government actions.[58] Indeed, when the Liberal government revived the institution in 1881 the hopefuls thought that this would be the case. By the 1890s, however, it had become clear that the institution did not work much better in the nineteenth century than it had done a century before. Moreover, the East Africa Company was only the beginning; the real troubles were yet to come through the South Africa Company, a charter of which was granted to Cecil Rhodes in 1889.

At first even Harcourt was thrilled about Rhodes. 'Even jingoism' was tolerable when it was done 'on the cheap', he declared after meeting Rhodes while visiting Lord Rothschild in 1892. According to the account of the meeting Rhodes was willing to

> take over Uganda and work it as a province of the South African Company for £24,000 per annum, though the East African Company want £40,000 per annum to keep it on. He also wants to take over the administration (as part of the Cape) of the Bechuanaland Protectorate from H. Loch, who is spending £100,000 per annum of British money in it, while Rhodes would run it for £40,000 per annum.[59]

Rhodes's proposal was rejected, but his eagerness to gain control over Bechuanaland began a new wave of expansion in South Africa. Simultaneously, an old border dispute between Venezuela and British Guiana worsened to the extent of affecting the hitherto cordial relations between the United States and Britain. After that had been settled, Britain was soon facing the danger of war with France when the countries collided in Fashoda, Central Africa. Strained international relations were seen as a consequence of British advancement in Central Africa which, many thought, had resulted from the occupation of Egypt.[60] When Britain was in 1896 once more advancing in the areas south of Egypt Wilfrid Scawen Blunt was at pains to explain that it was 'in no way due to Egyptian or Anglo-Egyptian initiative'; in contrast, the campaigns were generally condemned in Egypt.[61] It was all due to a changed atmosphere in Britain, he maintained. Similarly, a few months later another staunch 'anti-jingo', Goldwin Smith, wrote to a like-minded friend, John X. Merriman, that 'Jingoism is evidently rampant in England'. Smith thought that Disraeli was to blame:

> It is surprising that his Hebrew flashiness should have so dazzled a practical nation. I suppose he amused them; but they have paid pretty dearly for their amusement. ... The world is becoming embroiled in all quarters and upon all questions. Everybody shrinks from the unknown and dreads possibilities of a war with the new weapons and ships. This dread now keeps the peace. But the tension cannot last for ever. Somebody must break in the end.[62]

In economic terms, all the expansion was explained away by arguing that the empire provided safe and exceptionally profitable outlets for British capital. The reality was, however, different: from the 1880s onwards both foreign and especially domestic investments provided better capital returns than the empire.[63] Moreover, in practice even at the age of 'high imperialism' in the 1880s and 1890s British investments went largely outside the formal empire, especially to the United States and Latin America.[64] Patrick O'Brien has suggested that the only reason for the persisting belief in high capital returns from the empire was the growth of imperial sentiment and propaganda which 'created illusions of security and false expectations';[65] besides this, the fact that until the early 1880s the capital returns from the empire had indeed been greater than from the domestic or foreign sector,[66] undoubtedly maintained the faith in high imperial returns.

Even more popular – and equally flawed – argument for imperial expansion was that 'trade followed the flag'. Anti-imperialists argued that new conquests did not bring increases to the amount or value of trade and that there was no need for Britain to possess the territories with which it wanted to trade. As Richard Congreve, among others, stated, Britain had had commercial intercourse with India before British rule, and it would equally continue after British withdrawal.[67] Furthermore, the late-century competition for commercial 'spheres of interest' in China was thought to stir international tension far more than advance trade.[68]

Lord Farrer – a civil servant and a committed defender of free trade, who deeply resented the 'evil spirit' of Jingoism which had taken the form of 'lust of an extended Empire' – argued that Britain's economic decline and diminishing influence in the world had led to enormous military and naval spending and to a readiness 'to quarrel with the rest of the civilised world for any waste corners of the earth which are still left to scramble for, and for every "sphere of influence", however worthless'.[69] He reproduced a bunch of statistics from a Board of Trade Return showing that these 'new markets' did not compensate for their cost and that the existence of these markets did not even depend on British rule. He illustrated that during a fifty-year period, from 1854 to 1895, the proportion of trade with Britain's imperialist rivals had slightly increased while the proportion of trade with British possessions had slightly diminished.[70] In regard to Egypt, for instance, Farrer noted that Anglo-Egyptian trade had increased substantially both in quantity and in proportion until 1870; after that British trade with Egypt somewhat diminished and since the late 1870s had remained stationary, the occupation of 1882 bringing no changes.[71]

Lord Masham, an inventor of textile machinery, was quick to denounce Lord Farrer's figures.[72] He argued that it was indeed 'evident' and 'undeniable' that trade did follow the flag, since the true trade figures were revealed only when calculated *per head* instead of *per country*: in his opinion the point was not that in 1897, for instance, Britain exported goods worth £21 million to the United States and only £5.5 million to Canada – what mattered was that when the populations of those countries were compared, it emerged that Britain in fact 'exported more than three times as much per head of the population to that under our own flag'. The case was even clearer in Australasia, where the figure was twelve times more per head than in the United States.[73] Besides this peculiar way of calculating profit, it is worth noting that Masham's examples are from the settler empire and not from the areas where the expansion was supposed to advance trade.

William Clarke, who was one of the most committed anti-imperialists in late-Victorian Britain, continuously – especially as the editor of the New Liberal *Progressive Review* in the review's short lifetime, 1896–7 – accused 'the financial class' of encouraging aggressive imperialism and militarism for its own benefit and at the financial and moral expense of everyone else. He scorned the imperialists' view that the British empire was 'a valuable "commercial asset"', stressing that it was only natural that every British colony and dependency should wish to manufacture for itself and buy 'in the most convenient market', which put the mills of Yorkshire and Lancashire in the same line with those in Germany. 'The various countries composing the British Empire' could only be said to have common economic interests in the sense that 'the whole planet may be said to have a common economic interest'. Especially in regard to the dependencies, the view was gloomy:

England has been annexing territories which are, economically speaking, of no use. No effective demand can come from the Soudan or Uganda, or even from Rhodesia. One single first-class Continental city is of more value to England, from the economic point of view, than tens of thousands of square miles in Africa. As Macaulay said, an acre in Middlesex is worth a principality in Utopia – a hint for present-day expansionists.[74]

John Mackinnon Robertson was another prominent New Liberal anti-imperialist. In his book *Patriotism and Empire* Robertson attacked the three main explanations for imperial expansion. The imperialists argued that the expansion was necessary, as Robertson summarised it,

(1) To provide openings for the emigration of our superfluous population; and

(2) To 'open up fresh markets'.

    When answered that we need not own our markets, and that trade normally goes on between different States, he answers,

(3) That 'trade follows the flag'.[75]

Robertson then went on to contradict these statements one by one. He showed how the huge majority of emigrants headed for the United States instead of the empire and reminded that the latest imperial expansion – in China and tropical Africa – did not seem to offer any prospects for emigration at all.[76] Furthermore, in his opinion the empire increased *poverty* rather than prosperity: 'Imperial England has proportionally more and worse poverty than almost empireless France; much more than Switzerland, Holland, and Scandinavia. Such are the fruits of imperialism; and the prescription is, More imperialism!'[77] Indeed, Robertson predicted that 'the cheap labour of India and Japan' would eventually 'destroy the home industry' altogether: the only relevant sense in which 'trade followed the flag' was that the flag was 'the means by which the gamblers of trade can best find their way to new grounds of exploitation' after England was exhausted, 'leaving the seat of "empire" at home to sink ... like a deserted ship'.[78] Eventually the sources of British wealth would be 'outside of its proper soil' instead of in the home industry, and then decadence was sure to follow as had happened in Rome and Spain previously. Robertson still added that the cry 'trade follows the flag' implied that the commercial decadence had already begun, since 'when British trade was in a state of energetic expansion, no such cry was heard. In those days it was taken for granted that in the future, as in the past, trade would naturally go on between different nations, and that Britain was competent to trade with the subjects of other flags, as they with each other.'[79]

    J. A. Hobson's *Imperialism: A Study* was not published until 1902, but he had been developing the ideas for it at least since 1898. Clarke and Robertson both influenced him strongly in the process, Clarke with his fierce anti-imperialism and Robertson with his tentative ideas of oversaving.[80] *Imperialism* is generally regarded as the first study clearly arguing that the prime mover behind imperial expansion was overseas investment which resulted from underconsumption at home.

However, as it has been seen, this idea had been in the making for at least two decades, Robertson coming closest in formulating it before. Moreover, besides the City financiers Hobson pointed his finger at militant aristocracy, religious missionaries, and armament industry; and this sort of anti-imperialism had even longer pedigree.[81]

Hobson, too, attacked the notion that trade would 'follow the flag'. He ridiculed the free trade pretensions of 'open markets policy' since, as he wrote in 1898, the whole idea that 'England must be prepared to "fight for markets"' was 'nothing else than a direct repudiation both of the logic and the utility of Free Trade': 'in truth' it was 'the policy of forcing doors open and forcibly keeping them open'.[82] Like Farrer, Hobson demonstrated with statistics that the increase of expenditure on armaments was not attended by corresponding increase of trade. Moreover, Hobson declared that it was equally erroneous to concentrate only on foreign or colonial trade 'as an index of the real prosperity of a nation', since in fact *home* trade provided 'a more solid and substantial basis of industrial prosperity'. Instead of inciting the policy of imperialism, therefore, British politicians should stimulate home consumption.[83] In short, the issue was

> between external expansion of markets and of territory on the one hand, and internal social and industrial reforms upon the other; between a militant imperialism animated by the lust for quantitative growth as a means by which the governing and possessing classes may retain their monopoly of political power and industrial supremacy, and a peaceful democracy engaged upon the development of its national resources in order to secure for all its members the conditions of improved comfort, security, and leisure essential for a worthy national life.[84]

Hobson further stressed that this was no mere 'rhetorical antithesis, but the plain and very practical issue which Cobden and his friends strove to place before the Liberal party half a century ago'. Moreover, it was exactly the 'refusal to face this issue' which had 'crippled the principles and grievously impaired the working efficiency of Liberalism' at the end of the century, he argued.[85]

The South African War gave Hobson, who was the on-the-spot reporter of the *Manchester Guardian*, more insight into the workings of imperialism. He returned to Britain convinced that Britain had waged war on behalf of a 'small confederacy of international financiers' which contained 'a few Englishmen like Rhodes ... but chiefly foreign Jews'.[86] He was convinced that this financial oligarchy worked through 'a kept press' with the object of securing a regular supply of cheap labour for their mines.[87] H. M. Hyndman had written very similarly a year earlier, blaming the Jews, mine capitalists like Rhodes, and other 'blotters' to be only after cheap labour, in which 'the Jingo metropolitan press' assisted them by inspiring war spirit.[88] Frederic Harrison was thrilled to note that Hobson, too, had traced the imperialist war to 'a ring of international financiers' as he had always been saying.[89] But it was Hobson who finally, as Peter Cain has aptly put it, 'helped to establish, in the minds of anti-imperialists, the belief that the war was being fought at the behest of "alien financiers" who had hijacked the British state'.[90] This interpretation, however, widely accepted at the time as it was, was most likely not correct. After meticulous research Iain R. Smith has come to the conclusion that there is no convincing evidence to suggest that the British government would have gone to war to support the gold-mining industry or capitalists. Instead, the real, and simpler, reason was the British government's determination to establish firmer long-time supremacy over South Africa in general and the Transvaal government in particular.[91]

CHAPTER 2

ANTI-AGGRESSION AND ANTI-WAR MOVEMENTS

Wars are made, in short, by financiers and heads of trusts using the old words about patriotism and loyalty to cover their own practices and to throw dust in simple people's eyes.[1]
– William Clarke in 1901

It is often assumed that there was no anti-imperialism in the late nineteenth century because there was no significant and coherent movement of protest against imperialism. While the latter statement is correct, it nevertheless requires two clarifications. First, there was no coherent movement because the whole 'ideology' was so diverse – there were *various* anti-imperialisms, represented, for example, by intellectuals like John Morley or Herbert Spencer and practical propagandists like William Digby. Second, while none of the many late-Victorian movements declared to be anti-imperialist as such, two came very close: the Anti-Aggression League in the early 1880s and the Increased Armaments Protest Committee in the mid-1890s. The first was inaugurated by Herbert Spencer and Frederic Harrison and the latter by Sir Wilfrid Lawson and the journalist and peace campaigner George Herbert Perris.

Late-Victorian anti-imperialism was not far from anti-militarism. Many followed the arch-anti-imperialist Herbert Spencer's famous division between the militant and industrial type of society. Spencer had rather seen the militant society as part of a distant past when tyrants or oligarchies had ruled with martial law repressing proper liberal virtues. Only after centuries of progress, according to Spencer, had England changed from militant to industrial; and it was due to this change that England had prospered. In the late nineteenth century, however, this progress seemed to come to a halt and even turn into degeneration, when good old liberal and industrious England was fast becoming militant and imperialist Britain.[2]

Spencer was to describe later his involvement in the Anti-Aggression League as 'a grievous mistake'[3] and even 'the greatest disaster of my life – a disaster that resulted from doing more than I ought to have done'. He had recently spent many years writing his *Principles of Sociology* and focusing on 'the relation which exists between militancy and a social organization despotic in form and barbaric in ideas and sentiments', noting clearly 'the relation which exists between industrialism and a freer form of government, accompanied by feelings and beliefs of just and humane kinds'. In the climate of Midlothian in 1879 a further thought occurred to him 'concerning the possibility of doing something towards checking the aggressive tendencies displayed by us all over the world – sending, as pioneers, missionaries of "the religion of love", and then picking quarrels with native races and taking possession of their lands'.[4]

Two years passed and Spencer began writing *Political Institutions*, becoming even 'more profoundly impressed with the belief that the possibility of a higher civilization depends wholly on the cessation of militancy and the growth of industrialism'. In the summer of 1881 Spencer, strongly encouraged by Frederic Harrison, finally began organising a movement from these premises.[5] He knew that John Bright, who was now a member of Gladstone's Cabinet, agreed about 'the antagonism between industrial progress and war', and one of the first things he did was to inform Bright that he was finally gathering together 'the large amount of diffused opinion against our aggressive policy, which now tells but little because it is unorganized'.[6] Bright remained sympathetic and supportive towards the League but was not willing to get involved in it to any great extent.[7] However, John Morley and many others soon joined in. Spencer drafted the League's first address in which he mainly aimed to differentiate the Anti-Aggression League from the Peace Society by stressing the difference between the Peace Society's 'untenable' doctrine of non-resistance and the League's 'tenable' doctrine of non-aggression.[8] Whereas the Peace Society represented an intransigent pacifist position in its opposition to all wars, even defensive ones, the Anti-Aggression League represented 'pacificism' in its stand that most defensive wars should be supported until permanent peace was achieved.[9]

Frederic Harrison's active involvement in the Anti-Aggression League was a logical sequence in a long line of anti-imperialist activities since the Jamaica Committee of the 1860s. One public outcry he did not participate in, however, was the Bulgarian agitation in the 1870s, which under the charismatic leadership of Gladstone gave loud support to Christians in the Balkans against Ottoman rule.[10] Anti-imperialists like Harrison, Spencer, or W. S. Blunt did not see this as their campaign: to them it was 'a religious crusade' which only 'opened an era of general confusion and war', as Harrison put it. In their eyes the spirit which Gladstone inspired was not much less imperialistic than that of Disraeli's in its eagerness 'for the entire dismemberment of the Ottoman Empire and its partition amongst its rivals in Europe'. Harrison later noted that his 'Gladstonian friends' had dubbed him a 'Jingo' at the time – since he was not on Gladstone's side on the matter he supposedly supported Disraeli's policies.[11] This misconception, however, was only temporary, since when the Afghan War broke out Harrison proved to be one of its fiercest critics. He published two articles in the *Fortnightly Review* attacking the expansionist policies of the viceroy Lord Lytton and Disraeli.[12] Harrison later confirmed that he was at the time 'in daily communication' with Sir Arthur Hobhouse and Sir Henry Norman from the India Council as well as some 'other old soldiers and officials', who supplied him with inside information from the India Office.[13] Hobhouse was the legal member of the viceroy's council until 1877, but he nevertheless loudly denounced the war and imperialist policies.[14] When Hobhouse returned to Britain he, as Harrison testified, 'took a noble part in opposing this Indian system of expansion'. Harrison and Hobhouse even formed 'a small Afghan Committee on the lines of the Jamaica Committee',[15] for which they received some support even from two bishops and the Duke of Westminster.[16]

It was not difficult to persuade Hobhouse to join the Anti-Aggression League as well. After the Liberal victory in 1880, Hobhouse later stated, 'sanguine people proclaimed that the Jingoes – the party of aggression and "Empire" – were destroyed. I was one who thought them still the most powerful force in the country, as well as the most dangerous. Herbert Spencer thought likewise.'[17] The first tentative meeting of the Anti-Aggression League was then held at the house of Sir Arthur Hobhouse in July 1881.[18] During the winter the movement matured further and grew in size.

The first public meeting of the Anti-Aggression League was held on 22 February 1882 at the Westminster Palace Hotel.[19] The meeting was presided over by John Morley and it was a success: by March the League's council included thirty-six MPs and around forty other well-known politicians, professors, or writers.[20] The speeches from the meeting were published as *Anti-Aggression League Pamphlets, No. 1* in March. Frederic Harrison, in his speech, persuasively calculated in the meeting that due to the empire England had 'more wars than any other nation in Europe, not even excepting Russia'.[21]

On the evening of the first public meeting Herbert Spencer wrote in his diary: 'Anti-Aggression League meeting took place quite successfully. I spoke well, and was much complimented.'[22] He was, however, immediately disappointed by the obscure amount of press attention the League received. He blamed the simultaneous and 'tremendous disturbance in the House of Commons about the case of Mr. Bradlaugh' for not only having kept away 'very many members of Parliament who had promised to attend' but also 'occupying so large a space in the papers as to leave little room for the report of the meeting'.[23]

Moreover, the Anti-Aggression League had barely been formed when it faced the Egyptian problem. Spencer wisely pointed out that the League itself should be wary of expressing aggressive attitudes and show 'somewhat more sympathy with the Government in the difficulty of its position'; the right attitude might even do much 'towards conciliating those whose aid is important'.[24] After a meeting with Gladstone in June 1882 Spencer reported to John Bright that, in regard to the League, Gladstone had 'expressed his entire sympathy with its aims' and 'recognized the fact that our aims were in harmony with the progress of Liberalism at large'. Spencer was strongly encouraged by Gladstone's assurances, since thus far too many sympathisers had been 'deterred by the fear of hampering the ministry' – but 'if it could be known among such that not only do you sympathize with us', he wrote to Bright, 'but that Mr. Gladstone does so too in respect of our general aims, the difficulty would disappear and we should at once have ample and probably energetic aid'.[25]

The League had time only for another great meeting, on 26 June, before it collapsed at the beginning of the occupation of Egypt. Frederic Harrison addressed the representatives from Trade Unions and Labour Associations who had been specially invited. The address was published as *Anti-Aggression League Pamphlets, No. 2.*[26] On the occasion Harrison stressed that the League was not acting 'with any desire whatever to embarrass the Government'; on the contrary, it was 'seeking only to remind them of their principles'. The League's principles were, Harrison stated,

the principles of the Mid-Lothian campaign, of the Government of Mr. Gladstone: the principles that the nation ratified in May 1880. That is to say, that this policy of extending the Empire, aggrandising the power of Britain, thrusting ourselves as managers and masters of our weaker neighbours, backing up our adventurous people in every enterprise, just or unjust, bullying the weak tribes, making petty kings our vassals, opening markets by gunboats, and maintaining controllers by ironclads – this system must cease, once for all.[27]

In Harrison's view 'Mr. Gladstone and Lord Granville were personally most unwilling for war or for annexation – but politically they were thrust into both by others whom they could not control', since, 'as usual, financiers and money-dealers pulled the strings unseen'.[28] Wilfrid Scawen Blunt, who attended the June meeting was pleased with it and wrote in his diary: 'Sir Wilfrid Lawson, in the chair, was excellent. He is the pleasantest speaker I have listened to. Also

Sir Arthur Hobhouse was good. Frederic Harrison read a lecture in which he stated the Egyptian case fairly.'[29]

Nevertheless, after the bombardment of Alexandria in July and the occupation of Egypt in September 'nearly all' of League's most important members 'became tepid or neutral', as Harrison put it, declining to oppose Gladstone. Harrison, Hobhouse, Spencer, and Sir Wilfrid Lawson, among few others, were soon the only ones left in the League. Harrison bluntly concluded: 'From that day we have known that no member of the Liberal party, whether politician or publicist, could be counted on to resist unjust war and Imperial expansion.'[30]

Herbert Spencer's gloomy judgement was that 'Nothing at any moment came of our action':

> Though year by year filibustering colonists and ambitious officials, civil and military, were everywhere laying hands on the territories of neighbouring weaker races ('annexing' the wise call it) – though consequent chronic hostilities, and multiplying salaries to new governors and their staffs, were continually swelling the national expenditure; yet the elector at home, preoccupied by disputes about local option, hours of closing public-houses, employers' liabilities, preferential railway rates, and countless small questions, would give no attention to the fact that his burdens are being perpetually made heavier, and his risks more numerous, without his assent or even his knowledge.[31]

Furthermore, 'the organs of the upper classes' were even worse 'ever favouring a policy which calls for increase of armaments and multiplication of places for younger sons'. With hindsight, Spencer condemned it 'a foolish hope that any appreciable effect could be produced under conditions then existing, and with an average national character like that displayed': 'with a parliament and people who quietly look on, or even applaud, while, on flimsy pretexts, the forces of our already vast Eastern Empire successfully invade neighbouring States' the expectations had been 'irrational'. According to Spencer the only result of the League was that the vast amount of hard work he had poured into it had completely ruined his health.[32]

Organised anti-imperialism remained then buried for more than a decade, until Sir Wilfrid Lawson took the initiative. Like Spencer and Harrison, this second baronet and long-term Liberal MP was an anti-imperialist veteran – or, as he probably would have preferred himself, an anti-*jingoist* veteran. By 'a Jingo' Lawson meant 'an irresponsible, impulsive, ignorant shouter for war'.[33] The parliamentary session in 1878 was to him 'a miserable Session, jingoism triumphant and leading to mad and mischievous expenditure'.[34] When the parliament was called in December 1878 to provide for the expenses needed in Afghanistan, Lawson supported the vote of censure for the war; but 'of course we were well beaten by a majority of 101'.[35] In 1882 Lawson was one of the few MPs to condemn the occupation of Egypt. He also was a member of the Anti-Aggression League, presiding over the second public meeting in June. Moreover, after the bombardment of Alexandria he tried to get the Cobden Club to condemn it because 'peace throughout the world was a great object with Mr Cobden and should be a great object with the Club', he argued.[36] This, however, did not happen.

In the mid-1890s Lawson, together with George Herbert Perris, took the trouble of organising an Increased Armaments Protest Committee. The first meeting was held on 13 March 1896 and presided over by Lawson. The Committee was especially constituted to provide 'an effective antidote to the Jingo, militarist, and sham-patriotic sentiment which at present exerts an almost unrestrained influence upon the public mind'.[37] Robert Spence Watson was chosen as president and twenty-two other influential members of the community formed the executive committee. In addition to Lawson there were two other MPs in the committee, Robert A. Allison and Henry J. Wilson, and the committee also included Sir Robert Head as honorary treasurer, Perris as honorary secretary, and William Clarke.[38]

The Increased Armaments Protest Committee was not long-lived either, but it brought out one significant publication. This was titled *Empire, Trade, and Armaments: An Exposure* and published in the name of the Committee in 1896.[39] The publication indicated 'three closely related phenomena' which dominated the life of the people of Great

Britain at the time, 'perverting their development, wasting their resources, and filling all true patriots with anxiety for their future':

> We refer in the first place to the rapid and generally unreasoning expansion of an Empire which already overtaxes our capacity for good government. The second and derivative fact is the unconscionable increase of armaments claimed to be necessary for the defence of this Empire. Supporting these, and carefully cultivated by the classes which profit thereby, a new form of Jingo Imperialism has sprung up; and – because it makes a specious appeal to the more selfish instincts of an industrial nation – has obtained a certain vogue.[40]

Nevertheless, the Committee did 'not at all believe' that this sentiment had 'a real hold upon the mind of the people' – 'a great deal of corruption can be done with fifty million pounds a year'. The Committee's function, then, was to 'attack this pernicious sentiment by a candid examination of the expansion policy and its fruits'. The statement continued:

> Considering, too, the systematic misrepresentation carried on on behalf of this conspiracy of financiers, speculators, politicians and aristocrats – considering the superficial attractiveness of the commercial arguments with which Mr. Chamberlain and others have superseded the old-fashioned Jingoism of Lord Beaconsfield, it is hardly surprising that it should have obtained an apparent popular support. But we do not believe that the teaching of Cobden, Mill, Bright, and Gladstone is forgotten in the country that owes so much of its prosperity to those great statesmen.[41]

Empire, Trade, and Armaments explored the two major interrelated issues of the 1890s: the increasing cost of armaments and the thesis that trade 'followed the flag'. In regard to the first the Committee pictured the prevailing 'cold war' climate with the expanding military budgets and the hardening international competition for armaments as well as the argument that 'armed peace' was not a real peace but in fact 'civil war'.[42] The mantra of 'the trade and the flag' was confronted by statistics showing only 'stationary trade in a bloated Empire'.[43] The Committee argued that no one had even attempted to defend the increases of British armaments with reason: 'Instead of reasoning, we have had appeals to national cupidity and conceit, veiled threats, and the seeds of panic.'[44] The panic had resulted from some vague fears of invasion and 'the bogey of "Our Trade in Danger" ', but, the Committee asked, did anyone know 'what part of our commerce is in danger, and from whom?' In strong contrast to the imperialists who argued that the expansion of the empire increased trade, the Committee argued that the expansion only resulted in 'the disproportionate growth of armaments' which formed 'an increasingly severe strain and tax upon trade and industry'. Moreover, in contrast to the Jingo enthusiasts, the Committee stressed that British labour was 'losing, and not gaining, and will probably lose still more heavily by the extension of the Empire'. The terse conclusion was that 'we are suffering in both these ways: imposition at home and exasperation abroad is an excellent summary of the double-faced policy of Jingo Imperialism'.[45]

The problem was, however, that imperialism – and especially the 'mob-jingoism' – was not an ideology to be discussed by appealing to *reason*. It was a strong and emotional faith, as the late-century antiimperialists noticed in exasperation. Anti-imperialist reasoning with statistics could always be encountered with imperialist reasoning and statistics, interspersed with 'patriotic emotions'. Herbert Spencer's diminishing lack of faith was noted earlier, and even Lawson's old confidence in the political common sense of the people was shaken towards the turn of the century. He wrote bitterly: 'It may be laid down as a rule that all wars are popular in England. The longer I live the more incomprehensible does it appear to me, how people who call themselves Christians can take a pride and pleasure in war, which the *Times* newspaper once said was nothing more than "ornamental murder".'[46] Lawson began expressing himself more through satirical poetry instead of practical political action. An example from Easter

1898, when the partition of China reached one peak after the British occupation of Wei-Hai-Wei, illustrates well his touch:

> Ye Jingoes shout your very best,
>   Ye grumblers cease to cry;
> The East is conquered by the West,
>   We've taken Wei-Hai-Wei.
>
> We none of us know where it is,
>   But that's no reason why
> We should not feel heroic zeal
>   At taking Wei-Hai-Wei.
>
> George Curzon once has seen the spot,
>   And George is pretty spry,
> And George declared it must be got –
>   We must have Wei-Hai-Wei.
>
> German and Russian fleets, Ah ha!
>   Who cares for you, small fry?
> We laugh at all your warlike feats,
>   We're safe in Wei-Hai-Wei.[47]

Perris and Lawson were leading figures in the late-Victorian peace movement. Other major peace activists included the trade union leader Thomas Burt, Gavin Brown Clark, William Randal Cremer – who won the Nobel Peace Prize in 1903 – Hodgson Pratt, and Henry Richard.[48] As Paul Laity has summarised, the late-Victorian peace movement 'protested against imperial wars and pressed for arbitration, democratic control of overseas policy and limited arms spending'.[49] The gap between the peace activists and anti-imperialists was thus not wide, and especially at the times of major imperial wars the peace campaigners often joined forces with anti-imperialists. During the Zulu War in 1879, for instance, the Peace Society's protest to the colonial secretary was signed by, among others, John Morley, Herbert Spencer, Frederic Harrison, Lord Farrer, Sir Arthur Hobhouse, and even Joseph Chamberlain, whose 'jingo' days were yet to come.[50]

The first Boer War generated a Transvaal Independence Committee which was formed independently of peace associations in January 1881 and had the radical Scot Dr Gavin Brown Clark as its principal spokesman.[51] Lawson was also active in these anti-Transvaal War activities, declaring that 'If self-defence were right in war, then the Boers were right and we were wrong, for we were attacking them, and they were defending themselves.'[52] Leonard Courtney was another prominent MP to take a leading part in these so-called pro-Boer activities from the late 1870s and early 1880s onwards.[53]

Many activists belonged to the International Arbitration and Peace Association or the International Arbitration League. Both organisations had their own published organs: the first published *Concord* and the latter *Arbitrator*. The International Arbitration and Peace Association was founded in 1880 by Lewis Appleton as a secular and pacific-ist alternative to the Christian pacifist Peace Society. It was a rather moderate and 'respectable' middle-class organisation, including Clark, Lawson, H. J. Wilson, and Sir William Wedderburn as its members. Perris, as the editor of *Concord*, was the dominating figure in the Association in the late 1890s. Perris was also closely involved in the progressive Rainbow Circle and other ethical societies, thus knowing well eminent figures like William Clarke, G. P. Gooch, Ramsay MacDonald, John M. Robertson, Leonard T. Hobhouse and J. A. Hobson, many of whom also were active members in the Association. The International Arbitration League, on the other hand, was more radical and had more Lib–Lab members. It was first formed as the Workmen's Peace Association in 1870 by the carpenter William Randal Cremer. Due to its active and loud opposition to the Boer War at the end of the century, many of its members left the League and its meetings began to be poorly attended – which was not the case in the more middle-class Association.[54]

The second South African War gave rise to many new organisations, among which the South Africa Conciliation Committee was the leading one. Leonard Courtney was the Committee's president and Frederic Harrison and Lord Hobhouse were active members. Like the International Arbitration and Peace Association, the South Africa Conciliation Committee was a respectable and fairly moderate organisation with a large number of supporters, including the old and ill Herbert

Spencer.[55] In its manifesto the Committee deplored the 'expenditure of blood and money' in South Africa which brought 'misery to our Colonies at the Cape and grave peril to the Empire'. The Committee was formed to disseminate 'accurate information on the whole dispute' and to advance, 'as soon as a proper opportunity arises', 'some peaceable settlement of the great conflict between this country and the Boer Republics'.[56] The Committee looked forward to a time when, after the war, the British and the Dutch would govern together the natives in South Africa at least as justly as was done in British India. With this end in mind they demanded the chartered British South Africa Company to be deprived of its powers, 'just as we put an end to the East India Company in 1857'.[57] Frederic Harrison, though actively supporting the Committee, must have found it very tame: only few months earlier, in October 1899, he had grinningly written 'The rejected Draft of a Queen's Speech' which 'anticipated a scheme that Victoria would be one day proclaimed "Empress of Africa" as well as of India'.[58]

Those who found the South Africa Conciliation Committee too moderate – like Sir Wilfrid Lawson – found their place in W. T. Stead's extreme Stop-the-War Committee.[59] Stead, perhaps the best-known journalist of his time, might equally have been thought of as a radical imperialist: in the 1880s he was the leading exponent in the campaigns for strengthening the navy and sending General Gordon to the Sudan, and he was also a close friend and admirer of Cecil Rhodes.[60] The arms race of the 1890s worried Stead mainly because it seemed to jeopardise Britain's naval superiority, and it was thus logical to him to continue his 'navy scare' campaign of the 1880s with a 'peace crusade' a decade later. He was a strong supporter of the Hague Peace Conference and became a fierce opponent of the Boer War – for which he blamed Chamberlain and in which, unlike the majority of critics, he saw Rhodes as a victim. Stead's Committee's only aim was 'simply' to stop the war.[61]

The radical ideology of Stead's Committee attracted W. S. Blunt, too, although he was seemingly confused about the various anti-war bodies. In January 1900 Blunt wrote in his diary that he had written to Leonard Courtney, sending £50, to say he wanted to join the Stop-the-War Committee. This fierce anti-imperialist still added: 'This though with some qualms of conscience, for, if the war goes on another six months, it really may smash up the British Empire.' Blunt noted that while the British were fighting in South Africa, the Russians were 'advancing on India, where a huge famine is going on', and there were signs of change in Egypt as well.[62] Had Blunt fully realised how moderate Courtney's organisation was and that the more extreme organisation was in fact led by Stead he might have saved his money, for Blunt was always suspicious of Stead and his motives. Even after Stead perished in the Titanic in 1912, Blunt wrote in his diary:

> I cannot say I ever liked or respected Stead, he was too much of a *charlatan*. It is impossible that a man who has made himself the agent of the Russian autocracy, who has intrigued for the restoration of the ex-Khedive Ismaïl, and who has been named by Cecil Rhodes executor of his will, all the whole calling himself a friend of liberty, can have been quite honest. The Irish always refused to trust him, and they were right.[63]

In February 1900 yet another new organisation saw daylight, called The League of Liberals against Aggression and Militarism. This reputable League consisted mainly of Liberal 'pro-Boers'. The inaugural meeting declared that the League aimed for 'a clear lead to the Liberal party' on the lines of Cobden, Bright, and Gladstone and was against imperialism and increased state expenditure.[64] Liberal imperialists, on their part, responded with a counter-organisation, the Imperial Liberal Council, a few months later.[65]

The various anti-war or anti-military movements at the time of the Boer War were also overlapping to a great extent. Many were members in many organisations. Perris was in charge of press affairs for the Stop-the-War Committee, and other representatives of the International Arbitration and Peace Association's executive helped to form the Transvaal Committee in 1899. Perris was also involved in the League of Liberals Against Aggression and Militarism and sat in its committee along with J. L. Hammond, J. A. Hobson, F. W. Hirst, Fred Maddison, and H. N. Brailsford.[66]

William Clarke, who participated in the anti-war activities mainly by writing for the *Concord*,[67] saw the situation as desolate.

'Was ever greater satire known in history', he asked, 'than the aspirations and actual formal deeds of the Hague Conference, followed instantly by two needless and unjust wars in the Philippines and South Africa, waged by the very two nations which were foremost in urging methods of conciliation and arbitration at the Conference?' And like this was not enough, they had 'the Chinese expedition of the Allied Powers, in which the Western soldiers proved themselves quite the equals of the Chinese in ruthless barbarism, and more than their equals in wholesale robbery'. When the enormous increases of 'the already immense armaments of Europe' were added to the picture, nothing could be said to characterise the beginning century more than 'the recrudescence of brute force'. Clarke concluded: 'The prophet of the twentieth century is Friedrich Nietzsche, with his brutal "over-man" responsible to none, with no law but his pride and egoistic will. It is not a pleasant outlook for the friends of humanity and democracy.'[68]

CHAPTER 3

INDIA AND THE DRAIN THEORY

I admit at once that if it could be shown that India has retrograded in material prosperity under our rule we stand self-condemned, and we ought no longer to be trusted with the control of the country.[1]

– Lord George Hamilton, Secretary of State for India

India is not an organic part of our empire, but a foreign body, upon which we form a parasitic growth.[2]

– John Atkinson Hobson in 1897

This study has thus far concentrated on the critical debate on economy from the point of view of imperial expansion in the last two decades of the nineteenth century. This approach has minimised the existence of British India, the area which brought imperialism into the British empire in the first place by transforming it from the settler empire of 'Greater Britain' to an autocratic military empire. As one critic put it: 'The possession of India is the only argument ever used to enforce the claims of an Imperial policy for England. It was in India that the Queen was made to make herself Empress.'[3] Frederic Harrison pointed out how 'England is not herself, whilst she is forced thus to keep anxious and suspicious watch across Africa and Asia over her huge and precarious prize', British India. This watch was carried out only 'at the sacrifice of all that is truly great in England', since everything was subjected to the general rule 'Come what may, the empire must be saved'. This, according to Harrison, amounted to 'a system of slavery' where England was the slave.[4]

At the same time, however, the British involvement in Indian affairs had come to the point that very few saw it possible for the British to withdraw immediately. No matter how much they were against British imperialism in India they did not advocate that British troops should leave the subcontinent tomorrow. Since the British had caused damage there, they had to repair the damage before leaving, the argument ran. Harrison expressed the thoughts of many when he said:

> We have no crude project for abandoning the empire to-morrow like a leaky ship, or handing it over to confusion or chance, as a prey to new conquerors. ... We do not pretend that the blind conquests of former ages can be resettled in a day, or that we ought to fling off the tremendous responsibilities with which ages of history have burdened us. But this we do say: the heterogeneous empire must be regarded as a passing responsibility, and not as a permanent greatness of our country. ... To increase its burdens and its limits should be a public crime.[5]

Harrison added crucially that 'in the meantime it must be governed in the sole interest of the countless millions who compose it ... until the time shall arrive when, part by part, it may be developed into normal and national life of its own'.[6] Thus, the central issue causing critical debate in regard to British India – apart from the question of how efficiently it was prepared for self-government, which will be discussed in more detail later – was the question in whose interests the subcontinent was ruled while still in British possession. The most obvious way to calculate this was the state of Indian economy, and the debate on whether it was improving or worsening was continuous. The main factors in this often heated discussion were the famines, public expenditure, cotton duties, opium, and, in particular, the alleged 'drain' from India to Britain which summarised it all.

James Geddes was the one who set the tone for late-Victorian criticism on British India. Geddes had joined the Indian Civil Service in his youth and later become committed to positivism. Had he not died suddenly and prematurely in 1880 he would have without doubt been the most relentless among the critics; even as it was, his writings strongly influenced the later writings of H. M. Hyndman, Dadabhai Naoroji, and William Digby. He anticipated the drain theory as early as 1871 when declaring that 'like Ireland in the past, India is being impoverished by the rule of absentees and aliens.'[7] Geddes argued that Britain's moral image as a world power had weakened because of its unjust position in India. Moreover, he denied the existence of any real economic gain since British rule drained wealth away from the English at large as well as the Indians for the sole benefit of 'idle rentiers'. He predicted that British rule would end up in bankruptcy which would then fall the financial burden on the working class, causing eventually a social revolution in England.[8] Geddes testified that

> India costs in government more than it yields in revenue. At all times the English Exchequer in India has been in deficit. At no time has it defrayed the full charges of a single year out of a single year's regularly recurring revenue. The shortcoming is discharged by borrowing. The interest on old loans is paid out of new borrowings, or out of forestalments of coming revenue.[9]

The severe famines in the 1870s and late 1890s gave strength to Geddes' arguments and thus cast a long shadow over British rule. Many argued that the famines were due to British failings, the 'crushing weight' of its administration, and extensive public and military expenditure. The fact that both famine periods occurred at the times of expensive military crises in the north-western border – the Afghan War in the 1870s and the Chitral and Tirah campaigns in the 1890s – did not go unnoticed. William Digby, one of the fiercest critics, insisted, with plenty of statistics, that people in India were 'more subject to famine now than they were one hundred years ago'.[10] Moreover, he stated that native Indian administration had functioned much better in famine times compared to the British one, since they had important local experience and more suitable and flexible administration. He even argued that famines were more frequent in British provinces than in Indian states, aiming to convince his audience that India was overall much better off without British rule.[11]

Digby, a radical political organiser from Cambridgeshire, was quite a convincing critic of British famine administration, of which he gained first-hand experience in southern India in 1877–9. He had settled in Madras as the editor of an influential daily paper, *Madras Times*, in 1877, and before that he had lived six years in Colombo as the sub-editor of the *Ceylon Observer*. The horrors of famine he witnessed led Digby to question the rationale of British rule in India. He wrote his first major book on the famine campaign and used the *Madras Times* extensively, as well as *The Times* of London, to stir both the bureaucracy and the British public. As a result the Indian government began to organise public works and food shipments to southern India, and a substantial relief fund was launched in London.[12] After the famine campaign Digby, who had lost his wife in India, returned to Britain and launched a major campaign for Indian reform. Among the first things he went to meet John Bright, whose diary tells that they had 'much conversation on India' and that Bright considered Digby an 'intelligent and pleasant man'.[13] Digby became an active leader-figure in the Indian campaign, publishing ruthless statistics on the impoverishment of India under British rule until the early twentieth century.[14]

Critics suggested that the famine of 1877 was mainly due to too high land assessments which formed the basis for land taxation.[15] Anglo-Indian officials, however, defended the assessments 'on account of native laziness'. Strict taxation of land was the best way to make Indians work at all, the officials insisted. Sir Richard Temple, who administered the famine in South India rigorously in 1877 and became governor of Bombay the same year, assured the Famine Commission in 1880 that 'the obligation to pay has a stimulating effect on the apathetic native character'.[16] Temple's opinion was opposed by James Caird, member of the Commission but strongly supported by Lord Lytton and Sir John Strachey, the viceroy and the finance member of viceroy's council at the time of the famine.[17] Lord Northbrook, a previous viceroy, confided privately to the new viceroy, Lord Ripon, that he had always had his 'suspicions that the Land Revenue has been over-assessed, and always treated with great suspicion the opinion of Sir John Strachey, who was all for screwing up the land revenue'.[18] However, despite Caird's dissenting opinion, the Famine Commission of 1880 came to the conclusion that the land assessments were not connected to the famine.[19]

Nevertheless, the dreadful famine had revealed the appalling state of Indian finances and thus stirred the already loud opposition to the second Afghan War. Sir Arthur Hobhouse, who was the legal member of the viceroy's council in India in 1872–7, complained how the situation of famine and war was a clear example of how 'the ordinary moral law' was excluded from national policy. The British had been 'led by the excitement of a struggle for empire with Russia into wasting the resources of India, forgetting that our duty and our interest in India are confined to the good government of that country'. He was, however, partly pleased that the problems finally came into daylight and the 'question of Imperial policy' was 'fairly before the British nation' as well as the fact that India, which had always been 'a real burden' to Britain, had 'become so visible a burden as to require help from the British exchequer'. Hobhouse also pointed out that mere power was not enough for British 'subjugation' of Afghanistan; it required plenty of money. This money, he emphasised, could not be drawn from the resources of India but had to be paid by Britain, with the result that 'we shall be poorer, we shall be weaker, we shall be more degraded, as those are who have set up a false ideal of national greatness'.[20]

Frederic Harrison, W. S. Blunt, and John Morley, who all detested the British conduct in Afghanistan, were also close friends of the viceroy, Lord Lytton, who was the main target of criticism. These relationships were somewhat strained because of the differences, but in the end even Blunt managed to maintain cordial relations with Lytton. When Lytton returned to Britain in 1880, Blunt confided in his diary that the whole episode gave him 'a feeling of sorrow'. Yet he was reluctant to personify the issue by joining those 'who cry out on Lytton's policy' since, Blunt rather inconsistently stated, 'this policy was a necessary one & its execution was bold & successful'.[21]

Blunt was a staunch Tory at the time which, apart from the friendship with Lytton, may explain at least part of his inconsistency. Indeed, using poor India's revenues for a war was an easy target at the election campaign in 1880. William Gladstone led the way by blaming the government for increasing Indian taxation in the name of famine and then spending all the money on 'the ruinous, unjust destructive war in Afghanistan' instead.[22] Henry Labouchere used even stronger expressions in his campaign when insisting that the war should be paid by British taxpayers instead of the Indians who were not represented in parliament in any way.[23]

After the election, however, Labouchere was content with the government's decision to leave the costs generated by the Afghan War to be paid by the Indians as well as those generated by the employment of Indian troops in Egypt in 1882.[24] India faced enormous military expenditure within its own subcontinent already, but in addition to this India *de facto* ended up supporting a military reserve for the entire British empire. Lord Ripon, the viceroy, opposed vehemently the parliament's decision to make India pay the costs of the Egyptian campaign,[25] but the secretary of state for India, Lord Kimberley, pointed out the ultimate Indian responsibility of the occupation by answering to the viceroy: 'But for India, I feel certain that no Egyptian expedition would ever have taken place'.[26]

The officers and soldiers of the Indian Army as well as the civil servants were all paid by the Indian exchequer. Thus, unlike any other British possession, India was responsible for all of its administrative costs itself.[27] As B. R. Tomlinson has put it, India was in the late-Victorian era 'the largest purchaser of British exports, a major employer of British civil servants at high salaries', and 'the provider of half of the Empire's military might, all paid for from local revenues'.[28] In these circumstances it was not surprising that something like the drain theory – arguing that there was a constant drain of wealth from India to Britain – would develop. William Digby, Dadabhai Naoroji, and H. M. Hyndman were its most committed advocates in Britain.

Hyndman, in particular, had drawn his ideas from Geddes, as can be seen in his rather pessimistic writings on the finances of British India in the late 1870s.[29] Naoroji, too, had very likely read Geddes while developing the drain theory, first published in London in 1878. Naoroji argued that a large proportion of the yearly revenue that was raised in India was carried away to England, which resulted in continuous diminishing of the Indian national capital. He compared the situation to that of medieval England, which, as a tributary to the Pope, had suffered from 'a steady drain of money from every realm'.[30]

According to the drain theorists the drain's cause was the existing 'un-British' rule. The public expenditure on the day-to-day bureaucracy and basic infrastructure was immense, and due to the regressive system of taxation the main burden fell on the rural poor, causing 'internal drain'. The most important factor behind the 'external drain', Naoroji and Digby argued, was the fact that the huge Indian empire was administered by Britons, whose salaries and pensions were paid by Indian taxpayers but who then retired to spend their earnings in Britain. Thus, the cure for ending the drain was to establish benign British rule instead: better, fairer, and Indianised government with more moderate taxation and less obstacles for capital accumulation would show the way to the prosperity of India. It was pointed out that employing more Indians in the Indian government would be beneficial in two ways: Indians received notably smaller salaries than the highly paid British, and the money would stay in India.[31]

William Digby made it his special project to challenge the widely held view 'that India had no cause of complaint against Great Britain, as she was not made to contribute anything to this country'. In a pamphlet in 1881 Digby declared that England was 'draining India, not simply of its surplus, but actually of its very life-blood'.[32] As an example of this unequal partnership he listed seven occasions when India had been made to pay for English wars, when Britain had borrowed Indian troops for its imperial undertakings and India paid. In contrast, when reinforcements had been sent from Britain to India in the 1840s and 1857, India had been made to pay 'every fraction of the pay of the troops from the moment they left England'.[33]

Two years after Digby's pamphlet John Seymour Keay, who had made a successful career as a banker in India and returned to Britain in 1882, published the first of his three articles supporting the drain theory.[34] Following Digby, he blamed Britain for overtaxing the Indian people in order to make them pay for British wars. This he attributed to British greed for taking advantage of its stronger position. As

Sir Charles Trevelyan had put it ten years earlier: 'We charge Canada, Australia, the Cape of Good Hope, and the whole round of the British Colonies, nothing; why should we charge India anything? The only real difference is that Canada or Australia would not hear of it; whereas *India is at our mercy, and we can charge her what we like*.'[35]

Like Digby, Keay argued that this resulted in increasing poverty in India and that 'speedy collapse' would occur unless the expenses of the Indian government were significantly reduced.[36] Simultaneously Sir William Wedderburn and Florence Nightingale also took up the Indian cause. Both gave lectures on Indian village economy and together they wrote an article supporting Keay's assertions.[37] Furthermore, Blunt made an extensive tour in India in 1883–4 and subsequently wrote several articles for the *Fortnightly Review*, which were republished as a book in 1885. Blunt, too, testified 'the overwhelming poverty of the poor', 'the ever-increasing burden of taxation', and 'the ever-increasing selfishness of those charged with the expenditure'.[38] Moreover, Blunt felt quite certain that the official statistician Sir William Wilson Hunter's figures in his official handbook about India were 'enormously wrong' in regard to the burden of taxation. According to Blunt's calculations the only lightly taxed land was found in Bengal, which, consequently, was 'nearly the only' prosperous part of India.[39] Elsewhere in British India Blunt found 'hardly a village' which was 'not deeply, hopelessly in debt'. 'It is certain that all native opinion is against us, and that our present system is bringing India very near to ruin', Blunt warned.[40]

When the Liberal MP Samuel Smith visited India in 1885–6 he prepared for his task by reading Digby's recent book *India for the Indians – and for England* and Keay's articles.[41] He later wrote that he 'was staggered at the information' he got. On his voyage home Smith wrote out his conclusions, which were published as two articles in the *Contemporary Review* and soon also as a pamphlet.[42] In contrast to the general opinion that India was 'enormously indebted to British rule' and poverty was 'giving place to plenty', Smith testified that what he found in India was 'great dissatisfaction, and a widespread belief that India is getting poorer and less happy'.[43]

Sir Mountstuart Elphinstone Grant Duff, a recent governor of Madras, responded by ridiculing Smith's arguments and insisting that

India was getting more prosperous.[44] Smith urged that some Indian should answer Grant Duff's articles instead of him.[45] Naoroji then took the task and prepared thorough counter-arguments, published in 1887. He stated that the present material condition of India was 'the natural result of the non-fulfilment of the great pledges' of 1833 and 1858, which had promised to make the Indians equal to the British. He then illustrated with statistics that India was getting poorer, due to the drain which prevented India from acquiring any capital of its own.[46] These accusations, that Britain had impoverished India and done it even in direct contravention of its own pledges, sensitised the Indian government. Especially provincial governments became eager 'to assure both the world and themselves that India was not poor or disorderly'. Official reactions were particularly strong in South India.[47] Naoroji was pleased with the result: 'Friends now begin to ask me after reading my papers and those of Sir Grant Duff what I wanted, and that I should lay down some practical proposals. This, then, is a stage gained.'[48]

During the 1880s the land assessments continued to rise further. An Indian newspaper wrote ironically in 1888: 'There are, however, some things which are yet to be taxed, so that the triumph of the English may be complete. Among such things may be mentioned the skin of the Indian people and their atmosphere.'[49] Some Anglo-Indian officials, too, criticised the British Indian policies, most notably Wedderburn and Allan O. Hume. Sir C. Aitchison, the lieutenant-governor of Punjab, also saw the crushing effects of increasing land taxation first-hand but was unable to resist the Indian government in its revenue demands.[50] After he retired back to Britain he criticised the policies of the 'Strachey-school' severely in his biography of a former viceroy and his hero, Lord Lawrence.[51]

The Indian cotton duties issue made the already bad situation worse. It was no co-incidence that the determined battle to abolish the cotton duties had occurred simultaneously with the Afghan War. Amidst all the criticism Lord Salisbury thought that pleasing the Lancashire lobby in the cotton question was a good chance 'to detach the cotton lobby from the anti-imperialist front, drawing it into a conservative alliance committed to retention of the Indian empire', as Clive Dewey has put it. His 'most trusted councillor', Sir Henry Maine, formulated his views as follows:

> Amid all these disadvantages, what are the motives for preserving the connection? National pride in an empire once acquired is a strong one; so also, let us hope, is the sense of great benefits conferred by the British dominion on a huge portion of the human race. But after all, the one solid, tangible, material interest which Great Britain has in India is its interest in Indian trade. The importance of that trade has greatly increased. As market after market is blocked or closed by the reviving protectionism of the world, the Indian market becomes increasingly valuable. ... It is impossible to say what might happen if, in a great emergency, the English people formed, upon careful consideration, the opinion that they had no material interests of any kind in India.[52]

Subsequent secretaries of state for India, like Lord George Hamilton, believed equally in the policy of binding England and India together through commercial links.[53] This, indeed, was successful, to the extent that the Anglo-Indian cotton trade remained vital for Britain's balance of payments in foreign trade until the First World War – with the result that, in Dewey's words, 'no one could argue that the Indian connection was unprofitable to England: Manchester-style anti-imperialism was dead'. The other result was, however, that the policy of favouring Lancashire alienated educated Indian nationalists from British rule.[54]

Ever since the Indian import duties for cotton were abolished in 1882 under pressure from Manchester, the Indian nationalists advocated their re-imposition. The principle of free trade cost an important source of revenue for the Indian government and forced the undeveloped Indian industries into a premature competition with the highly developed British industries.[55] Digby criticised the decision severely: in his opinion it stimulated the destruction of Indian industries which led to the 'British monopolisation' of Indian trade and subsequently increased the drain.[56] Blunt concurred,[57] but most Liberal friends of

India did not. They – like Wedderburn, the Cobden Club's India-expert – favoured the abolition of the cotton duties since it would enhance the supply of Indian cotton for British industry as raw material and enlarge the Indian market for British manufactured goods. It was also because of this favoured position of India as a producer of raw materials for British industry that the Indian government guaranteed railway construction and undertook numerous public works, even the experimental cultivation of cotton. This policy, then, increased Indian public expenditure on the one hand, while on the other it made the Indian economy appear as an ideal complement to Britain's economy in the eyes of the Lancashire cotton interests.[58]

There were, however, notable Liberals who considered this maladministration. The ardent free-trader and economist Henry Fawcett stressed continuously that India's financial situation required the application of different rules, not those of free trade. Fawcett had been a staunch advocate of Indian interests in parliament since 1865, and he campaigned hard for the retention of the Indian cotton duties.[59] As Lawrence Goldman has well put it: 'Fawcett was no anti-imperialist ... but he was passionately concerned that British rule in India should be competent, cheap and fair to the native population.'[60] Fawcett's main reason for the defence of the Indian duties was in fact non-economic, for he did not want Indians to think that they were unfairly treated in order to please English manufacturers.

John Bright was another prominent politician who considered India's interest more important than British economic advantage. He continuously emphasised that India was not committed to British control 'to be held as a field for English ambition and for English greed',[61] and that it was vital to convince Indians that they were not governed 'for mere selfish objects'.[62] 'Our right to India and the rule of it at present must depend upon the services which we render to the millions of her people', Bright declared; 'It cannot depend permanently on our imports from India of rice, jute, tea, cotton, and wheat, or exports of calico from the mills of Lancashire.'[63]

The experiment on free trade in India was not successful, but the reasons for its failure had more to do with financial reality than moral criticism. When Lord Ripon repealed the duties he believed that frontier wars had been left behind; but this was far from the truth. A few years later Britain faced yet another serious crisis in the north-western border, in Penjdeh, coming close to war with Russia, and the Indian borders were simultaneously expanded to include Burma in the northeast, thus annoying France. These military operations led to the re-imposition of income tax in 1886 which was much opposed in India. The continuously falling price of the Indian silver rupee in relation to the gold-based sterling added to the problems, since it increased the amount payable in England as interests and pensions – the 'home charges' – enormously.[64] Soon the detested salt tax, successfully abolished by Ripon in 1882, was also re-enforced, and by the early 1890s one after another viceroy kept asking the British government to re-institute the cotton tariffs, too.[65] The British parliament became convinced that, due to the disastrous state of Indian finances, the cotton duties were important for fiscal reasons, and despite vigorous opposition from Manchester the duties were re-imposed in 1894, stressing in particular that India had to be ruled according to the interests of India and not Britain.[66] Nevertheless, Lancashire was still able to put considerable pressure on the government in regard to Indian tariffs – Clive Dewey has even used the word *dictate* – until the end of the First World War.[67]

It was equally for fiscal reasons that the widely disapproved opium trade was allowed to continue until 1910. The revenue from the opium trade between India and China formed the second largest source for the Indian government after the land revenue.[68] Indian nationalists defended the trade together with Anglo-Indian officials on the ground that if the opium trade were ended other financial sources had to be found, which would most probably mean new heavy taxes. Anti-imperialists, however, insisted that the money gained from the opium trade could easily be saved if only the political will were found. Richard Congreve, who saw that 'the evils of the opium trade' degraded Britain's reputation in the East and jeopardised Britain's relations with China,[69] pointed out that the simplest way to end it was to transfer the 'home charges' 'to English shoulders', as Congreve's close friend James Geddes had 'boldly advocated' at the meeting of the Famine Commission in 1879.[70] In this way 'the Salt Tax should be utterly extinguished, and that crime against Humanity, the opium transactions of Government, should be wound up', Geddes had explained.[71] Congreve noted that 'the sacrifice is a heavy one – so was that for the slave owners. But it is even more imperatively demanded than that was.' Britain should 'offer to the Indian Government full compensation for the sacrifice of revenue which a new policy would necessitate', and in justice the burden should fall 'on that portion of the taxpayers of England which has derived advantage from our Indian possessions', i.e. 'the upper and middle classes'.[72]

Another way to save the money gained from the opium trade was, of course, to reduce public expenditure. Indeed, the critics argued that the costly bureaucracy and lavish projects might have been well reduced to the point that not only the opium revenue but also the land tax could have been reviewed. Blunt's opinion was that there was not 'much difference between making the starving Hindoos pay for a cathedral at Calcutta and taxing Bulgarians for a palace on the Bosphorus'.[73] He wrote to a friend from India in the late 1870s:

The *natives*, as they call them, are a race of slaves, frightened, unhappy, and terribly thin. ... I have been studying the mysteries of Indian finance under the 'best masters', Government secretaries, commissioners, and the rest, and have come to the conclusion that if we go on *developing* the country at the present rate the inhabitants will have, sooner or later, to resort to cannibalism, for there will be nothing but each other left to eat. I do not clearly understand why we English take their money from these starving Hindoos to make railroads for them which they don't want, and turnpike roads and jails and lunatic asylums and memorial buildings to Sir Bartle Frere, and why we insist upon their feeding out of their wretched handfuls of rice immense armies of policemen and magistrates and engineers. They want none of these things, and they want their rice very badly, as anybody can see by looking at their ribs. As to the debt they have been saddled with, I think it would be honester to repudiate it, at least as a Debt on *India*. I never could see the moral obligation governments acknowledge of taxing people for the debts they, and not the people, have incurred.[74]

Blunt had been mainly instructed in India by the finance member of the viceroy's council, Sir John Strachey, who was a leading exponent of the extension of the public works and the government's duties. In Strachey's view it was 'a most imperative duty of the governors to the governed' to provide 'an intelligent extension of the great public works which the country requires'.[75] Strachey's views collided sharply with those of Digby and Naoroji, and he was one of the severest critics of their drain theory.

There was, however, one aspect which all three were able to agree to some extent: the heavy burden of the guaranteed railway system. The Indian railways were financed by British private capital with a guaranteed five per cent return. The actual earnings rarely came to this, and the Indian government had to pay the difference. Thus, although India suffered from paucity of capital, the investments for railways were not welcomed by the drain theorists, who only saw further drain and increased indebtedness in the guaranteed returns. Digby was a determined opponent of Indian railways as waste of public money,[76] in which he, again, followed in the footsteps of James Geddes.[77]

Strachey, on his part, argued that – while the benefits of the railway policy had been great to India – the guaranteed returns had 'placed a burden on the home financial administration of India that could hardly have been anticipated... its gravity increases year by year, and the importance of removing or alleviating this constantly growing burden cannot be exaggerated.'[78] Davis and Huttenback have put similar emphasis on the railway expenditure: they have calculated that expenditures in British India were in fact lower than those of the Indian princely states if the railways were excluded.[79] In other words, to put it crudely, what made British rule expensive, in their calculations too, was the system of guaranteed returns for railway investments.

Along with India's financial decline, the tone of the debate grew harsher. William Digby put his message noticeably more bluntly in his open letter to MPs 'on the dark side of British rule in India: a side so dark as to make it doubtful if British rule has been and is a blessing to the masses of India' in 1891.[80] The editor of *Greater Britain* magazine described Digby's letter as 'one of the most terrible indictments ever probably written of a governing race'.[81] Digby explicitly blamed British Indian policy for selfishness: Britain prospered at the expense of India. He felt 'compelled to assert, on the strength of official statistics alone, that England, without meaning to do so, by want of foresight and through thinking mainly of her home industries and the interests of her own sons before those of her distant subjects' had caused that the Indian nation was 'being stupefied, demoralised, and starved. Starved!'[82]

Before British rule the subcontinent had been self-contained and prosperous, Digby argued. Britain had first destroyed nearly all Indian industries and then began to drain the profits made in India to Britain. Moreover, according to Digby, the increasing import trade of India was not a sign of native prosperity, as 'the other side' argued: 'only a mere fraction' of the trade profits went to Indian people, since European capital and European firms commanded the trade. Even the trade, then, merely increased the drain. The editor of *Greater Britain* observed: 'Yet, ironically observes Mr. Digby, so righteous and so considerate are we in our dealings with a helpless community, so high is our notion of honour, that we make India pay the cost of the India Office here (£220,000 a year), while the rich Colonies pay never a penny towards the maintenance of the Colonial Office.'[83]

Digby expanded the debate further in the following issue of *Greater Britain*, which contained Digby's article 'British Rule in India: Has It Been, Is It Now, a Good Rule for the Indian People?', subsequently also published as a pamphlet.[84] The pamphlet elaborated on the drain from India to Britain, the need for the Indianisation of the Indian civil service, the destruction of Indian industries, the British monopolisation of Indian trade, the maladministration, and the breaking of the pledges of 1833 and 1858. Apart from economic exploitation, Digby found serious moral, intellectual, and social consequences arising from the fact that all chief positions in India were filled by foreigners. 'How should we feel if all the best positions in every department in our national life were filled by, say, Russians?', he asked provocatively.[85] In regard to the poverty, he insisted that Indians were so weak that 'from fever alone there have been more additional and preventible deaths during eight years than there have been deaths from all the wars in every part of the world in the past hundred years'.[86]

By the 1890s the poverty of India had become a more commonly acknowledged fact, and the critics were not always radicals. A retired Madras civil servant, J. B. Pennington, wrote a weighty attack against the British salt monopoly in India, declaring it a far greater evil than either opium or alcohol. Pennington argued that the monopoly led the people to live permanently in the want of an abundant supply of salt, which in Indian climate led to the virulence of cholera and cattle disease. Thus, 'the case for the prosecution is simple enough', Pennington declared: the British destroyed 'untold millions of the wealth of the people' only in order to gain a rather small annual revenue.[87] Moreover, even an old arch-enemy of the Indian agitators, Sir Auckland Colvin, began to criticise the 'perilous growth of Indian state expenditure'.[88]

On the other hand, while the costliness of British rule was largely acknowledged, the impoverishment of India or the existence of drain as largely denied. General Sir George Chesney, like many other Anglo-Indian officials, argued that India was 'extraordinarily prosperous'.[89] He denied the existence of any drain since, after all, any wealth in India was according to him the creation of British rule at any rate: 'We found India poverty stricken as it always had been before, and as doubtless it would still be if we had not appeared on the scene'. Although there were indisputable money transfers from India to Britain, they were only natural. The majority of the transferred capital consisted of the payment of interest on the British capital invested in India to establish tea and jute industries and provide railways 'which have enriched India more than anything else, and brought about her present prosperous condition'. The salaries and pensions paid to English officials on the other hand were 'obviously a necessary condition of the maintenance of a stable government of any sort in India'.[90] Without British rule there would be no internal peace and prosperity in India, Chesney argued. He summarised his position on the matter:

All that can be said is that a good government by foreigners is more costly than would be an equally good government by the people of the country. So it would be cheaper for a man to cure himself when sick, if he knew how to do so, than to call in a physician. And the fact needs to be plainly stated that the capacity of the Indians to govern themselves has yet to be established.[91]

Nevertheless, despite the efforts to assure otherwise, the extent of the impoverishment was once more revealed when India was again struck by disastrous famine in 1896–7. The Lord Mayor of London and the Lancashire Indian Cotton Duties Committee were anxious to start private charity work already in December 1896, but the secretary of state for India, Lord Hamilton, when asked for a formal permission, requested them to wait. Many were angered at the India Office and attacked Hamilton in particular for his reluctance to appeal for charity; before the end of the year even the Queen had urged Hamilton to undertake a campaign on behalf of India.[92] William Digby, who had been the secretary of the Indian Famine Relief Committee twenty years earlier, offered his services to the constitution of a similar committee, also requesting Hamilton to start a charity fund.[93] The India Office declined Digby's offer, stating that, since the 1870s, major improvements had been made in the methods of organising government relief and no help was needed.[94]

The famine of 1896–7 had barely ended when the most devastating famine of the century began in 1899. Belief in the Indian government's official statistics was strongly shattered, since it had been argued that great famine would not occur more often than approximately once in twelve years.[95] In early 1900 the India Office was again pressed to seek financial assistance. Sir William Wedderburn and Samuel Smith kept the issue alive in the House of Commons by their repeated inquiries in February, March, and April about the help from the imperial treasury towards the Indian famine. Each time they were answered that the Indian government was able to meet the expenditure and there was no need for British help.[96] Hamilton wrote to the viceroy, Lord Curzon, that he opposed the idea of British official assistance mainly in principle, since it would destroy the independence of the Indian exchequer and lead to further British parliamentary interference with Indian affairs.[97] Curzon, however, considered it odd that the British government was not willing to help India while foreign governments were contributing to the Indian Famine Relief Fund.[98]

The press, too, was unhappy about the situation and quickly pointed out how the government was not willing to give a penny to India at the time of distress but was simultaneously spending fortunes for expeditions in China and war in South Africa. Moreover, many found it confusing that the parliament could vote a grant for Tirah campaign in the Indian north-western border, but when it came to famine the same procedure was pronounced impossible. Hamilton, however, kept insisting that Indian finance should be kept separate from the British,[99] and during the Indian budget debate in the Commons in July 1900 a motion for a grant of £5 million to India towards the famine expenditure was defeated by 112 against 65 votes. Britain was in the middle of the Boer War and suffering from a budgetary deficit of its own.[100] The refusal to assist famine-stricken India was, nevertheless, criticised by the press, which rather unanimously thought the decision would weaken the ties between Britain and India.[101] Furthermore, it was quite a tactical blunder on Hamilton's part that while he refused to appeal for charity in England and rejected Curzon's request for an imperial grant, he at the same time requested Curzon to launch an official campaign for a war fund in India due to the imperial wars in China and South Africa.[102]

The situation at the turn of the century made anti-imperialists desperate. J. L. Hammond wrote in 1900: 'If India is to be treated as an end-in-herself, and not merely as a means to the aggrandisement or the enrichment of England, we have little to hope for from the hysterical, unintelligent, bombastic tumult of speech and counsel which calls itself Imperialism.'[103] Blunt commented in his diary that 'the British Empire, playing double or quits again and again, should go entirely bankrupt. It is the greatest curse the world has ever suffered & it is time it should cease to be. The famine in India is a new judgment of God upon it, &, just as in old times, the strength of the punishment falls upon the innocent.'[104] In the summer of 1900 Blunt spent several days 'writing a letter to *The Times* about the Indian Famine' but then 'decided after all to let it alone'. He thought it was 'of course a monstrous thing that the Home Government should refuse to subscribe a penny'. He was convinced that now, at least, Britain's 'shameless self-ishness' was 'ear-marked for ever', when Britain had first 'upset the old economical system of India' thus causing famines, and then refused to help India financially.[105]

By this time Romesh Chunder Dutt, a Bengali publicist and former Indian civil servant, had also travelled to England to advocate the drain theory alongside Digby and Naoroji.[106] In his book on Indian famines Dutt listed the traditional famine remedies: the moderation of the land tax, the advancement of irrigation works, and the reduction of public expenditure and the annual drain from India by making England share the cost of the Indian army and 'giving effect to Queen Victoria's Royal Proclamation of 1858, and admitting the people of India to all offices in India without distinction of race or creed'.[107] Dutt stressed that his criticism was not directed at British rule as such, but at its *nature*. He wrote:

> Englishmen have not done worse, but have done better, than any other nation could have done in India under any form of absolute rule. The British administrators of India are not incompetent men, they are competent and able administrators, but they have failed because a system of absolute rule *must fail* to secure the interests of the people. It is not in human nature for one set of people to work for the interests of another, and without some sort of representation the people of India can only be held, in the words of John Stuart Mill, as 'a human cattle farm', worked for the benefit of England. Even as a farm India has not prospered; the 'human cattle' are dying, and England's trade with a famine-stricken nation is declining![108]

Digby and Naoroji, too, published in 1901 the final results of their theses which they had been developing for over twenty years.[109] In *Poverty and Un-British Rule in India* Naoroji put the finishing touches on the drain theory. Digby's satirically entitled *'Prosperous' British India: A Revelation from Official Records* was his most significant indictment of the financial and economic impacts of British rule. Perhaps the most notable argument in Digby's book was his notion of the nature of the drain in different periods. For this purpose he divided British rule in India into three phases of conquest. The first phase was 'conquest by trade', covering the period of 1700–83. At that time the British East India Company 'exploited India undisguisedly' – 'naked and not ashamed'. The second phase, from 1783 to 1833, was a period of 'conquest by deliberate subjugation: India for England first and last'. The last phase, labelled as 'conquest by "Pousta"' had begun in 1833. By the expression Digby meant the contemporary 'show of fair dealing accompanied with the maintenance, rigidly and uncompromisingly, of Indian national inferiority'.[110] The drain had thus always been there; it had only become more disguised as time progressed. The main difference between the second and the third phases was that earlier in the nineteenth century the British had at least been more honest in their dealings with India, Digby argued. He pointed out that the way James Mill had argued in favour of keeping 'the Indian people in a condition of subjection' in his *History of British India* appeared 'brutal' at the end of the century, when people had begun to practice 'smooth phrases and periphrastic disguises' instead. Digby maintained that 'the majority of Anglo-Indians and Britons, who take any interest in India, still think as James Mill thought and spoke. The difference is that Mill was frank; the others are disingenuous.' James Mill had 'said exactly what he meant', whereas Digby's contemporaries were 'masters in the use of language which deceives'.[111]

Digby also emphasised, referring to a book on 'the Indian tribute' published in Calcutta in 1884, how the drain from India to Britain was in fact 'arranged in such a way as to disguise its real purpose from everyone but an expert'.[112] He disparagingly quoted Sir George Campbell's comment that what was 'sometimes called the "tribute" paid to England' was 'not tribute, but it is paid for civil and military services, loans, railways, industrial investments, and all the rest; and the result is that a large part of the increased production is not retained by the Indian peasant.'[113] In Digby's opinion this was

the merest juggling with words, and is unworthy of so notable a public servant. Those 'civil and military services', were India governed with strict justice, could, all but a bare modicum, have been performed, have been well performed, at any time within the past fifty years, by the natives of the country. For, every pound sterling which has been paid to a foreigner for services which a native could have rendered is in itself an unjust charge and, in addition, is a gross injury to the country in an economic sense. Such payments and pensions constitute a tribute of the worst kind with a grievance attached.[114]

The drain theory more than anything else in the late-nineteenth-century debate on imperialism anticipated the tone of the debate in the following century. In regard to the economic dimension the mid-Victorian generation, like Robert Lowe, criticised British rule in India from the British point of view arguing that it was an extremely costly affair for *Britain*. In contrast, the late-Victorian generation, like William Digby, emphasised that British rule in India was a costly affair for *India* impoverishing it by draining Indian resources abroad.[115]

Modern research has quite conclusively stated that the extent of the supposed drain was far exaggerated. B. R. Tomlinson has pointed out that British rule did not in fact change the structures of Indian economy as radically as may seem to have been thought at the time; in addition, quite a number of Indians gained considerably from British rule.[116] Moreover, Neil Charlesworth has argued that the conditions for Indian material development were favourable throughout the latter half of the nineteenth century, and whatever drain there was must have been very small. In his opinion it would be more accurate to criticise British imperialism in India for the fact that it neglected Indian industrialisation by squandering opportunities for promoting it instead of focusing on the 'drain'. Thus, according to this view, rather than blaming British rule for being too destructive in regard to Indian industries it might be nearer the truth to deplore it for being too weak in modernising them.[117]

PART II

THE ETHICS OF IMPERIALISM AND ANTI-IMPERIALISM

CHAPTER 4

PATRIOTISM, 'LOYALTY', AND MORALITY

Oh! bravo, British Patriot!
   Your words were sound and true:
We have beaten wicked Kruger,
   And we've burned his Bible too.

God save and bless this noble land!
   Whatever we may do,
All foes we'll stubbornly withstand,
   And burn their Bibles too.

Then History's pen some day shall write
   What now we say and do,
How we with pride fought, stole, and lied,
   And burned our Bibles too![1]

                – Sir Wilfrid Lawson in 1900

Patriotism, morals, and two contrasting views on the desirable progress in society and the world in general were at the very heart of
the debate between imperialists and anti-imperialists. The latter followed the lines of argument laid down by Auguste Comte, the founder of positivism; H. T. Buckle, the author of *History of Civilization in
England* (1857); and W. E. H. Lecky, the author of *History of the Rise
and Influence of the Spirit of Rationalism in Europe* (1865). Like Herbert

Spencer, Comte, Buckle, and Lecky were certain of 'the ceaseless march of intellectual progress, which made the triumph of the pacific spirit over militarism a certainty', as Bernard Semmel has put it.[2] Lecky's work, in particular, stated that military achievements as the primary source of prestige belonged to medieval Europe, whereas the nineteenth century and the era of free trade saw the advance of civilisation and democratic spirit, and the decline of 'great heterogeneous empires' and the passion of war.[3] While this mid-Victorian optimism faded notably towards the end of the century, the basic understanding of the nature of progress – from militarism to industrialism – remained central in the anti-imperialist minds.

Imperialists, on the other hand, found their ideas of progress in the continuous expansion of the British empire. In their view this did not result in militarism as the anti-imperialists argued but in the strengthening of patriotism. Indeed, imperialists linked imperialism so closely with patriotism that they did not hesitate to label anti-imperialists 'unpatriotic' or 'un-English'. This rhetoric was at first directed at Liberals in general by the Conservatives, to which the Liberals responded by labelling Disraeli and his imperialism 'un-English' instead.[4] At the end of the century the debate on 'patriotism' was not confined to party politics anymore, and Liberal imperialists accused Liberal anti-imperialists as easily as Conservative or Unionist imperialists did. In the long run, however, as Hugh Cunningham has argued, even the Conservatives failed in their 'attempt to promote the empire as a focus of loyalty': 'If empire contributed so little towards patriotism, of what then did the latter consist?' Cunningham has asked.[5] One answer would be to follow the more traditional line of Englishness, which defined 'patriotism' as respect towards the English liberal virtues.

The contradiction in these two definitions of patriotism – one centring on the empire and the 'manly military values', and the other on the 'humane liberal values' – was more or less understood at the time. This is obvious when one looks at the amount of propaganda which was considered necessary to highlight the humanitarian and liberal elements in the imperial project; 'the white man's burden'. Many became convinced that British imperialism was justified and even desired, but many remained doubtful, asking like the *Pall Mall Gazette* did at the time of the Royal Jubilee in 1887: 'Does our Empire stand everywhere for peace, for liberty, for justice, and for right?'[6]

Herbert Spencer devoted in 1873 a whole chapter to 'the bias of patriotism' in *The Study of Sociology*.[7] He stressed that anyone who entertained the sentiment 'Our country, right or wrong' did not have 'that equilibrium of feeling required for dealing scientifically with social phenomena'. In Spencer's view these people were blinded by 'personal and national interests' and thus incapable of seeing how things really stood. In this way, Spencer pointed out, people with 'the bias of patriotism' could not be expected to reach any 'balanced judgments respecting the course of human affairs in general'.[8] He did not, however, oppose patriotism as such since he made it clear that some patriotic sentiment was needed for 'the very existence of a society': 'A nationality is made possible only by the feeling which the units have for the whole they form.' Spencer argued that 'patriotism is nationally that which egoism is individually'; and 'a duly-adjusted egoism' as well as 'a duly-adjusted patriotism' were 'essential'.[9] Too much patriotism would lead to 'national aggressiveness and national vanity'.[10] On the other hand, 'the bias of anti-patriotism' was almost equally serious, since, in Spencer's opinion, it led to 'the wish for a strong government, to secure the envied benefits ascribed to strong governments abroad'. Spencer saw this as a result of undervaluation of proper English cultural and political traditions and overestimation of anything 'foreign'.[11] True patriotism, for Spencer, meant respect for English liberal virtues, and this definition excluded both imperialism and socialism; the first because it contained too much patriotism, the latter because it was anti-patriotic.

Robert Lowe, too, highlighted the importance of morality in politics in 1878, stating that his objections 'to the doctrine of imperialism ... turned very much on its immorality'. Lowe denounced the whole imperialist 'principle, if anything so utterly unprincipled can deserve the name', which 'resolved itself to the oppression of the weak by the strong, and the triumph of power over justice'.[12] Annie Besant wrote in similar vein at about the same time:

It is said to be unpatriotic to blame one's country. But not so have I read the history of England's noblest patriots. Love of England does not mean approval and endorsement of the policy of some Oriental adventurer whom chance and personal ability and unscrupulousness have raised to power. Love of England means reverence for her past, work for her future; it means sympathy with all that is noble and great in her history, and endeavour to render her yet more noble, yet more great; it means triumph in her victories over oppression ... it means condemnation of her bullying, boasting, cruel imperialism since Lord Beaconsfield seduced her from her purity, and regretful remorseful turning back to the old paths of duty, of honor, and of faith.[13]

Likewise at the time of the British occupation of Egypt, Besant declared that 'the most sacred principles of Liberalism' were being 'trampled under foot': 'We have commenced a war to enforce a foreign yoke on a people striving to break it; to crush back into slavery a nation trying to shake it off; to stifle the aspirations of a race awaking into national life; to re-establish a despotism over a community endeavouring to create a system of self-government.'[14]

The events of 1882 were, indeed, a defining moment in the history of liberalism and imperialism, for until then anti-imperialism was linked with Gladstonianism and imperialism with Beaconsfieldism. While the main lines of disagreement after 1882 were within the Liberal party, it has to be remembered that one of the sternest anti-imperialists was the Tory poet, Wilfrid Scawen Blunt. A week before the bombardment of Alexandria, Blunt wrote in his diary how he at a dinner party of some forty people 'sat next to Harry Brand and had a grand row with him about Egypt'. 'I felt myself in rather an unfriendly atmosphere politically, as most of those present were Jingoes', Blunt confessed. In his drunken and not-too-serious after dinner speech Blunt declared that 'some served their country in one way and some in another, but that as long as one served it and did one's duty, it did not much matter what one did'.[15]

John Morley expressed the same idea much more eloquently in his memoirs: 'Chamberlain always said that Little Englandism was not a term of reproach; it only means a particular view of policy. Imperialism means a totally different view. This ought to have been recognised as true, for after all there may be two different ways of loving one's country.' In Morley's opinion the contradiction was there only because 'in foreign affairs everybody thinks it a duty to have a point-blank opinion, and the nearer it comes to pure guesswork on complex and obscure affairs, the more violent is the point-blank'. Morley did not quite accept the centrality of the empire in Chamberlain's definition of 'love of country':

> The very word empire is in history and essence military; emperor means soldier; all modern history and tradition associate empires with war. Asked at a meeting what I meant by a Jingo, I tried to define the genus mocked by that terse designation as men who held that territory was territory, and all territory was worth acquiring without regard to cost. We held the purse of Fortunatus, and were free to fling our millions abroad, with the certainty that benignant fairies would by magic make them good. ... The advancement of the people of our own country in the note of civilised well-being was important but comparatively secondary.[16]

The imperialist notion of patriotism equalled the 'love of country' with unquestioned loyalty towards the nation and the empire in every enterprise. No criticism was tolerated especially in regard to British India, which remained 'the centrepiece of the empire' until the very end. As Sneh Mahajan has put it, the Indian empire 'could not be peripheral to anything' and was therefore 'jealously guarded' and defended 'whatever the risks, costs, and enigmas of doing so'.[17] Imperialists argued that the 'unpatriotic' critics of British rule in India – like those who could not see the importance of strategic railways in the borderland or adequate military expenditure – failed to understand the bigger picture. If the military expenditure were reduced, they argued, India – and many even thought that Britain, too, at least economically – would face a serious danger from Russia. Some, like Charles Marvin in 1885, argued that Britain had already given too much in for the critics: when England merely 'played with diplomacy' Russia was building railways near the Afghan borders.[18] The Penjdeh

crisis further sharpened the question of whether England was able to
defend India against the Russian threat at all, like a Conservative MP
Ellis Ashmead Bartlett asked in 1886. Bartlett argued that it was certain knowledge 'that Russia means to have India, if, and whenever, she
can get it', and only British troops with British statesmanship could
safeguard India from Russian rule. Bartlett's pamphlet on the Russian
threat was still considered topical in 1897 by the then viceroy, Lord
Curzon.[19]

The Russian threat was taken seriously indeed and could be used as
a counter-weapon by someone who had a grudge against British rule.
A good example is the case of the Maharajah Duleep Singh, who had
as a child been the Maharajah of Punjab under British guardianship.
Punjab had been annexed to British India in 1849, after which the boy
Maharajah had been brought to England to live the life of a country
squire. Despite the generous allowance from the British government,
Singh met continuous financial problems, due to his lavish lifestyle,
which resulted in worsening relations and arguments with the India
Office. In the early 1880s the Maharajah lost his patience and wrote
angry letters to *The Times*.[20] Major Evans Bell was quick to defend
Singh's case and testify on his part that the annexation of Punjab had
been illegal and the Maharajah had been deprived of his land and
fortune – including the famous Kohinoor diamond – by the misdeeds
of the British government.[21]

The most telling part of the story is that when Singh finally decided
to rebel openly against Britain, he used the Russian threat extensively
in his demands for more money and 'compensation for his private jew-
els and estates'. Although this method did not work, it caused increasing anxiety both in the India Office and the Indian government. The
Queen's private secretary, Sir Henry Ponsonby wrote to the secretary
of state for India, Lord Kimberley, that Singh had 'felt it his duty to
warn me that if justice was not done to him, the news of his ill treatment would spread through India and if we again found ourselves in
difficulties the Sikh soldiers who had saved India for us in the Mutiny
would be found among our enemies'.[22] Kimberley sent copies of Singh's
letters to the viceroy, Lord Ripon, noting that Singh was indeed 'in
a very unsatisfactory state of mind' and was possibly 'engaged in a

seditious correspondence' with some other Indian princes.[23] In his letters Singh assured the officials: 'There is a terrible storm gathering
in India ... I know that the advent of Russia is hailed with intense joy
both by the people and Princes of India in their secret hearts whatever they may say outwardly and they are all prepared to rebel as soon
as that Power advances a little nearer.'[24] The government's main aim
was to keep Singh away from India as long as possible, as Kimberley
had promised to Ripon,[25] and in this they succeeded, for Singh never
returned to India. Nor were his attempts to befriend the Russians any
more successful either and he died as a bitter, poor, and lonely man in
France in 1893.[26]

The likes of the Maharajah Duleep Singh made the India Office
and the Indian government extremely sensitive towards any criticism;
to them it was treason. Anti-imperialists, however, detested the use
of the 'Russian weapon' in stirring the imperialist patriotic–militarist
spirit. In spring 1885, when the Egyptian campaign led to General
Gordon's death in the Sudan and there was extreme military pressure
in the Indian borders, John Morley expressed his tiredness on the talk
of 'inevitable wars': 'I utterly hate and distrust all this talk about manifest destiny and inevitable conquests. It is nothing else but the most
stupid fatalism. They say the conflict is written in the stars. I do not
believe in governing by astrology.'[27] Henry Labouchere, on his part,
pointed out that Britain was equally to blame for the strained relations between Britain and Russia.[28] Leonard Courtney, like Morley,
did not believe in the danger of war with Russia but stressed that the
expansion of the empire in Africa led to danger of war with France.[29]
He complained:

We are distrusted if not detested by every European Power. And
we are so weak with swollen Empire that we are under hostages
for at least 20 years to come. The weary Titan has become a fat
Falstaff, obese and floundering, gorged beyond digestion, incapable of action.

Why are we so distrusted and detested? ... What have we been
doing the last twenty years? Snatching at continents, 'pegging
out claims', interfering as missionaries of order and peace, and

then settling down in permanent possession; in short, making up those 2,600,000 square miles of 'undigested empire' which satisfy so powerfully the Imperialist instinct and reduce us to abject impotence.[30]

Imperialism and Russophobia became thus closely linked in both imperialist and anti-imperialist minds. John M. Robertson commented on this connection pointedly in his *Patriotism and Empire* in 1899, when stating that the only reason for the hatred for Russia was British 'megalomania, which regards relative smallness of territory as a ground for contempt':

> Our imperialist Russophobes must be gnawed hourly by the worst of pangs, when they reflect that Russian territory in Europe and Asia outbulks British; and the thought that little Scandinavia can be made great by literature must appear to them as preposterous as the opinion that little Athens availed more for human enlightenment than imperial Rome.[31]

The argument that true greatness was greatness in humanity and morals was common among anti-imperialists. 'Without Justice what are Empires but Companies of Brigands on a large scale', was the motto of a French writer called 'Peter the Hermit' in an indicting pamphlet on the Egyptian question. 'No nation has the right of interfering in the internal government of another nation, any more than the father of a family has any claim to regulate the domestic affairs of his neighbour',[32] the pamphlet declared. Positivists, in particular, advocated this view that same moral laws should be applied to the relations between nations as to those between individuals.[33] These English followers of Auguste Comte maintained that only the termination of all colonial relationships would bring peace to the world.[34]

Auguste Comte established the foundations of the new 'religion of humanity' between the 1830s and 1850s by developing his ideas of the intellectual development of human race into the more specified scheme of moral and social regeneration of mankind.[35] Most of all Comte wished to enhance the growth of altruism as opposed to egoism both in public and private life; his main problem was 'how to make social feeling prevail over self-love, to the end that man's activity may become ever more social in its character'.[36] The most fundamental principle of positivism was therefore 'Love for Humanity'.[37] This required not only that France and Britain were to proclaim the independence of their colonies and dependencies but also that they were to break up into smaller countries themselves. France, for example, was to become seventeen independent states, since the 'transition to a family of small countries' would end aggression and imperialism and would harmonise and pacify international relations.[38]

Richard Congreve, the leader of British positivists, laid the foundation for positivist anti-imperialism in his famous pamphlet on India, written in 1857 and reprinted in 1874, in which he demanded complete re-evaluation of British foreign politics. He argued that there was little commercial gain, and that India was a military, political, and economical burden to Britain. Optimistically Congreve believed, however, that no violence would be needed before the British realised this: he thought that they would leave India as a result of 'an improved moral judgment – the outcome of a new religious impulse' – not because of any threat of war or violent revolution.[39] Congreve wrote that he was as ambitious as others for his country, 'but not with the common ambition'; instead of being 'in the first rank in the conflict of interests' he would rather see Britain 'in the first rank in a new and nobler policy of repentance, restitution, and disinterested moderation'.[40] In 1879, inspired by Gladstone's Midlothian campaign, he declared with Henry Crompton that 'the time is ripe now for action on this great question' of imperialism:[41]

The Anti-Imperialists, long in a small minority but never silent or inactive, are not likely to be quiet now that they have gained so great an accession of strength, now that their views have begun to penetrate and move the working-classes and many of the Liberals themselves. The Government has by its conduct made Imperialism ridiculous, and has given additional prominence to the evils and dangers of Imperialism, by their device of making the throne the symbol of empire – that is, of all the

injustice, wrong, war, conquest, and annexation, which are day
by day more and more associated with the word empire.[42]

Even when the early anti-imperialist optimism turned into pessimism after the occupation of Egypt under the leadership of Gladstone
himself, the positivists stood firm in their opposition. When Britain's
position in Uganda was debated in 1892, Congreve declared that positivists objected to 'the whole enterprise, whatever the reasons assigned'.
He argued that all the claimed commercial advantages were 'a delusion', but even if they were true the positivists would still oppose
British occupation of Uganda. The reason was clear and straightforward: 'We think this partitioning of Africa by the Western nations
wholly wrong in principle – a violation of all the obligations conferred
by superior strength. *This moral objection supersedes all others.*'[43]

Frederic Harrison was an even more dynamic propagator of positivist anti-imperialism throughout his life. Like Congreve, Harrison was
galvanised by the Indian Mutiny in 1857, and was actively involved in
the Jamaica Committee in the 1860s denouncing Governor Eyre's 'martial law' in the Jamaican massacre. The notion of 'martial law' remained
central in Harrison's conception of imperialism later as well; most notably he employed it in the connection of the Afghan War in 1879–80.[44]
'By what title are we treating the Afghan people as rebels? By what law
are our generals hanging men on charges of leading the enemy's forces
to battle?' Harrison asked. There was no public law or any moral justice
which would give Britain the right to act as it did, he insisted:

> That our armies have invaded Afghanistan, and in two expedi-
> tions have crushed the soldiers of Kabul, we all know. That we
> have broken up what shadow of state existed; that we have its
> titular ruler as prisoner; that we have seized its treasures, and
> destroyed the centre of its capital – all this is very true. It is
> what invaders and conquerors usually do, or at least have done
> in former ages.[45]

Harrison also chose the theme of 'Empire and Humanity' for his
annual address to the Positivist Society on the New Year's Day 1880.[46]

The address was published in the *Fortnightly Review* and republished twenty-eight years later because, as Harrison then put it, 'in all its essential principles it is now as true as it was then, and because succeeding events have proved how real were the dangers which it deprecated, and how continually the same evils are bred by the Imperialist system'.[47] Harrison asked his audience: 'Who is a patriot, filled with the high memories of our glorious name, staunch to make every sacrifice to continue that heroic tradition to our children and our children's children to the twentieth generation, if we … are not amongst such men?' Indeed, the anti-imperialist policy of 'peace, the active maintenance of the actual settlement, the protection of the weak, the resistance of the strong' was 'an English, not an Asiatic policy', in contrast to that of the imperialists. To be sure, Harrison announced, 'We are against *all* oppression of conquered by the conquerors; we look for the dissolution of these empires of conquest; we desire decentralisation of vast political communities, and not a never-ending system of annexations; and, above all, we protest against military government in every form.'[48] Harrison's definition of patriotism was thus notably different from the imperialist definition:

> No! It is not that we have outlived the spirit of patriotism and care nothing for the bond of country. It is that we earnestly cling to the idea of country, and honour to the utmost the brave men who so nobly maintained that sacred trust. Those who have wantonly crushed the Zulu nation and broken up the Afghan kingdom are they who have trampled under foot the duty of patriotism. … It is we who defend the sacred name of country; it is the invader and the conqueror that drag it to the dust.[49]

'This inheritance of empire', Harrison concluded, 'forms for our England of to-day as great a moral peril as ever tasked a great people'.[50] Indeed, the Boer War at the turn of the century was seen to illustrate 'so clearly the evils of vicious policy abroad', as Harrison put it.[51] Once again he stated that 'I prefer the name of a just, peaceful, and righteous England to that of an Empire scrambling for half a continent at the bidding and in the interest of cosmopolitan gamblers and speculative companies, in search of bigger dividends and higher premiums'.[52]

Richard Congreve and Frederic Harrison had strong disagreements inside the positivist movement, but in regard to British imperialism they always agreed in public. Herbert Spencer, too, was at one point in private and public dispute over positivist dogmas with Harrison, although they on the whole were close friends.[53] At the time of Spencer and Harrison's public argument in the mid-1880s Richard Congreve wrote to Spencer regretting 'anything which tends to alienate you', since, after all, 'your utterances on social and, especially imperial questions have been of a nature to obscure other differences between us'.[54] Spencer, too, who had befriended Harrison during the Jamaica Committee in the 1860s, summarised their friendship in 1901: 'While we have sundry points of difference we have many and more important points of agreement.'[55]

Goldwin Smith and John Morley were close to the positivist circles as well and similarly veterans of the Jamaica Committee.[56] Harrison and Morley, in particular, were good friends, and the long correspondence between them forms the largest entity in Harrison's archive.[57] While Harrison and Morley mainly discussed literature or private matters in their letters, Harrison's correspondence with Smith was more political. The committed stance against imperialism combined them especially at the turn of the century, when Harrison noted to Smith: 'I have observed with much sympathy and great admiration the powerful protests that you have made against the prevalent Imperialism – the great moral plague of our time, it seems, on both sides of the Atlantic.'[58] Smith subsequently tried to get Harrison to visit Canada to galvanise his lonely anti-imperialist campaign there, unsuccessfully. 'I will not say that I have been crying in the wilderness', Smith wrote disappointedly about his attempt to stir an anti-Boer War campaign in Canada, 'but I have been crying in an apparent wilderness'.[59]

Harrison's closest positivist friends, Edward Spencer Beesly and John Henry Bridges, argued the anti-imperialist case in similar positivist vein. Bridges, when examining the question of patriotism in 1898, declared that 'between Imperialism and Patriotism there is a gulf set which no sophistries can bridge'. 'A common country, a common government, common memories, traditions, enthusiasms, these things constitute patriotism', Bridges wrote. Imperialism, in contrast, referred to an *empire*, which in the strictest sense could mean only India or other territories governed 'by material force', since 'such colonies as Australia, New Zealand, and Canada' Britain could not be said 'in any ordinary sense of the word to govern at all', even less so imperially. Moreover, that India would have been a wealth to Britain was 'an illusion long since dispelled', Bridges argued; even the argument that the subcontinent was becoming more prosperous under British rule had become 'strongly doubted'. His conclusion, therefore, was that 'no one who knows what patriotism really means can pretend to feel patriotic exultation at the maintenance of our Indian empire. We may accept it as a duty inherited from the past. We may recognise its necessity. ... But to be proud of it is another matter altogether.'[60] When the Boer War began Bridges complained of 'the misery that we have been spreading in South Africa', wondering 'whether the Positivists are not the only people left who have not forgotten their Bibles, and who retain dim memories of an avenging angel on the threshing floor of Araunah the Jebusite'.[61]

Beesly was the editor of the *Positivist Review*, of which the first issue was published in 1893. The *Review*, in Beesly's own words, 'consistently and continually opposed the extension of the British Empire in all parts of the world'. It 'especially and frequently condemned the occupation of Egypt, not only as a wrongful interference with Egyptian independence, but as creating a formidable danger for England herself, because it tends to embroil her with France'. Beesly added further that 'not a single member, as far as I know, of any English Positivist group has defended the British occupation of Egypt' and 'English Imperialism and Jingoism, in all their manifestations, have found nothing but determined opposition from English Positivists'.[62] Although this critical approach tended to make positivism unpopular in Britain, 'none of the principal misdeeds of our country in India, Afghanistan, Burma, China, Zululand, the Transvaal, Matabeleland, Egypt, and many other regions, have been allowed to pass without protest', Beesly proudly listed.[63] He was certain that 'the true primacy of Europe will belong in a not distant future not to military strength, but to intellectual, moral, and social eminence'.[64]

Beesly also stressed that the positivists had continuously advocated gradual withdrawal from India. The London Positivist Society stated the principle clearly in its manifesto 'The Russian Approach to India' in 1885, and Beesly restated the case in 1894 with the additional warning that 'things are worse now than they were nine years ago, and worse they will become as every year passes'.[65] The manifesto deplored the situation where Britain held 'India not by the assent of the peoples that inhabit it, but by the sword': 'To the English people the position of conquerors has been and is deeply demoralising; tainting what should be the noblest of virtues, patriotism, with the poison of greed and injustice, and incapacitating us for taking an upright and elevated view of all questions of foreign policy.' Beesly believed that British withdrawal in friendly terms and without chaos was possible, if the Indians were freely admitted 'to the highest civil and military functions in order to train them for self-government' and the various Indian provinces were simultaneously raised 'to the position of protected allies, as a preparation for ultimate independence'.[66]

The notions of patriotism, imperialism, and jingoism were much debated at the end of the century. In Beesly's view the era of imperialism was the result of a 'lamentable interregnum between the decay of the religions of God and the rise of the religion of Humanity';[67] he was convinced that once positivism gained the hegemony, imperialism would also disappear. He considered an imperialist more dangerous than a mere 'jingo', since not many took the latter seriously. By a 'jingo' Beesly meant 'the bellicose person who would by preference settle every dispute with other nations by the sword' and who said 'there must be wars from time to time to keep up the martial spirit of the nation'. Luckily enough, Beesly stated, 'their disease' was not 'catching', since 'the vast majority of Englishmen are immune, being saturated with the antidote of industrialism'. All jingoes were imperialists, but the majority of imperialists were not jingoes. Unlike the jingo, an imperialist was not keen on 'fighting for fighting's sake'. Some imperialists were 'simple megalomaniacs, rejoicing in every fresh acquisition of territory, however extravagant the cost or invisible the profit', while others had 'an eye to profit, either seeking their way to direct gain for themselves, or deluded by the often refuted maxim that trade follows the flag'. Thus, Beesly argued, 'The Imperialist is really far more dangerous than the mere Jingo, because his policy is not in obvious antagonism to the industrial spirit, but is represented as favourable to and even necessary for the development of industry, and therefore enlists very wide support.'[68]

Nevertheless, Beesly continued, both jingoes and imperialists were equally confused about the right notions of patriotism. 'True Patriotism', in Beesly's view, consisted 'in maintaining the liberty and promoting the progress of our own country, in subordination to the general welfare of mankind, and in developing its friendly and harmonious relations with all the other peoples of the world'. Furthermore, no nation was 'warranted in interfering with the freedom, domestic policy, or possessions of other nations, either for the spread of its religious opinions, for scientific exploration, for the accomplishment of political or supposed philanthropic purposes, or for the extension of its trade'. Most important:

> All attempts at the extension of empire are to be condemned, as tending to prolong militarism, to imperil the peace of the world, and to retard the industrial, political, and moral progress of mankind; and in the case of existing empires it should be an object of policy to gradually and prudently grant complete self-government and independence to the various nationalities and colonies included in, or held in subjection to them, with a view to their free and voluntary co-operation on a basis of common interests and opinions.[69]

As Beesly rightly pointed out, the imperialist patriotic rhetoric was indeed powerful and persuasive – and, from the point of view of their opponents, thus 'dangerous'.[70] Imperialists represented their policy not only as favourable but also necessary, stressing how the South African republics, for instance, lacked British liberties and how it was Britain's duty to 'bring liberty' to the Boers, thus justifying the war. Moreover, this patriotic imperialism was epitomised as the manly fulfilment of duty, while their Liberal opponents were depicted as unpatriotic and unmanly cowards due to their preoccupation with domestic issues at the expense of the empire.[71]

This distinction between manly military values and humane cosmopolitan values was drawn by both imperialists and anti-imperialists, but what was valued by one group was despised by the other. The anti-imperialist William Clarke was sad to see the old 'cosmopolitan Europe' of the late eighteenth century having turned into the 'national and particularist Europe' of the late nineteenth century.[72] While nationalism as such was a positive feeling, Clarke wrote, the late-nineteenth-century jingoism represented 'the excess of that feeling carried to a point of absurdity where its victim becomes wholly irrational as well as immoral'. This excess of sentiment was then 'artfully worked on in every country on behalf of sinister interests which have nothing to do with any normal or healthy national feeling'.[73] Notably echoing the positivist view, Clarke argued that 'humanity as such, and not any particular group of humanity', should be 'the real object of our affections and its good the real end of our endeavour'.[74] Bismarck, in particular, Clarke argued, had generated the transformation in the European ideals from humanitarian liberalism to militant imperialism and 'hard cynicism'. Clarke pointed out that while all the powerful nations had become imperialist, it was left to the smaller European nations to 'keep alive the democratic instincts of the European peoples'.[75]

Lord George Hamilton, a staunch imperialist, agreed with Clarke about the importance of Bismarck; but far from blaming him, Hamilton gave him credit. Even after the Great War he wrote admiringly about the German 'blood and iron' patriotism and disparaged the 'unpatriotic' Britain, where 'patriotism is untaught, commemorations of great victories are unknown, the Union Jack is unflown, the celebration of Empire Day until recently was forbidden, and little or nothing is taught to the rising generation of the wonderful heritage in store for them – won by the courage and fighting power of the British race'. All this was the fault of the anti-imperialists and Cobdenites, Hamilton argued; but Bismarck had wisely 'determined that no ideas such as were taught by the Cobdenite political economy should get into the higher education of Germany' and had 'utterly repudiated the idea of cultivating cosmopolitan amity as a substitute for a love of your own country'. The result was, Hamilton applaudingly but rather ominously wrote, that 'Germany has been drilled into one solid mass of patriotism, ready to bear and to brave for its Fatherland anything it is asked to do.'[76]

J. Lawson Walton confessed in 1899 that attempting to define imperialism was treading 'consciously on thorny and delicate ground'. His intention was to avoid the 'spheres of malign influence' into which Chamberlain and Morley had 'sought to thrust each other' when using 'the malodorous names' of 'Jingo' and 'Little Englander' for one another. Walton, instead, aimed 'to describe in outline the intermediate and more fortunate region of popular opinion which avoids the indefinite but conscious objections which attach to either limbo'.[77] This 'intermediate' way of defining imperialism was to see it, Walton argued, 'as a principle or formula of statesmanship for interpreting the duties of government in relation to empire'. He emphasised how he as an imperialist took 'a profound pride in the magnificent heritage of empire won by the courage and energies of his ancestry, and bequeathed to him subject to the burden of many sacred thrusts', and how he was convinced that 'the spread of British rule extends to every race brought within its sphere ... incalculable benefits'. Furthermore, the imperialist always believed 'that the strength and resources of our race will be equal to the weight of any obligation which the sense of duty of our people may call upon our Government to undertake', Walton argued, with a strong sense of 'imperial destiny'.[78]

It is difficult to see, then, how Walton's 'intermediate' approach to the question of imperialism was any different from the 'imperialist' position of, for instance, Chamberlain. Indeed, R. Wallace was quick to point out that Walton's account of imperialism contained 'a larger number of Beaconsfieldian features about it than seems desirable to such a Liberal as myself'.[79] Wallace's pride in empire was 'somewhat dashed by its history', and the 'disadvantages to which it exposes the Kingdom and our own highest progress' discouraged him further: 'It notoriously involves us in an enormous expenditure of money and service which is seriously marring our own civilisation and prosperity', Wallace argued.[80] The 'general lesson taught by our military empire', he summarised, was how 'to add meanness to lawlessness'. Moreover, the experience of empire encouraged the ruling classes to act despotically at home as well as abroad, he insisted.[81] This all was against the doctrines of the Liberal party, who had taken up 'the cause of the oppressed masses':

> On that footing of the rights of man as man they fought the battle of the people, and their toast was civil and religious liberty *all over the world*. But all that is changed now. The Liberal Imperialist holds that man as man has no rights if he is in another country, and is weaker than ourselves, and has anything which the Liberal Imperialist can put in his imperialist but not liberal pocket.[82]

Wallace's interpretation of the whole process of imperialism was simple:

> Nowadays, if there is a whisper of some conceivable thousand pounds to be made anywhere, even in such a desert as the Soudan, a thousand firms, financiers, adventurers, and company promoters, will start up out of the Invisible. ... The terrible clamour made by a thousand people touting for it simultaneously creates the impression that there is really something valuable and important going; and, apparently to meet such an emergency of demand, a distinguished occupant of our Liberal front bench has in effect declared that it is a sound Liberal doctrine that you may set to and conquer a backward race without more ado, and exploit them, if they have anything, provided you civilise them afterwards – by teaching them, I suppose, the Nicene Creed and possibly algebra up to quadratic equations.[83]

The time had come to 'make a stand for the sake of the Kingdom', Wallace declared, since enough had been sacrificed for the empire. 'Every triumph of expansionism' was a further 'rebuff to Democratic Liberalism', for 'expansionist Imperialism means more Despotism abroad and more Aristocratic recrudescence at home'.[84]

Despite the heated discussion on the concepts and their meanings, the confusions and disagreements remained. To anti-imperialists 'imperialism' represented militarism, despotism, and autocracy summarised in one word. While they accepted the concept of the British 'empire' as a figure of speech, any attempts towards imperial policies in practice were fiercely opposed. Imperialists, in contrast, regarded 'imperialism' as larger patriotism which embraced the whole empire with its colonies and dependencies, and were therefore eagerly looking forward to further expansion in the name of 'empire patriotism', or 'imperialism'. The main differences between anti-imperialists and imperialists were, indeed, in definitions and principles, but even there the contradiction was not necessarily as stark as it may have seemed at the time. Anti-imperialists were not against the existing British 'empire' as long as it was self-governing, democratic, and liberal – i.e. not an *empire* in any literal sense. Moreover, there was not one single committed imperialist who would have even proposed that the British empire should really be an empire; the Queen was an Empress *only* in India and remained so.

In the minds of the contemporaries the contradiction was there, however, and, for a while, it was significant. Imperialists considered it a vital question to enhance, in Lord Rosebery's words, 'the larger patriotism that I have called Imperialism',[85] and disparaged the 'unpatriotic Little Englanders' who did not accept this view. Sir William Harcourt, in contrast, asked:

What is this Imperialism which, in the slang of the day, is paraded as the highest form of patriotism? I laugh sometimes when I hear myself and others denounced as 'Little Englanders'. I confess I did not know that there was a 'Little England' to belong to. I always thought that England was the greatest, the most extensive, the most powerful, the most famous nation in the world; that it was one of which any man might be proud to be a citizen … Little England, forsooth! Where is it?[86]

Harcourt, as his friend and biographer A. G. Gardiner put it, loved England 'not for its possessions, but for itself, for the beauty of its countryside, the qualities of its people, the splendour of its intellectual achievements, the inspiration it had given to the world in the conceptions of social order and human liberty'. This 'true' patriotism he contrasted starkly with 'the vulgar notion that patriotism consists in a desire to paint the map red and whip unwilling peoples into obedience to our rule'.[87] However, the wider the 'true liberal spirit' of England spread over the world the more Harcourt was content. As Gardiner testified,

> there was nothing in which he took greater pride than in the triumph of the Liberal doctrine of self-government which had made the overseas Dominions equal partners in a community of free nations inspired by the English spirit of liberty. But Jingoism and Imperialism were the negation of the English spirit. They aimed, not at widening the borders of freedom, but at imposing by force the will of a conquering race over subject peoples, and the fact that the conquering race was one whose chief contribution to the world was the idea of liberty added to the wrong the sense of *disloyalty to the soul of England*.[88]

On the other hand, John St. Loe Strachey, editor of the *Spectator*, is a good example of someone who in practice was against imperialism in its *literal* sense but did everything in his power to avoid the label of a 'Little-Englander'. Throughout his memoirs he stressed every now and then how he always was 'an ardent Imperialist' or 'a strong democratic Imperialist'.[89] Indeed, so 'Imperialist' was he that he had 'hundreds of ... grounds for saying that, if the British Empire had not existed, it would have had to be invented in the interests of mankind'. Despite this 'empire-patriotism', however, Strachey became at the end of the century disgusted at 'Mr. Rhodes's practical methods of expanding the British Empire', which were 'so dangerous and so little consistent with a high sense of national honour and good faith that I felt it was part of my job to protest against them with all my strength'. Strachey despised Rhodes's corruption: he depicted him as a man 'who bought policies as other men buy pictures', and was 'a kind of throw-back to the eighteenth century': 'The chief trouble with him was that he really believed that all men were buyable.'[90] Strachey's imperialist friends were amazed at his 'opposition to the great empire-builder':

> I told them that it was just because I was an Imperialist, and did not want to see the Empire destroyed, that I opposed Rhodes. I pointed out to them that he was an arch corrupter, and insisted that corruption destroyed, not made, Empires, I was told that I did not know what I was talking about. I was a foolish idealist who did not understand practical politics.[91]

Curiously, this experience of 'an ardent imperialist' was not that different from the experiences of explicit *anti*-imperialists at the same time. John M. Robertson, for instance, wrote in 1901 how the corruptive and despotic 'imperialist' policies in South Africa were 'wrecking' the whole empire.[92] Moreover, when anti-imperialists usually grew more steadfast if they were disparaged and ridiculed, Strachey's opposition to Rhodes's policies, too, was only strengthened by the criticism he met. As he himself put it: 'This talk, instead of putting me off, made me feel it was absolutely necessary, however disagreeable, to pursue my policy' of 'exposing Rhodes'.[93]

CHAPTER 5

PROGRESS AND CIVILISATION – OR DEGRADATION AND RE-BARBARISATION

Will England be loyal to her love of truth and her hatred of oppression, or has she begun to tread the path of disregard of all duty, of contempt for all morality, the path that inevitably leads to national decay?[1]

– Annie Besant in 1879

England, then, must keep India ... because India offers to England an unequalled scope for giving effect to the purest philanthropy, the noblest ideas, the loftiest aspirations by which the English people can be moved and actuated; and because England herself is elevated morally by the obligation of caring humanely and unselfishly for the good of a vast population which Providence has committed to her charge.[2]

– Sir Richard Temple in 1880

Imperialists believed strongly that the British empire and its expansion advanced progress and spread civilisation throughout the world. Anti-imperialists, in contrast, were convinced that pursuing imperialist policies resulted in the 'degradation and re-barbarisation' of England. In the late-Victorian era, the imperialist rhetoric was notably more persuasive and successful than the anti-imperialist, and this led to wide disillusionment and pessimism among anti-imperialists at the turn of the century.

The early imperialist rhetoric defended autocracy, pride of race, and the cult of force explicitly. Sir James Fitzjames Stephen, the famous critic of democracy, regarded the British governance of India through disinterested and gifted elite as an almost ideal model of government.[3] His cousin Edward Dicey, too, defended the autocratic imperial spirit fiercely, arguing consistently that the British empire was established for the sole benefit of Great Britain and not to expand any notions of liberal or democratic values.[4] This 'illiberal' imperialism was confronted by Gladstonian anti-imperialism until 1882; after that the imperialist rhetoric began to change notably more liberal and the early anti-imperialist optimism subsequently began to fade. Although the strategic and economic reasons for imperialism remained important alike, the liberal imperialist rhetoric, putting special emphasis on the imperial humanitarian mission, gained considerably more strength in the 1880s and 1890s. This liberal notion of imperialism amounted to a huge and responsible duty to spread progress and western civilisation around the world through the benevolent, Christian, and anti-slavery British empire.[5] Even scientific anthropology, which turned critical towards the westernisation project in the twentieth century, provided its wide support. The connections between imperialism and anthropology were greatly enhanced by Sir Richard Temple, who served as the President of the Anthropological Institute after his retirement from the Indian Civil Service.[6]

The pride of race was important, but it was not merely a notion of black and white. The contrast was drawn for the benefit of the British and for whatever reason between them and whoever was the opponent at the time. Fighting against the Islamist Mahdi in 1884–5 highlighted the notion of *Christian* imperialism.[7] In the South African context, on the other hand, the manly Briton was mainly compared to the Dutch Boer, who, according to George Baden-Powell's testimony in 1885, was 'slow to act, averse from change, greedy of land', and 'disdainfully ignorant'.[8] Unlike the industrious Briton, the Boer did 'not succeed in making himself prosperous'; and, even worse, was 'a drag on the prosperity of his neighbours' as well, being 'the firm enemy of all co-operation'.[9] Furthermore, when Britain's interests became in conflict with those of France in mid-Africa in the 1890s, it was argued that Britain was by far the better civiliser of the two: this was mainly because, as Henry Birchenough pointed out, 'the colonial movement in France is not directed and controlled of any well-informed public opinion'.[10] In this sense, then, even some imperialists acknowledged that critical debate – on imperialism, too – was indeed part and parcel of British political culture in a positive way.

The concept of humanitarian and civilising imperialism implied the eventual end of empire, for the whole ideology was based on the notion that some day the dependencies would become like England. The more racist and conservative notion of imperialism regarded British rule as more or less permanent, since no progress on the lines of western civilisation was to be expected. This was because the 'subject races' were thought to be incapable of progress along the western lines. A good example is Lord George Hamilton, the Conservative secretary of state for India, who was certain that Indians would never be able to govern themselves according to western ideas; the whole idea of 'educating them' was doomed. 'There is a fixed gulf between European and Asiatic mentalities which will always remain', he argued. He despised the ideas of Macaulay, the founder of the literary system of European education in India in the 1830s, who had predicted 'that in course of time his educational system would eliminate heathenism'; in Hamilton's view 'a literary system of European education, when engrafted upon Asiatic mentality and fanaticism' merely upset 'the mental balance of some of its recipients' to the point that they became 'ruthless and senseless perpetrators of outrage'.[11] While many Indians spoke English 'with great fluency and ease', the words simply meant different things to them than to the British, Hamilton insisted. According to his experience at the India Office the 'many distinguished natives' he met 'somehow or other failed to gauge fully' what he meant to say to them. 'This feeling was not due to subtlety or disingenuousness. It was inherent in the mental remoteness one from another of the talkers,' Hamilton formulated.[12]

The notion of British liberal imperialism played successfully with the old enthusiasms for anti-slavery campaigning and religious missionary work. Anti-imperialists' remark about British hypocrisy on humanitarian issues was not new, either. Richard Cobden had declared in 1858:

> What a pretentious and hypocritical people we are in our dealings with the outside world! How we abuse and bully King Bomba because he will not govern his lazzaroni according to our notions of constitutionalism! But when you propose to apply a little of our love of liberty to our own fellow-subjects in India 'oh! oh!' is the reply you meet with in the House. Yet you would have no difficulty in carrying the cheers of the said House for any proposal to put the slaves in America or Cuba immediately on the same political level as their masters. This nation will meet with a terrible check some day, unless it makes a little better progress in the science of self-knowledge.[13]

Neither did Herbert Spencer, though a philosopher of progress, ever believe in Britain's mission to civilise the world. For Spencer, there was only one way to global progress, and this was peace between nations. He took this notion to the extreme that he opposed not only aggressive imperialism but also government colonisation already in the mid-century, when it was generally and strongly supported by others.[14] His main reason for this was moral-economical, since he considered it against the law of equal freedom that one portion of subjects was taxed at a higher rate in order to give protection to another portion which emigrated to the colonies.[15] Thus, 'the political union of a parent state with a colony' was, in Spencer's opinion, inadmissible, unjust, and 'absurdly unfit'.[16] Anticipating the much later debate on the 'trade and the flag', Spencer wrote in 1851:

> But not only do we expend so much to gain so little, we absolutely expend it for nothing; nay, indeed, in some cases to achieve a loss. All profitable trade with colonies will come without the outlay of a penny for colonial administration – must flow to us naturally; and whatever trade will not flow to us naturally, is not profitable, but the reverse.[17]

Even in the colonies the system of colonisation brought 'nothing but evil results', Spencer argued.[18] 'May we not reasonably doubt the propriety of people on one side of the earth being governed by officials on the other? Would not these transplanted societies probably manage their affairs better than we can do it for them?' he asked. Furthermore, Spencer stated that 'the evils entailed by government colonization upon both parent state and settlers' were nevertheless nothing 'compared with those it inflicts upon the aborigines of the conquered countries'.[19] Thus, while the protection of the settlers was an expensive policy for Britain to adopt and morally wrong on the principle of the law of equal freedom, in practice 'this so-called protection' also turned out to be 'oppression'.[20]

Spencer repeated the statement in 1880, when he was invited to sign an address to Lord Kimberley 'on the native question in South Africa'. The address was in favour of transferring the government of Basuto territory from Cape Colony to the British government; Spencer, however, did not agree. He replied:

> So long as it is felt by colonists that when they aggress on native and get into quarrels, the home government will come to their defence, and so long as men who initiate aggressive policies, which end in the annexation of territory, get titles and honours, notwithstanding their unauthorized actions and even their disobedience to orders, the filibustering policy with all its atrocities will continue.[21]

A few months later he wrote to the poet Algernon Charles Swinburne, asking him to write a 'scathing exposure of the contrast between our Christian creed and pagan doings, our professed philanthropy and our actual savagery', 'in condemnation of our filibustering atrocities all over the world'. Spencer hoped that an indicting pamphlet by Swinburne would amount to 'holding up to the English people a glass in which they might rightly see themselves and their doings'. Swinburne, however, politely refused, which was a major disappointment to Spencer.[22]

Africa was at the heart of the debate on the civilisation project. It was not considered to contribute to the dignity of the empire in the way India did; it was not suitable for colonisation, the southern part notwithstanding; moreoever it was not considered that important for trade reasons, either. The major reason left to justify British imperialism in mid-Africa was the humanitarian one. Indeed, supporters of autocratic and 'illiberal' imperialism, like Dicey, did not see sense in British expansion in the African tropics: it was not beneficial for Britain, which should be the sole motive for expansion.[23] Liberal imperialists, on the other hand, had the Christian and anti-slavery ideology close to their heart; the critics, however, were not persuaded by appealing to humanitarian and religious reasons. 'The welfare of the native, be he Christian or pagan, is the last argument that should be adduced in favour of our presence anywhere, least of all in Africa. Those whom we have civilised we have ruined by the contamination of our vices', declared one.[24] Although Britain had spent fortunes on African wars there were hardly any converts to British rule, the critic argued. According to him, the story of the necessity of British rule in Africa was only believed because it flattered national vanity.[25]

Wilfrid Scawen Blunt, too, argued that while the slave trade in Central Africa 'had for many centuries been a terrible scourge upon the indigenous black race',[26] western interference only brought along 'other evils ten times more destructive than those it cures'. Thus, in Blunt's opinion, 'the only true humanity towards the negroes of Equatorial Africa would have been to leave them unvisited, uncivilized, and severely alone with their own local troubles'. He pointed out that rather than applying military force it would have been more efficient to encourage 'Mohammedan reform in the Mediterranean Moslem states, and with it to secure the abolition of slavery as a legal institution and so the demand of slaves from the interior. This policy, however, was never one at all popular with the anti-slave-trade associations.'[27] Sir Charles Dilke, from a different point of view, came to same conclusions. He wrote in 1893:

> We shall never get back the money that we may spend in the heart of Africa, and when we are assured that it is our duty as Christians or as men to intervene there, at any distance, at any cost, for principle, regardless of prudence, without thought

of calculation, reason answers that our action – in withholding arms from the negroes where the Arabs have them in perfection – leads only to the destruction of the negro kingdoms for the benefit of the slave-traders, and that our intervention increases rather than lessens the sum of human suffering. We break up bad but comparatively settled governments and we put nothing in their place.[28]

Even the missionary enthusiasm was sometimes thwarted by news of European cruelty towards the Africans. In the early 1890s, for instance, the case of Major Barttelot, who had been a member of Stanley's expedition in 1887–8, was debated. Many genuine altruists were shocked by the news of Barttelot's behaviour in Africa, the nature of which was revealed by Stanley himself in 1890.[29] Reginald Bosworth Smith, schoolmaster at Harrow and staunch supporter of Britain's Christian 'civilising mission', was extremely upset and strongly criticised the way the British 'hushed up' disagreeable truths and used patriotism to justify any behaviour of their countrymen. British acts of violence and wrong were always tried to 'deny or explain away', and this method, Smith argued, led to 'the deterioration, slow but sure, of all those qualities on which Englishmen, as an Imperial nation dealing with weaker races, have hitherto had most reason to pride themselves'.[30] 'In all Imperial races', Smith stated, 'there is an element of the wild beast':

It seems almost like a law of Nature that civilised men, when thrown amongst uncivilised, should assimilate themselves to their surroundings, and should catch something, and at times – as in the case of the Spaniards in America and the West Indies – a double measure of their ferocity and their barbarism. Great Britain is no exception to the rule.[31]

Thus, Smith was willing to condemn 'all expeditions into barbarous and unknown countries, which are prepared, in the last resort, to have recourse to force'; nevertheless, he remained confident that if only 'proper precautions' would be taken, 'the evil' would be 'outweighed by the good' in the end.[32] The British empire, after all, was superior to any other because of 'the safeguards which a sensitive and enlightened public opinion at home' provided. Indeed, Smith concluded, 'Of all the Imperial races which have ever existed, there is not one – as the history of our Indian Empire, rightly viewed, will prove – which is more disinterested, more merciful, more just, more anxious to serve those whom she rules, and to rule by serving them.'[33] In Smith's opinion influencing, controlling, civilising, and assimilating 'barbarous tribes' was a noble job, as long as it was done by 'men who have a conscience which is keenly sensitive to right and wrong' as well as 'the more distinctively Christian virtues which we expect to find in the philanthropist and the missionary'.[34]

Smith's optimism and firm belief in the ultimate justification of British rule made his criticism very different from that of the committed anti-imperialists. Grant Allen represented the other extreme, condemning even the purchase of diamonds as symbolising the British slaving of the Africans. 'To buy diamonds is sin against the creed of humanity', he declared; 'a diamond, viewed as an æsthetic object alone, is distinctly vulgar',[35] and 'the love of diamonds, of precious stones, of silver plate, of costly raw material is essentially a taste that goes with the slave-owning and slave-driving temperament', he argued.[36] He compared the modern 'occidental barbarism' of 'vulgar profusion of diamonds' to the similar love of 'costly and purposeless baubles' in 'the lower and earlier grade of culture', like 'the barbarism of Indian princes and of Peruvian Incas, of the Red Indian in his war-paint and the South Sea islander in his necklet of shells', who all 'regard warfare and slaying as the highest task of our race, and who love to be arrayed like Solomon in all his glory'. Therefore, Allen argued, 'No true Liberal would even own a diamond.'[37] To encourage the diamond industry amounted in Allen's eyes to encouraging 'the barbaric tastes' of 'hunting, warfare, the predatory life, militarism: while the civilised tastes encourage steady labour, peace, the industrial life, socialism'.[38] Any righteous man should always ponder over 'What effect will this act of mine have upon human progress and human freedom?'; 'He should never use silk where well-printed cotton will serve his purpose as well … he should encourage good handicraft, honest trades, elevating occupations: he should refuse to be implicated, remotely or closely, in filibustering, cruelty, land-grabbing, sweating.'[39] Despite his socialism, Grant Allen greatly looked up to the anti-socialist Herbert Spencer, with whom he was in continuous contact from the 1870s onwards.[40] He was also a friend of Frederic Harrison's, who gave the funeral address when Allen died in 1899.[41]

The positivists, in order to prevent any further violent mischief, advocated a joint European protectorate for Africa.[42] Indeed, their enthusiasm 'to assist such races to reach a higher [positivist] civilisation', as Beesly put it in 1898, was not very different from that of the Christian missionaries; however, they continuously emphasised how they had learned and 'set forth better ways of fulfilling the duty' – not violently and forcefully, but advancing peace and harmony; 'without compulsion by British admirals, generals, and administrators'.[43] In the instance of the clash of British and French interests in Fashoda, for example, the positivists were quite exceptional in their stress on the rights and interests of the African inhabitants, whereas people in general debated whether it was France or England who had 'the title to Fashoda'.[44]

Similarly, the debate on British imperialism in South Africa was overwhelmed by the relations between the British colonists and the Dutch Boers. When Elisabeth Lecky, for instance, complained how the English people were 'strangely deficient in the power of putting themselves in the place of others' and how every question was always examined from the British point of view only,[45] she, being of Dutch origin, was only concerned about Britain's relations with the Boers and not with the black inhabitants of South Africa. Some critics, like Annie Besant and Charles Bradlaugh, ended up supporting the 'pro-Boer' movement in the late 1870s mainly because of their admiration towards the Boer republicanism.[46] Another 'pro-Boer' approach was well summed up by Kate Courtney at the time of the second South African War: 'No, I will not read a paper on the "treatment of the Native races in S. Africa" at the Christian Conference. While we are sinning so deeply in S. Africa it seems to me to be mere hypocrisy to be condemning other peoples' sins.'[47] H. M. Hyndman, in contrast, combined a fierce 'anti-Boer' attitude to his anti-imperialism, a position which at least implied a 'pro-native' stance. To Hyndman, the Boers were 'for the most part a coarse, ignorant, cruel, and bigoted set', who 'treat the natives more cruelly and slave-drive them more relentlessly even than our people do, which is saying a great deal'.[48] In practice, however, Hyndman did not argue the black African case any more than others, for his energy was exhausted by arguing against both the Dutch and the British. Although there was 'cause for remonstrance' and 'ground for complaint' against the 'greedy, overbearing, corrupt, impolitic, and in some respects unjust' Boers, there still was no legitimate cause for war, Hyndman argued – only the British greed 'to get gold' out of the Transvaal.[49] Thus, whether one was imperialist or anti-imperialist, pro- or anti-Boer, the result was the same: to a large extent the black Africans were forgotten.

Nevertheless, not all critics argued the cases purely from the western points of view. William Digby always declared to be on the side of the Indians first and the English second; Wilfrid Scawen Blunt, too, regarded himself primarily as the advocate of Muslims. Their concern for Britain was mainly concern about Britain's reputation in the eyes of their foreign friends, and neither of them hesitated to tackle the defects they witnessed. When Blunt, for instance, was travelling in India in 1884, he witnessed a racist attack against 'some thirty of the chief noblemen and notables of the city' of Patna by 'a middle-aged Englishman', who had shouted rudely to Blunt's friends and even 'struck at them with his cane'.[50] Blunt wasted no time in reporting the incident to the viceroy, Lord Ripon, in the hope that Ripon would pay 'serious attention' to it.[51] 'The violence of the offender was absolutely without excuse', he testified. Blunt suspected that the attacker considered that he had 'unwarrantably interfered with his time-honoured privilege of ill-treating men of an inferior race to his own', 'but I do strongly resent the daily wrongs suffered by the Indian people at the hands of men of his class', he maintained.[52] The news of Blunt's interference spread fast and he soon wrote again to inform Ripon that he had 'received numerous letters & personal communications from Mohamedans who have suffered indignities of a somewhat similar nature'.[53] Ripon was sympathetic and to a large extent agreed with Blunt, but, against Blunt's wishes, the matter was quietly laid to rest.[54] On the other hand, Blunt,

like Hyndman, was equally flawed with stereotyping, for his strong
pro-Muslim sentiment turned him into anti-Semitic. He met once in
Egypt a friendly man who invited him to his home, and Blunt noticed
only there that the family were Jews. Their company and servings 'disgusted' Blunt; and once the man accompanied him back to town and
asked for a coin, Blunt was more than happy to give him one in order
to get rid of him, for he was so 'ashamed to be seen with him'.[55]

British rule in India was more difficult to justify on the ground
of the civilising mission. Even Christianity failed to take root there,
for, unlike African tribal religions, the ancient Asian religions of
Hinduism and Buddhism were strongly institutionalised contest-
ants. Thus, in regard to India, the more prevailing notion of imperialism was the authoritarian one, stressing India's conservatism. John
M. Robertson summed up the notion of this school of Sir James
Fitzjames Stephen and Rudyard Kipling – 'who may be defined as
barbaric sentimentalists' – 'that Asia in general, and India in particular, are absolute exceptions to all the principles of European politics.
The East, they say, is unprogressive, unchangeable, unimprovable.' In
Robertson's opinion these were 'foolish generalisations', since 'India can
no more than any other land resist the laws of social transmutation' of
which the western-type Indian National Congress was his primary
example.[56] Annie Besant, on the other hand, became enchanted by
India exactly because of its 'unchangeable' culture.[57] After converting
to the new religion of theosophy in 1889, Besant regarded India as her
spiritual home. She visited India in 1893 and soon moved there permanently. First this staunch anti-imperialist refused to get involved in
Indian politics, campaigning only for 'spiritual renewal' which she by
then considered more important.[58] Moreover, because of her eagerness
not to criticise Indian culture, this fierce feminist denied that Indian
women were suppressed and insisted that they were 'for the most part
content with their secluded life'.[59] She declared to the British that 'in
dealing with a highly civilized nation you must learn to rule according
to its traditions, not according to yours'.[60] Later Besant did, however,
change her mind and began advocating radical social reform and political self-government for India, becoming the first female president of
the Indian National Congress in 1917.[61]

The notion of the civilising mission gained strength alongside British expansion in Africa from 1882 onwards. When this humanitarianism, rather than authoritarianism, became the defining character of British imperialism its popularity grew simultaneously. In the 1880s the activists of the Anti-Aggression League laid the blame for their disappointments on the indifference of the public, but in the late 1890s anti-imperialists reluctantly confessed that imperialist rhetoric was more powerful and more popular. Bernard Porter's thesis on the indifference of the British public towards the empire can therefore be well applied to the 1880s, but not quite so well to the late 1890s by which time the propaganda was already working efficiently.[62] Indeed, it seems that much of the Liberal imperialist rhetoric of the early 1890s resulted from the unpopularity of imperialism in the 1880s. The British, both the public and the politicians at large, had been reluctant expansionists in Egypt in 1882 and the Sudan in 1884–5: the prevailing element in the imperialist rhetoric at the time was the excuse of the temporary nature of the occupation. By the time the situation in Uganda was debated in the early 1890s and the 'temporary' occupation of Egypt had continued for ten years, there was a new sense of inevitability in British presence and expansion in Africa. Combined with the missionary and anti-slavery pressure, the humanitarian justification became the cornerstone of this 'new' imperialism. Until then the critics had contrasted the traditional liberal values and imperialism, but the notion of humanitarian, liberal, and civilising imperialism was like tailored to thwart these arguments.

None other than W. E. H. Lecky – the historian whose mid-Victorian views of the progress towards an era of liberty, industry, and peace had inspired anti-imperialists – paved the way for this more popular imperialism. Half of his address on the British empire at the Imperial Institute in 1893 was dedicated to denouncing the 'Little-England' approach. Lecky began by referring to

the great revolution of opinion which has taken place in England within the last few years about the real value to her both of her Colonies and of her Indian Empire. Not many years ago it was a popular doctrine among a large and important class of politicians that these vast dominions were not merely useless but detrimental to the Mother-country, and that it should be the end of a wise policy to prepare and facilitate their disruption.[63]

The Manchester School, especially, and its view that the 'empire should be gradually but steadily reduced to the sweet simplicity of two islands' were the main targets of Lecky's criticism. He disparaged the way Richard Cobden had amounted the question of colonies to 'a question of pounds, shillings, and pence; he proved, as he imagined, by many figures that they were a very bad bargain'. Even worse, in Lecky's view, was the way Cobden had described the Indian empire 'as a calamity and a curse to the people of England' which 'was destroying and demoralising the national character'.[64] Luckily enough, Lecky continued, these views had 'within the last few years steadily lost ground' and given way to 'a far warmer and, in my opinion, nobler and more healthy feeling towards India and the colonies'.[65] The empire increased trade and provided extensive markets for British products as well as various employment opportunities, Lecky argued.[66] The problems of Indian administration, in particular, were 'peculiarly fitted to form men of a kind that is much needed among us – men of strong purpose and firm will, and high ruling and organising powers', he pointed out, in addition to which India was 'the great seed-plot of our military strength'.[67] Furthermore, and most important, the empire patriotism could not be 'reduced to a mere question of money', for 'an England reduced to the limits which the Manchester School would assign to it would be an England shorn of the chief elements of its dignity in the world'.[68] 'Nothing in the history of the world is more wonderful than that under the flag of these two little islands there should have grown up the greatest and most beneficent despotism in the world', Lecky stated.[69]

Benjamin Kidd's *Social Evolution* and *The Control of the Tropics*, published in 1894 and 1898, respectively were utterly significant in shaping the public opinion more endorsing of humanitarian imperialism.[70] Kidd's arguments in favour of western paternalistic interference in the matters of 'un-civilised' territories in order to develop vital tropical resources for the benefit of world economy at large influenced Joseph

Chamberlain and American expansionists alike.[71] Kidd explicitly argued that it was the *responsibility* of the more progressed western nations to administer the tropical resources as a trust for the whole civilisation; at the same time he argued against the more traditional idea of imperialism as 'purely military subjection of indigenous peoples'.[72] He had an especially low opinion of the Roman empire, which to him was 'the highest example of the military state', where 'universal conquest was the recognised and unquestioned policy of the state' and 'the national policy was in reality but the organised exploitation by force and violence of weaker peoples'.[73] Christianity had then generated a more altruistic ideal of human existence, which had developed further throughout centuries.[74] The emancipation of the individual, Kidd argued, had not led to selfishness but to the strengthening of altruistic and humanitarian feelings.[75] 'It is the resulting deepening and softening of character amongst us which alone has made possible that developmental movement whereby all the people are being slowly brought into the rivalry of life on equal conditions', Kidd stated, stirring the feeling that western imperialism indeed was a genuine service to the world.[76] He explored the results of British rule in India and Egypt: under British guidance, both countries enjoyed a steady development of their resources, huge improvements in their public infrastructure, and general increase in trade and wealth. Although Britain gained enormously by administering the countries it was not exploiting them, he argued, for India and Egypt benefited even more, as, indeed, and most important, did the whole world.[77]

Kidd, like Lecky, implied that the idea of imperialism was not in a particularly high reputation in England, and he set out to change people's minds about it. His emphasis that modern western imperialism did not amount to militarism but civilisation and progress confused the whole debate from the anti-imperialist point of view. It made anti-imperialists seem like cowards who wanted to 'shirk the grave responsibility' which lay upon the English-speaking peoples, as Kidd pointed out.[78] His ideas were soon echoed all around:

> To us – to us, and not to others, – a certain definite duty has been assigned. To carry light and civilisation into the dark places of

the world; to touch the mind of Asia and of Africa with the ethical ideas of Europe; to give to thronging millions, who would
otherwise never know peace or security, these first conditions of
human advance.[79]

Interestingly enough, Benjamin Kidd and the arch-anti-imperialist William Clarke became close friends around the same time, and
Clarke introduced Kidd into radical Liberal circles.[80] Not surprisingly,
their diverging views on imperialism and civilisation caused some hot
debates every now and then. Clarke advised Kidd in 1895:

> Do not use the cant phrases of that charlatan W. T. Stead: you
> are too much of a thinker to wear his cast-off rags. ... Stead's cant
> of 'Little Englander' is claptrap. England is England, and you can
> neither add to nor take away from it: what you can do is to enable
> capitalists here to grab at regions in other parts of the world,
> enrich themselves and reduce the natives to virtual slavery. This
> is what is going on in Africa, and I will fight it as long as I live.
> Unlike you I do not desire to see English race everywhere. I do
> not like the creature well enough.[81]

In the mid-1890s, at the latest, the critics despairingly realised
that anti-imperialism could not become a popular movement. To
them, imperialism had always represented *de*-civilisation and degeneration. *Imperium et Barbaries* was what Annie Besant alongside Frederic
Harrison suggested should be the motto of the 'new Empress of Asia'
in the late 1870s, instead of the old *Dieu et mon droit*.[82] 'By the light of
flaming villages may be traced the blessings of the Empress of India's
advancing rule', Besant formulated in 1879.[83] Harrison, as a positivist,
noted in 1880 the major role of the Church in spreading the enthusiasm for expansion. 'Christianity in practice, as we know it now, for all
the Sermon on the Mount, is the religion of aggression, domination,
combat. It waits upon the pushing trader and the lawless conqueror;
and with obsequious thanksgiving it blesses his enterprise', he declared.
Nevertheless, back then Harrison was still convinced that the 'sound-
hearted people' of England would not 'for ever continue in this career

of evil', for there was 'a national conscience; and when it stirs, the most imposing empires totter and break up beneath it'.[84] Any arguments for humanitarian missions were 'indeed mere self-delusion' for Harrison, since in reality the British only went on 'from one outrage on justice to another, in the vague hope that some day we may begin to do our duty, when all our subjects are perfectly submissive and all our neighbours are perfectly friendly'.[85] In less than twenty years Harrison's optimism faded notably. His depression reached its low point at the turn of the century, when he 'declared England was no longer fit to live in, and threatened to move the family to Ireland'.[86] Goldwin Smith, too, who in 1878 had noted to Gladstone that 'With you, the tide seems at last to be turning against Jingoism',[87] asserted at the turn of the century that England had 'been put in a worse moral position since the burning of Joan of Arc'.[88] He cancelled his plans to visit England on his way back to Canada from a holiday in Italy because 'the Jingoism there' would have 'sickened' him.[89]

It was most ironic that the one who had first coined the phrase of 'the survival of the fittest', now put in new use in the 1890s, was none other than the arch-anti-imperialist Herbert Spencer in his *Principles of Biology* in 1864.[90] Spencer was strongly of the opinion that human character showed more signs of degradation than progress in the late nineteenth century. He gained his first 'evidence of the popular estimate of the relative importance of events' when launching the Anti-Aggression League in spring 1882: as his friend and biographer David Duncan pointed out, Spencer noted 'that the *Times* of February 23 had no notice of the meeting [of the Anti-Aggression League] at all, and that the *Daily Telegraph* devoted half a column to report of the meeting, and about three columns to Jumbo, the elephant'. Three weeks later, 15th March, *The Times* published Alfred Tennyson's poem glorifying the empire and its noble burden, which made Spencer, in his own words, 'very angry'.[91]

The popularity of militant imperialism contradicted Spencer's theory of progress from the militant society to industrial. Moreover, the emotional 'mob-jingoism' made him doubt his former belief in the eventual hegemony of reason over passionate emotion, too. Towards the end of the century, then, Spencer became disillusioned about the power to persuade people by reasoned arguments, denying 'that human beings were rational creatures at all'.[92] He employed the concept of 're-barbarisation' to describe the 'ethical evolution in reverse' which he observed in the society.[93] 'At present there is an unusual resurgence of the passions of the brute', he wrote to a friend, when men 'pride themselves in approaching as nearly as they can to the character of the bull-dog'.[94] Spencer's thoughts about this turn-of-the-century imperialism were most clearly formulated in his last book, *Facts and Comments*, which was published in 1902.[95] In it he argued that imperialism represented slavery to both the master and the captive, for they were tied to each other in many ways. He warned that because of its imperialist policy Britain too was in danger: 'in proportion as liberty is diminished in the societies over which it rules, liberty is diminished within its own organization.' Thus, 'a society which enslaves other societies enslaves itself', as it had been in Rome and other empires before.[96] Lord Hobhouse expressed the same idea in a private letter at about the same time when complaining how the new catchphrase of '*Imperium* et *libertas*' was 'the fantastic quip of a fantastic politician whom the irony of fate induced the magnates of England to put at their head'. In his opinion

> '*Imperium* aut *libertas*' fits the case better; for the two are contradictory to one another. It is obvious that the military habit necessary for a conquering nation must crush individual freedom. And where is the instance in history of a people who set themselves to subjugate their neighbours and have remained free themselves? ... I fear that we have chosen *Imperium* and rejected *Libertas*. We are fast becoming a military empire.[97]

Spencer's stance in regard to the Boer War was clear. When asked to sign a protest he declined on the ground that it was not 'sufficiently strong, and not sufficiently concise'. In his opinion the British outlanders who had moved to the Boer territory were 'a swarm of unwelcome intruders and had no right to complain of the social regime into which they intruded themselves, since nobody asked them to stay if they did not like it'; moreover, 'they were proved traitors trying to overturn the government which gave them hospitality, and ... were long contemplating a rising and a seizure of the government of the country'. He wanted the protest to clearly emphasise that 'the Boers have done no more than would inevitably have been done by ourselves if similarly placed, and in doing which we should have regarded ourselves as patriotic and highly praiseworthy', and that 'the advocacy of annexation is nothing more than a continuance of our practice of political burglary'. 'We are rightly vituperated by other nations, as we should vituperate any one of them who did similar things, and as we are now vituperating Russia for its policy in Finland, carried out in a much milder manner', Spencer concluded.[98]

Spencer found it useless to appeal to reason when the public was passionate. The only way to attack the emotions which Tennyson, among others, had stirred was to write a powerful anti-imperialist poem. Unable to write one himself, Spencer looked for a suitable person to do this from the mid-1890s onwards. What he wanted from the poet was a clear expression of power and 'a due amount of burning sarcasm'. Having seen quotations from Blunt's *The Wind and the Whirlwind*, he decided to approach him on the matter in autumn 1898. Spencer suggested an adaptation of the theme from Goethe's *Faust*, 'an interview and dialogue in which Satan seeks authority to find some being more wicked than himself, with the understanding that, if he succeeds, this being shall take his place. The test of wickedness is to be the degree of disloyalty – the degree of rebellion against divine government', he explained to Blunt.[99]

Blunt was only pleased to write the poem which he named *Satan Absolved* and dedicated to Spencer. According to Spencer's wish, Blunt did not indicate the origin of the idea to Spencer, for Spencer thought this would have only aroused 'still greater antagonism' towards him and prevented the spread of his evolutionary views, which would have been 'a greater evil than any benefit to be gained'.[100] Months later Spencer wrote to Blunt to tell that there was in fact a 'wide difference between the general conception as embodied by you and the conception which I had myself formed and suggested' for the poem. It was, he thought, unquestionable that 'Satan's description of Man and his doings is given with great power, and ought to bring to their sense millions of hypocrites who profess the current religion', Spencer stated – for instance, the devil explained to the Lord God that 'The white man's burden, Lord, is the burden of his cash'[101] – but he still wished that Blunt 'would emphasize more strongly the gigantic lie daily enacted; the contrast between the Christian professions and the pagan actions, and the perpetual insult to one they call Omniscient in thinking that they can compound for atrocious deeds by laudatory words'.[102]

Blunt, like Spencer, had suffered from political depression for some years. At the end of 1895 he wrote in his diary: 'I am tired of polit-ics, even Eastern ones, I shall never write anything of value again.'[103] Only five days later, however, he was thrilled about the 'excellent news' from South Africa, where 'those black guards of the South African Chartered Company under ... Jameson have made a filibustering raid on the Transvaal & have been annihilated by the Boers, Jameson a prisoner. I trust devoutly he may be hanged', Blunt wrote with pleas-ure.[104] For a while it seemed to him as if the incident would cause a decline in the popularity of the empire, but his joy was premature. Spencer still tried to see some light at the end of the tunnel, assuring Blunt that although they were

> commencing a long course of re-barbarization from which the reaction may take very long in coming, I nevertheless hold that a reaction will come, and look forward with hope to a remote future of a desirable kind, to be reached after numerous move-ments of progress and retrogression. Did I think that men were likely to remain in the far future anything like what they now are, I should contemplate with equanimity the sweeping away of the whole race.[105]

Blunt's respect for England, and European civilisation in general, could not have been any lower than it was at the turn of the century. He noted in desperation how the British empire was 'playing the devil' in the world 'as never before an Empire did on such a scale'. Spencer's assurances may have done some good, however, for optimistically he added: 'I am convinced however that the decline has set in & we may even live to see the fall.' Nevertheless, for the moment there was no doubt that an age of re-barbarisation had come:

All nations of Europe are making hell upon Earth in China, massacring and pillaging & raping in the captured cities as outrageously as in the Middle Ages – the Emperor of Germany gives the word for slaughter & the Pope looks on & approves. In South Africa our troops are burning farms under the command of the scoundrel Kitchener, & the Queen & the two houses of Parliament & the bunch of Bishops thank God & vote money for the work. The Americans are spending 50 millions a year on slaughtering the Filipins. ... The French & Italians for the moment are playing a less prominent part in the slaughter but they are grieving at their inactivity. The whole white race is revelling openly in violence as though it had never pretended to be Xtian – God's curse upon them all & may God doubly confound our precious British Empire its church & Parliament & Queen-Empress & all the Royal family! So ends the famous XIXth Century into which we were so proud to have been born.[106]

Most of all Blunt despised the British 'self-worship': the never-ending praises for the imperial expansion and its glories and Britain's 'mission of freedom and justice'. He wrote a long public letter to point out 'the huge vulgarity of pretending to be other than the miserable sinners we are' by examining 'the broad facts' of the past century.[107] Britain had impoverished once wealthy India, Blunt insisted; China and Africa were equally doomed; the once 'happy races' of the Pacific Isles as well as Maoris were 'dying out' – 'Are these things, I ask, things to be proud of, to be the subject of our boastings...? Surely, on the contrary, we should hide our heads in shame,' he declared.[108] Anyone who claimed that 'out of all this good will come!' was heavily mistaken, for the subjected nations certainly did not benefit, and neither did England, Blunt stated. According to his observations during the past fifty years there were 'changes in England indicative of moral and material decay corresponding very closely with the ruin we have inflicted on others', similar with imperial Spain: the industriousness of the British had collapsed, for 'the Imperial Englishman needs his imperial amusement too much'.[109] The whole world ridiculed Britain, Blunt argued, for there never was a more amusing spectacle known than the one when 'high-minded England, with her traditional love of liberty' was 'now given wholly over to the rage of destruction, outraging the whole decent feeling of the world by a war of extermination against a people which, whether right or wrong at the outset, is now fighting only for its existence! What a spectacle is this, and what a moral degradation!'[110] In his view the end of the century should be the time of silence and humiliation rather than arrogance; Blunt therefore advised all 'to sit with ashes on our heads, mourning for what it [the nineteenth century] has brought us in the loss of our old virtue'.[111]

Edward Spencer Beesly was equally disappointed by how easily the British public swallowed the 'noble notion' of the 'white man's burden'. In his view, it was 'an ignorant and shallow conception of civilisation to suppose that the religion, morality, and manners prevailing in one part of the world are also suitable to another which is subject to very different conditions'. These imperialists recognised only one norm of civilisation, he asserted: 'that which prevails in England in the year 1899'.[112] Moreover, in reality the conquests were never made 'in an altruistic spirit', Beesly argued, for 'if they were undertaken as a "burden", and were expected to furnish "no profit beyond fair pay for honest work", they would never be attempted' in the first place.[113]

Sir Wilfrid Lawson, too, ridiculed the naïve public in his inimitable style:

> The British flag shall ne'er be furled,
> We'll be the bullies of the world.
> How have we made our glorious name?
> From Heaven the great commission came:
>
> 'Go rule the earth, ye Britons, go,
> Led by your mighty leader "Joe".'
> From rank to rank the watchword flew,
> With echoing 'Cock-a-doodle-doo!'[114]

Anti-imperialist pessimism reached its peak at the time of the Boer War but the war also turned out to be the turning point, beginning the new century of somewhat more popular anti-imperialism. The twenty-seven-year-old Bertrand Russell was among those who at the outbreak of the war in 1899 were, due to the patriotically appealing rhetoric, staunch defenders of British imperialism. By the end of the war Russell, like many others, had, however, abandoned the view,[115] and he later became one of the most prominent anti-imperialists and pacifists of the twentieth century.

David Blitz has pointed out how Russell was greatly influenced in this change by Louis Couturat, a French philosopher. In December 1899 Russell, too, was 'so crushed' by Britain's 'disgrace' that he was 'unable to think of anything else', he wrote to Couturat. Unlike Blunt and others, however, Russell was depressed by the British defeats in South Africa. Embracing the imperialists' notion of 'empire-patriotism', he could nothing but 'hope for the success of our armies, in the first place because of stupid and instinctive patriotism, but also for more profound reasons'. He explained to Couturat how 'intellectuals' 'for the greater part' did not oppose English imperialism, since they considered it was inspired 'by the idea of Rome, by the history of Mommsen (whose maxims will justify anything), by Carlyle and by Nietzsche, and finally by Darwin and evolution'.[116] Couturat accepted that Russell's patriotism was 'the legitimate love of one's own country', but he warned of chauvinism and jingoism, which he regarded as 'perversion of patriotism used to justify conquest of other countries'. 'The philosophy which inspires' imperialism, Couturat wrote, was 'especially hideous', for it was all about 'the Bismarckian maxim: force takes precedence over law and rights' and 'the adoration of ... brutal force'. 'This also, unfortunately, is part of your national traditions, and in practice is translated into egoistic and aggressive chauvinism, an insatiable thirst for conquest and domination; though it may invoke the glorious (but hardly enviable) memory of Rome, it necessarily provokes the antipathy and the distrust of the other nations', the French wrote, revealing a very different notion of 'traditional Englishness' than the anti-imperialists with their emphasis on English liberal values.[117]

Russell did not give up that easily but continued arguing his case for imperialism.[118] Couturat, too, continued his counter-arguing, accusing Russell for being 'duped by imperialist propaganda' in his sixteen-page-long letter in April 1900. He insisted that the right principles of international law were those of Immanuel Kant 'and not those of Bismarck or Napoleon'; he even added that the peaceful notions of Kant were 'in conformity with the most noble and generous traditions of the French spirit'.[119] It is worth noting that Herbert Spencer was equally a disciple of Kant;[120] moreover, Couturat used a very Spencerian language to condemn the British 'crime against humanity' when Britain, 'through arrogance, ambition, and egoism', had negated the results of the Hague Peace Conference, thus taking 'a step back for civilization, a return towards barbarity'.[121] Russell disagreed, insisting that, in contrast, British liberal imperialism spread civilised government and gradually improved the lives of the 'savages'.[122] Two years later, however, Russell was ready to agree with Couturat, finding himself 'much less imperialistic than before' and 'disgusted' at the British concentration camps in South Africa.[123] Many, indeed, felt the same.

CHAPTER 6

OLD AND NEW LIBERAL ANTI-IMPERIALISM

The real question is not of the amount of England's power in the world, but of the nature of that power: whether it shall be physical or moral.[1]

— John Atkinson Hobson in 1897

A nation, roughly speaking, must be ruled either by moral ideals or by appetite; by the critical spirit or by the acquisitive spirit, by its reformers or by its self-seekers.[2]

— John Mackinnon Robertson in 1899

Anti-imperialists approached the issue of imperialism primarily from the point of view of ethics and only secondarily from that of politics. John Morley, for instance, considered aggressive imperialism and military expeditions as moral questions, but those inclined to Liberal imperialism, like Joseph Chamberlain, regarded them as political questions. To Morley it was the moral principle that mattered; to Chamberlain it was the political context.[3] This difference of approach at least partly explains Chamberlain's seemingly inconsistent opinions on British imperialism: by the mid-1880s he mostly opposed imperialism because he wanted to focus the political attention to domestic grievances, but as the political context changed he too changed his approach.

Interestingly, in the domestic context this ethical element manifested itself in two, seemingly opposite, ways. According to the law of equal freedom, as formulated by Herbert Spencer, many older critics made a combined stance on behalf of individualism and liberalism against both imperialism and socialism. To these 'Old Liberals' – like Spencer, John Morley, Goldwin Smith, and Lord Hobhouse – imperialism and socialism, or collectivism, were representations of the same problem: the growing powers of the state over the individual. In contrast, the younger generation of 'New Liberals' – like William Clarke, J. M. Robertson, and J. A. Hobson – advocated advanced leftwing social reforms in domestic politics, while they opposed imperialism with equal strength. The transition from the individualist to the collectivist Liberal anti-imperialism was perhaps the most notable change in the anti-imperialist principles in general in the late-Victorian era.

'Modern Imperialism, wherever tried, has produced *Socialism*,' declared Frederic Seebohm when he examined the issue of imperialism and socialism in its larger European context at the time of the election campaign in 1880:

> Democracy is the claim of a self-reliant people for equal rights and fair play for every man, standing on his own feet, to guide his own life unfettered by needless interference on the part of the State. Socialism is the sad opposite of this. It is the cry of a helpless and enfeebled residuum unable to run alone, calling for a State which ... shall do everything for it – feed, clothe, and amuse it. ... This terrible result seems to be the logical consequence of a necessary course of action on the part of modern Imperialism – viz., the subordination of internal development to external military ascendancy. It would seem that the two ends cannot both be attained.[4]

Imperialism, i.e. the policy of military ascendancy abroad, necessitated more personal rule in order to be successful, which resulted in depreciation of representative institutions, Seebohm argued. 'The rulers take the reins into their own hands, and the nation expects everything from them and less and less from itself. ... This results in an alliance of the monarch and the mob. The popular will is invoked by appeals to popular passions rather than by argument addressed to the best minds of the nation,' he warned, strongly anticipating the later anti-imperialist accounts described in the previous chapter. According to Seebohm, imperial interests led inevitably to the neglect of domestic questions and the increases in taxation, thus causing wide discontent and spread of socialist ideas among the working classes. This had already occurred in Russia, Germany, and France, Seebohm stated.[5] He continued:

> But there was one nation free from this necessity, which seemed to be committed to a policy the reverse of Imperial. Its government was not a union of the monarch and the mob, but a free Parliamentary government under a Queen. ... Through a long reign of this enlightened policy it had grown in freedom and respect for law, as well as in population, commerce, and wealth. ... And yet this moment, when Continental Imperialism is everywhere confronted by Socialism, it is chosen by the ruling party of the English nation – the party calling itself conservative – to let itself be drawn by its leader into a policy which he himself has cynically and theatrically recommended to the nation under the ill-fated name of 'Imperialism'![6]

England, then, under Liberal guidance, was the hope of whole Europe; England remained, for Seebohm, 'the only great European nation' which could reverse this course of history towards imperialism and socialism by persisting in maintaining its traditional liberal values and institutions. 'Is it too much to say that the future of civilisation depends upon whether the great problem of democracy, which it seems to be the chosen destiny of England and her children to grapple with, can be fairly solved?' Seebohm asked. He stressed, right before the election, that 'the home and foreign policy of a nation with so unique a destiny must be consistent. This fact alone excludes Imperialism.'[7]

Herbert Spencer was at least as committed in his anti-socialism as in anti-imperialism.[8] His conception of *laissez-faire* was, indeed, all-embracing. As he clarified his stance to J. E. Cairnes in 1873: 'I do not think that *laissez-faire* is to be regarded simply as a politico-economical principle only, but as a much wider principle – the principle of letting all citizens take the benefits and evils of their own acts: not only such as are consequent on their industrial conduct, but such as are consequent upon their conduct in general.' Accordingly, something like a Poor Law would be 'a gross breach of *laissez-faire*', Spencer stated.[9] While the rising tide of imperialism depressed him later, so did the increasing popularity of collectivist policies in the Liberal party. In 1881 he was still hopeful that this process could be reversed: 'In our day Toryism and Liberalism have become confused, and the line between them has to be drawn afresh. Toryism stands for the coercive power of the State *versus* the freedom of the individual. Liberalism stands for the freedom of the individual *versus* the power of the State. At present the Liberal party has to be formed to re-assert it.'[10] Like Seebohm, Spencer condemned the 'influences of various kinds' which 'conspired to increase corporate action and decrease individual action'. 'The numerous socialistic changes made by Act of Parliament, joined with the numerous others presently to be made, will by-and-by be all merged in State-Socialism', he predicted in 1884; and, like imperialism, 'all socialism' involved 'slavery', for 'that which fundamentally distinguishes the slave is that he labours under coercion to satisfy another's desires', Spencer formulated.[11] He even declined to become a member of the League of Liberals Against Aggression and Militarism in 1900, since he did not want 'to be classed among those who are in these days called Liberals' because of their eagerness to extend the power of the state and restrict the freedom of the individual. 'In the days when the name came into use, the Liberals were those who aimed to extend the freedom of the individual *versus* the power of the State,' he repeated again.[12]

Goldwin Smith, too, complained of the 'increased interference of government' in all matters of life and, instead, advocated 'individual effort, free association, and the same agencies, moral, intellectual, and economical, which have brought us thus far'. In 1894 Smith even claimed that England was 'apparently drifting towards socialistic revolution'.[13] At the same time he equally denounced the imperialist spirit, referring similarly to traditional English policies and 'the spirit of her free institutions' instead. 'There is surely no disparagement in saying that England's real strength was always in herself', Smith maintained, persisting that 'when the advocate of prudence is flouted as a "Little Englander" his answer is that bulk is not sinew and that he prefers the strong man to the stuffed giant.'[14]

Lord Hobhouse, Sir Arthur Hobhouse until 1885, was yet another 'Old Liberal' who criticised the 'modern tendencies' of imperialism and socialism.[15] 'It was with the deepest regret that he witnessed the defection of a large portion of the Liberal Party from its old principles in relation to these matters,'[16] his biographers, both anti-imperialists of the younger Liberal generation, put it in 1905: in Hobhouse's view 'a profound change had affected the national temper, and the only hope of permanent and genuine improvement lay in the return to the better ideals of an earlier day'.[17] During the Boer War Hobhouse, like Spencer, felt unable 'to join in electoral operations merely because they profess to be on behalf of "Liberals"; seeing that many who call themselves Liberals (I fear the great majority) are merely competing with the Tories which shall make the most show in doing the work of the Primrose, or the Army and Navy Leagues', he complained. He declared that at least since the mid-1890s he had 'been convinced that the Liberal Party will do nothing as long as they try to conciliate men whose ideals of national welfare and greatness are directly antagonistic to Liberal ideals, at least, as I have always understood them'.[18] A couple of years later he joined the League of Liberals against Aggression and Militarism, still regretting that there were 'as many subdivisions of men called Liberals as there are of Methodists, or more'. He recalled how

> just twenty years earlier Herbert Spencer and others, who saw deep into the main currents of thought, tried to form a similar organization, and a meeting was convened at this house. But it all came to nothing. Nearly all the Liberals were supine, saying, and I suppose thinking, as Sir William Harcourt openly boasted, that the election of 1880 had finally crushed the Jingoes.[19]

Despite the serious blow that William Gladstone gave to antiimperialism in 1882 these 'Old Liberals' looked back to his era with deep nostalgia. This was especially true in the case of John Morley, who was also a friend of Herbert Spencer. To Morley, opposition to both imperialism and collectivism amounted to safeguarding the principles of true Liberalism. This was despite the fact that in regard to foreign affairs and anti-imperialism Morley in fact identified with Edmund Burke more than with any Liberal thinker; Burke, as a great literary talent 'taking active part in great events', was, in this sense, his role model.[20] John Stuart Mill's influence on Morley was enormous in general, but it is noteworthy that in regard to imperialism this influence was clearly visible only when Morley had to *defend* his policies as the secretary of state for India in the early twentieth century.[21] The Liberal Mill, then, provided the model for defending Liberal imperialism while the more conservative Burke was his anti-imperialist exemplar.[22] Nevertheless, Morley connected anti-imperialism as well as anti-collectivism tightly with true Liberalism. Furthermore, even after the British entanglements in Egypt, the Sudan, and elsewhere under Gladstone's premiership, Morley equalled anti-imperialism with Gladstonianism; the Liberal imperialists, then, amounted primarily to 'anti-Gladstonians'.[23]

Morley saw imperialism in direct contravention of democracy and English liberty. 'Parliamentary government' and 'an imperial policy' were 'absolutely and for ever incompatible', he maintained in 1878; for the 'very essence' of imperialism involved 'a vast fabric of military administration and a thousand secret schemes of military movement', which made it the exact opposite of 'an open democracy of free people, such as ours is'.[24] Imperialism as well as British coercion in Ireland represented thus severe threats to British Liberalism and democracy, and opposition to them was, to Morley, the natural 'test of definition of true Liberalism', as David Hamer has put it.[25] Based on the election results of 1880 Morley was convinced that British working men were against imperialism, and in 1885 he suggested anti-imperialism as 'the great Radical cause' for the next parliamentary election as well.[26] He argued that opposition to imperialist policies was much more significant than Chamberlain's radical social programme, since continuous military and imperialist interventions abroad would necessarily delay any domestic reform.[27] He repeated this argument in 1899, pointing out that as long as the major part of public expenditure and political attention were diverted abroad any talk of financial and social progress at home was 'complete moonshine'.[28]

Morley greatly detested the popular working-class imperialism of the turn of the century, and he continuously emphasised, in contrast to Lord Rosebery and the Liberal imperialists, that imperialism abroad and social progress at home were incompatible. He was particularly concerned about the fast increasing imperial expenditure, for he feared that once the taxation had been readjusted to pay for the war, it would never be returned back to the pre-war level after the conflict. This would result in major changes in Britain's economic and social structure and, since some people would be taxed more heavily than others, in introducing dangerous class distinctions into British politics. Imperialism was thus closely connected to the undesirable increasing power of the state and central government, and by the 1890s Morley had become a doctrinaire opponent of state intervention. In order to prevent 'mischievous and dangerous' experiments to please sectional or class interests, he even argued in favour of transferring more power from the state to local governments.[29]

This combination of anti-imperialism and anti-collectivism separated Morley to some extent from other prominent Liberal anti-imperialists like Sir William Harcourt and Henry Labouchere. They, too, opposed imperialism on the ground that it diverted attention from reform in Britain; however, although Morley wanted to prevent widespread radicalism, Harcourt and Labouchere advocated it. For them it was genuinely a political matter, it was not about moral principles. Morley, who particularly disliked Harcourt's support for the Eight Hours Bill in 1892, regarded both Harcourt and Labouchere as opportunists who were only after 'the Radical vote' with their 'extreme' visions.[30] He preferred the more elitist Rosebery to Harcourt as the next party leader in 1894, for he hoped that Rosebery would 'take Collectivism boldly by the throat',[31] but he was to disappoint. At the turn of the century, when Morley's disappointment with the Liberal party was at its widest, he considered Rosebery, with his 'slippery' statements 'with no firm political substance', to be a good enough leader 'for a party without principles'.[32] By this time the earlier differences between

Morley and Harcourt had been put behind; anti-imperialism was, in the end, more powerful in combining than the issues of collectivism were in separating. After all, Harcourt, too, considered himself as the disciple of Richard Cobden and William Gladstone, advocating peace and goodwill in international relations; and, like Morley, Harcourt felt, amongst the 'high and aggressive mood of the country' at the end of the century, to be 'something like a survival of a past age'.[33]

Indeed, for a brief period in the 1890s Morley came to regard anti-imperialism as a policy which had the potential to unite the Liberals. He hoped that the clear principle of anti-imperialism would prevent any further disruption inside the Liberal party and would advance its reconstruction.[34] David Hamer has pointed out that there was 'an element of continuity' in the transfer of Morley's interest from home rule to anti-imperialism when 'denial of self-government to Ireland had become bound up in the larger issue of imperialism'. Anti-imperialism, in Morley's view, provided the Liberal party with 'simple, clear-cut definitions of liberal principles' and 'a firm and distinctive ground of its own', as Hamer has put it.[35] Morley stressed that the party could survive only if it stuck to its traditional values of peace, economy, and reform, instead of trying to outdo the Tories and the Unionists in popular imperialism.[36] He warned that the day when those traditional principles were forsaken 'the Liberal party would have to disband and to disappear', and 'the Socialists would take its place'.[37] Despite his hopes, Morley, like many other anti-imperialists, became 'disgusted' at the jingoistic imperialism of the turn of the century. It seemed to be a 'new world into which you and I have survived', he wrote to Frederic Harrison; and, like Harrison, he, too, pondered over going abroad because of the 'really hellish' moral and political atmosphere in England.[38] He became increasingly inactive and withdrew to write his *Life of Gladstone*, which Francis Hirst, Labouchere, Harcourt, W. S. Blunt, and other kindred spirits were disappointed to note.[39] By 1902 Morley had thus given up of his idea to revive the Liberal party around one principle, accepting it as 'a coalition of interests'.[40]

Apart from these 'Old Liberal' critics there were many who linked anti-imperialist and socialist opinions essentially together. At the time of Blunt's campaigns for Egypt and India in the early 1880s, the

Marxist critic H. M. Hyndman sent him socialist literature in the hope that Blunt would 'join their ranks', too. 'I think it must be clear to you that the infamous capitalist system under which not only the workers but all of us suffer is responsible for the existing miserable state of India, Egypt and other countries, as well as for the awful situation of degradation of our working population at home,' Hyndman argued,[41] unsuccessfully. The more moderate – and also more popular – way for the left-wing critics was to contrast imperialism abroad with social reform at home, as Harcourt and Labouchere as well as, indeed, even John Morley from a different point of view, did. Sir Wilfrid Lawson caught the mood of these collectivist anti-imperialists neatly in a poem which examined the Britons' relations to imperialism:

> For this we eat, for this we drink,
> For this to idiocy we sink,
> To bursting point our Budgets swell,
> And in our slums gaunt paupers dwell.
>
> But who to heart such things would take
> When glorious Empire is at stake?[42]

This question appealed especially to those Christian ethicists who were more concerned about the welfare of the British poor than missionary work in Africa. James Guinness Rogers, for instance, expressed at the time of the Uganda debate his surprise at how 'Radicals with Socialist proclivities should declare themselves in favour of an aggressive Imperialism'. He declared that if the people's attention was called away to the 'buccaneering expeditions' in Uganda it was 'tolerably certain' that 'the social reforms so much needed at home may be postponed till the Greek Kalends'. Rogers strongly agreed with those who held 'that in opposing these aggressive tendencies they are showing the truest patriotism' and that it was 'neither territory nor prestige, but righteousness, which exalteth a nation'. Rogers predicted, like Hobson later, that the empire might 'well become a danger to a State' through 'the creation of a class of men accustomed to rule, and alien in spirit from the people whose authority they represent', for eventually these 'prancing proconsuls' returned home 'to carry out in domestic politics the arbitrary principles on which they have acted in our dependencies', and the British liberal democracy would be ruined.[43] Rogers acknowledged that while he had never been 'in sympathy with the views of the extreme Manchester school' he had become more and more convinced of 'the peril of that Imperialist policy' with its 'deeds of high-handed aggression'. 'Of course, those who take this view will be charged with wishing to belittle England. It is a well-worn cry which we can afford to treat with indifference,' he advised his kindred spirits.[44]

An even better example of Christian social anti-imperialism was Charles F. G. Masterman's and nine other writers' book *The Heart of the Empire*, published in 1901, which discussed the various 'problems of modern city life in England', from housing to temperance and from church and industry to imperialism. The book began by pointing out that, due to imperialism, enthusiasm for social reform had waned significantly during the past twenty years.[45] G. P. Gooch, whose chapter on imperialism deplored the increasing intolerance, glorification of war, poverty of India, and Britain's disrespect towards native rights, summarised their position:

> To carry out the transformation detailed in the foregoing chapters of this volume are needed time, money, and resolve. But these indispensable conditions are not at the present moment forthcoming, principally owing to the domination of certain theories of foreign policy. Until this attitude is modified, ethical democracy has little chance of asserting or establishing its claims.[46]

Masterman and Gooch, both young Cambridge academics, belonged to the younger generation of 'New Liberals' which became particularly active at the end of the century. New Liberals argued that true liberty was not in 'the absence of restraint' as the Old Liberals understood it, but in 'the presence of opportunity', as William Clarke put it in 1893.[47] Clarke, like so many other anti-imperialists, had been influenced by positivism in his youth and was a friend of Frederic

Harrison's.[48] Similarly, like so many other anti-imperialists, Clarke 'had a positive distaste for the mechanism of politics, regarding it as concerned too much with measures and politicians, too little with principles and ideas', as his friend Herbert Burrows described him. One of the chief reasons for this was 'his sense of disillusionment with regard to public affairs', Burrows suspected: 'The slowness of the march of progress seemed at times almost to chill his blood.' Clarke – again like so many other anti-imperialists – 'had firmly convinced himself that, outwardly at any rate, England was on the down-grade, and that, as with the Cities of the Plain, retribution in some shape or form was surely awaiting her', Burrows formulated. Nevertheless, even though 'the eternal verities' were for the time being 'clouded ... by the folly and ignorance of humanity', 'never did he lose his ultimate faith in man'.[49]

Clarke chaired the first meeting of the Rainbow Circle, the new informal but regular meeting point for progressive New Liberals, on 7 November 1894.[50] The whole first session of 1894–5 was dedicated to discussions on 'the Old Manchesterism and the New Radicalism'.[51] The Circle attracted not only many other young anti-imperialists like J. M. Robertson, G. H. Perris, and J. A. Hobson but also progressive imperialists like Herbert Samuel and Douglas Morrison. They all agreed about the importance of social reform, but the disagreements on British imperialism became more dominant year by year and significantly de-capacitated the whole enterprise. This was obvious by 1896, when Clarke began editing the Circle's journal, *Progressive Review*. In a letter to Ramsay MacDonald, with whom Clarke had an additional 'nasty dispute' about the *Review*'s funds, Clarke declared the imperialists' view on foreign policy as 'bastard Liberalism'.[52]

The *Progressive Review* lasted only a year, but its collapse made Clarke even more committed in his anti-imperialism. He abandoned socialism and resigned from the Fabian Society in 1897 due to the Fabians' support to imperialism.[53] 'I have given up all work of the reforming kind, for it is useless', he wrote to a friend: 'The masses are just fools and just as greedy & material as the rest of the community. They won't let one do anything. England is growing more & more rotten every day.'[54] To the Fabian Sidney Webb he declared that 'I detest bureaucratic imperialism so much that I can scarcely trust myself to speak on it'.[55] In public, too, Clarke argued:

> Thirst for empire, thirst for gold, thirst for amusement have eaten deep into the heart of the English character, and in my opinion have largely transformed the national life. Until England is delivered from the moral hypnotism under which she is enslaved at the present time, she can do nothing for progress, nothing for humanity.[56]

Nevertheless, the meetings of the Rainbow Circle continued, and imperialism was boldly chosen as the theme for the session of 1899–1900.[57] At the first meeting, on 4 October 1899, J. M. Robertson suggested that, for clarity, the meaning of empire should be restricted 'to the rule of a state over a subject aggregate' only. The imperialist relationship was thus a relationship between the conqueror and the conquered. The discussion which followed was 'prolonged'.[58] Clarke addressed the Circle on imperialism and democracy a month later. He referred to the Roman example and argued that imperialism always led to conditions 'which no democracy could survive': 'to militarism & Caesarism, to slaughterings & conquests, to centralisation & officialdom, to an economic parasitism & exploitation, to the separation of economic classes at home'. The imperialist spirit was always accompanied by the military spirit, which was seen as much in the increase of armaments as in the increase of bureaucracy in general and 'the secrecy with which public affairs are conducted', Clarke stated. Democratic power was therefore declining.[59] His views were summarised in the minute of the meeting: 'It is a mere delusion to believe that it is our love of freedom & uprightness which makes us an imperial people. We are suffering from a combination of the capitalist & the soldier which in the course of a generation or two will kill democracy in this country.'[60] In the following discussion it was interestingly noted that the self-governing colonies were in fact more democratic but at the same time more imperialist than Britain, due to their expansive nature and treatment of native inhabitants.[61]

The imperialist reverend Douglas Morrison addressed the Circle at the third meeting of the session, on 6 December 1899. Morrison

argued that the British empire promoted civilisation and liberty, and
if this work was condemned then the existence of the United States
and Canada should be condemned, too. The Circle's anti-imperialist
members were quick to criticise Morrison's concept of empire and to
point out that moral individuals were better civilisers than nations
which imposed law and order.[62] The division between imperialists
and anti-imperialists became equally clear at the Circle's next meeting, when Herbert Samuel argued that imperialism and social reform
were completely compatible and even supplemented each other. 'The
"Little Englandism" of many Progressives stands in the way of Social
Reform' in Britain, Samuel argued, for imperialism generated wealth
and 'poverty can best be fought where riches are most accumulated'. In
the dependencies, too, he continued, 'the excellence of British administration' contributed to social reform by 'uplifting the native'.[63] In the
following discussion, in contrast, it was stated that 'Empire produced
pride & contempt; materialised the Imperial people'; and 'increased
the volume of trade without increasing the organisation of industry'.[64]
Moreover, later in the spring Hobson further emphasised that civilisation could not be imposed; it could only grow. Unlike the imperialists
seemed to think, he stated, the upholding of law and order by coercion
did not amount to civilisation.[65]

William Clarke's alienation from socialism and Fabianism because
of their imperialism brought him interestingly closer to the individualist argument. He warned about the dangers 'of making the State,
instead of the individual, the end of policy'. In the case of Germany,
for instance, Clarke saw no difference whether it was ruled by despots
or social democrats 'in their present temper', for in either case 'the
means would justify the end, and "reasons of State" would determine
policy'.[66] He wrote in 1900:

> The idyllic State dreamed of by some of our good Socialist friends
> is a very different thing from any actual Socialist State that could
> be framed now, with men as they are. The latter would be a State
> armed with vast military power, able to crush all opposition to
> its will, and, above all, 'run' in the interests and modelled after
> the ideals of the average sensual man – not a very attractive

picture to those who think our existing States of Europe far too strong already, and who would be glad to see a rehabilitation of the individual.[67]

Clarke also resigned from the *Daily Chronicle*, for which he had worked for nine years, when the paper began supporting the Boer War.[68] He died suddenly in 1901, but many of his ideas were later developed by J. A. Hobson and Leonard Hobhouse.[69]

Unlike Clarke, who had for a while been enchanted with socialism, John M. Robertson had always kept a distance from it. He criticised socialism for its class antagonism and maintained that liberalism, in contrast, recognised broader needs than those of any 'class'.[70] At the same time his stance in regard to the importance and urgency of social reform was unshaken. In his most important anti-imperialist work, *Patriotism and Empire*, Robertson stated that it was 'the ancient schism of rich and poor' which formed 'the fundamental evil which made militarism still possible'. This was most clear in France where the revolutions had paved the way for the first and second empires, and still in the third republic the social problem pressed 'hard and steadily'.[71] In Britain 'the strife of classes' had been less marked than in the continent, but to Robertson the rise of the imperialist movement represented 'a half-distinctive reckoning' on the fact that a crisis lied ahead in England, too. He quoted the famous catchphrase of 'opening up new markets in the waste places of the earth' to illustrate his point that

The primary object is not to buy, but to sell, and receive goods in return to sell again; all to the end of heaping up more capital for investment. Our own toilers are not to do more consuming, to begin with: it is not their lot that is in question; at most it is assumed that they can prosper only through the prosperity of capital.[72]

Through the decisions made in parliament, the British imperialist policy deliberately subsidised the interests of 'the speculative trading class, the speculative capitalist class, the military and naval services, the industrial class which supplies war material, and generally those who look to an imperial civil service as a means of employment for themselves and their kin', Robertson argued.[73] The same parliament, he declared, rejected any appeal 'for the relief of masses of unemployed men' stating 'that such provision is outside the proper functions of Parliament'; 'The proper function of Parliament, as now conceived, is to spend as many millions as possible in the interests of the moneyed and well-to-do minority,' Robertson stated. He summarised his conclusions bluntly:

> As against all the sophistries we have passed under review, the central truth falls to be stated thus: imperial expansion is substantially a device on the part of the moneyed class, primarily to further its own chances, secondarily to put off the day of reckoning as between capital and labour. It does not and cannot bring a socially just solution any nearer: it does but secure a possible extension of employment for labour on the old terms.[74]

In Robertson's opinion imperialism and social reform were therefore strictly incompatible; they even excluded each other. Moreover, he accused 'reactionary Ministers' of 'playing the game of militarist imperialism' exactly in order to 'push aside the appeal for such reform'. He maintained that the British working classes were wooed by telling them that they were heirs to an empire and 'of a dominant race', sharing in 'our possessions'.[75] This was a dangerous policy, Robertson argued, as anyone could see from 'the lesson read to us in age after age, in civilization after civilization, by empire after empire that has left only its ruins behind to warn us against the errors by which it perished'.[76]

Morality and love of liberal values – as comprising the 'true' patriotism – were as important for the younger generation of critics as they were for the older one. Robertson emphasised that 'wisdom and righteousness for a nation are not vitally different from what we esteem as wisdom and righteousness in individual men'.[77] J. L. Hammond also argued that domestic reform had 'nothing to hope for until the language of England abroad shall be once again the language of morality', 'till England shall honour her old ideals in the larger affairs of

humanity' and 'the love of country and the love of liberty, divorced today, shall be brought back into their old glorious association'.[78] Francis
Hirst and Gilbert Murray, Hammond's co-authors in *Liberalism and the
Empire*, concurred. In the preface to their book the three young intellectuals declared that there was 'no sentiment so dangerous' and 'easy
to stimulate' as was 'the false excess of patriotism': the whispering of
'the sub-conscious voices of national egotism' that 'we are the pick and
flower of nations, and (in one sense or another) the chosen people of
God!'[79] As opposed to these 'jingoes' or 'chauvinists' there was another
party 'in most civilized countries', the trio wrote, which was inspired
'by the older school of English Liberals' who

> judge of national honour by more or less the same standards as
> they apply to private honour; who believe in international mor-
> ality and in the co-operation of nations for mutual help; who, if
> they are to dream at all, will dream not of Armageddons and
> Empires, but of progress and freedom, and the ultimate frater-
> nity of mankind.[80]

The South Place Ethical Society served similar function as the
Rainbow Circle: the members examined political problems from an
ethical point of view and formulated the ideas of progressive New
Liberalism. The Society's journal, *Ethical World*, largely condemned
imperialist expansion and 'militaristic tendencies', arguing in favour of
native organisations and organic progress 'from within'.[81] The membership in the South Place Ethical Society and the Rainbow Circle was
largely overlapping. J. A. Hobson was particularly prominent in the
Society from 1897 onwards and participated actively in the editing
process of the *Ethical World* after the collapse of the *Progressive Review*.[82]
Edited by an American-born socialist Stanton Coit, the weekly paper
included contributions from a wide range of intellectuals: Herbert
Spencer, J. Ramsay MacDonald, G. H. Perris, J. M. Robertson, James
Bryce, William Clarke, S. G. Hobson, H. M. Hyndman, and George
Bernard Shaw.[83] Indeed, the sharp division between imperialists
and anti-imperialists became clear among the South Place ethicists
as well: Hobson and Ramsay MacDonald criticised imperialism,

while, for instance, the philosopher David George Ritchie and Eduard Bernstein – a revisionist Marxist and German social democrat exiled in London – defended it.[84]

J. A. Hobson's development into an anti-imperialist New Liberal was gradual and not completed until about 1898. In the early 1890s Hobson was much closer to the emerging Liberal imperialist camp than to the anti-imperialists;[85] and even later, as Cain points out, 'Imperialist sympathies of a rather surprising kind remained a part of Hobson's intellectual baggage.'[86] Hobson's New Liberalism came first, and he was an active member of the Rainbow Circle from its start in 1894. Once in the Circle, he became under the anti-imperialist influence of William Clarke and G. H. Perris, especially when assisting Clarke in editing the *Progressive Review* in 1896–7.[87]

Hobson's first attack against aggressive imperialism came in the form of a review of Benjamin Kidd's *Social Evolution* in 1895.[88] A more profound criticism appeared two years later under the disguise of a pseudonym 'Nemo' in an article on the 'ethics of empire' in the *Progressive Review*.[89] Hobson argued that Britain was not a civiliser but a parasite in the conquered territories like India, obstructing their free and natural development. Moreover, England, too, suffered from this parasitic imperialism through the introduction of corruption and authoritarianism back into English politics and, most significantly, through the distraction from domestic problems.[90] Imperialism, then, for its absorption of resources and distraction of attention, became to Hobson '*the* great barrier to social progress', as Peter Cain has pointed out.[91]

Hobson denounced the concept of a 'manifest destiny' as not only 'a wrong view of national conduct' but also 'the negation of all conduct'. In Spencerian terms he maintained that under the guidance of a 'manifest destiny' a nation became itself conducted rather than the reverse. He continued in the same Spencerian vein, stating that territory was 'needed for the self-realisation of a nation: national life is expressed through the character of its population, and this population obviously demands means of physical support'. Bigness, however, was not greatness, if morality was lost in sight; 'are we certain that a free policy of territorial expansion may not enfeeble rather than strengthen national life?' Hobson asked.[92] The only pronounced ethical defence of empire, he noted, was that it contributed 'to the elevation of humanity, to the fulfilment of a rational cosmic plan' by extending 'the bounds of civilisation' and educating 'lower races in the arts of government and commerce'. But 'no one, of course, seriously suggests that our recent advance upon Chitral, our seizures in the Soudan, our crooked policy of grab in South Africa, are consciously undertaken with these lofty motives', Hobson declared. In his opinion British rule was indeed beneficial to India and Egypt but to use that as ethical defence would be 'strange', for the primary reason for the conquests had always been British 'own private ends'.[93] Moreover, he questioned whether it was in fact good for the world to impose 'upon the largest possible area of land certain uniform types of civilisation' as the European empires did.[94] From a different point of view it could even seem to many that India, with its ancient cultures and history, might as well 'have a mission to civilise us', Hobson pointed out.[95]

It is interesting to note how much the New Liberal Hobson was influenced by the theories of Herbert Spencer.[96] The influence was obvious not only in Hobson's ethical condemnation of empire but also, and even more, in his socio-economical arguments. In 1898 Hobson wrote of 'the larger meaning of Free Trade ... as a phase of social evolution by which, on the one hand, militarism is displaced by industrialism, and, on the other hand, political limits of nationalism yield place to an effective internationalism based upon identity of commercial interests'. Needless to say, imperialism and militarism were wholly incompatible with this 'battle of Free Trade' and freedom in general.[97] Moreover, in *Imperialism: A Study* Hobson effectively developed Spencer's division of militant and industrial societies into his famous binary opposition of 'parasitism' and 'industry', the latter representing 'energy, creativity, manly independence, peace, and civic virtue', as Peter Cain has put it, and parasitism and militancy 'the corresponding vices'.[98] Hobson considered imperialism a severe threat to British liberal values first and foremost because it supported militarism and parasitism. Parasitism in general referred to any 'unearned income' in a situation where one group of people lived at the expense of another, and what differentiated Hobson from Spencer was, of course, that Spencer regarded social reform as 'parasitic' as well: to him it amounted to poor people living at the expense of the wealthier and more industrious people. This caused him to oppose fiercely even minor public relief for the poor and free education, which New Liberals could not accept.

Besides Spencer, Hobson was much influenced by the French sociologist Gustave Le Bon.[99] Hobson reviewed the English translation of Le Bon's *The Psychology of Peoples* in the *Ethical World* in February 1899; two years later, when examining the 'mob passion' which excited imperialism and jingoism, he wrote, 'A recent French writer, discoursing on the nature of "a crowd", attributed to it a character and conduct which is lower, intellectually and morally, than the character and conduct of its average member.'[100] This is what Hobson thought happened in Britain during the Boer War, when, in his opinion, irrationality became a commonplace and 'the war-spirit in non-combatant mass mind' differentiated 'savage from civilized man'.[101] Following both Spencer and Le Bon, Hobson declared how the work of 'the mob-mind' staggered 'any confidence one might have held in man as a rational and moral being';[102] indeed, 'no more convincing proof of its mental collapse' could be found.[103] Although these manifestations were completely irrational, Hobson stressed that the manipulation behind them generated from a wholly rational policy of the financiers and politicians who gained from imperialism.[104] Their 'patriotism' was only a 'screen' for pursuing private interests 'under the name and pretext of the commonwealth', he argued.[105]

Ethics and ethical debate served a major combining purpose among the various anti-imperialist groups, significantly narrowing the gap between 'Old' and New Liberals. Anti-imperialists from Herbert Spencer to J. A. Hobson were active ethicists, not even to mention the positivists. The *Ethical World* declared in 1899: 'We believe that Mr. Frederic Harrison may claim the honour and responsibility of the word *ethicist*. He is its father. He did not mean to describe only members of Ethical Societies, but all persons whose supreme interest is in ethical truth as distinct from metaphysical theory about it.'[106] Moreover, although the New Liberals argued that Liberalism ought to be radically reformed to place primary emphasis on social reform and redistribution of income, they also sought to emphasise the continuity within Liberalism. They maintained that their Liberalism was a natural development from the older Cobdenite premises, and in regard to the anti-imperialist ideology in particular they acknowledged their intellectual debts to the Manchester School. They did, indeed, look up to the 'Old Liberals', especially John Morley, and even more so when Morley at the turn of the century became more tolerant towards their social programme of old age pensions and national insurance.[107] Lords Hobhouse and Farrer were equally respected among the New Liberal anti-imperialists.[108]

The old and young Hobhouse, uncle and nephew, illustrate well this rapprochement. Leonard Hobhouse, too, had 'admiringly' read Spencer in his youth and become alienated from the Fabians because of the group's support to imperialism.[109] He was more inclined to follow 'the Gladstonian principle of internationalism' than the 'Cobdenite doctrine of non-intervention' because of the Gladstonian emphasis on morality as the basis of all relations between nations and individuals alike.[110] Hobhouse detested the Liberal imperialists despite their support to social reform, for he regarded them as 'anti-Gladstonians' because of their attacks on Gladstonian morality. He especially admired John Morley, due to Morley's respect for principles and morals in politics.[111] Lord Hobhouse wrote to his New Liberal nephew in 1904:

I should like to see some passages of history put together with the view of showing how certainly, and how quickly, a nation which throws itself into the business of conquest loses its own liberties, and with them its power of initiative and its general health ... The same survey would show how the lust of conquest is habitually disguised under the names of Liberty, Religion, and Peace.[112]

The uncle had just read Leonard Hobhouse's manuscript 'Democracy and Reaction' which was published a few weeks later.[113] Lord Hobhouse suspected that the book could

have none but a good effect, if it has any at all. I add this proviso, because I feel convinced (I dare say you have heard me say so

before) that our countrymen are so besotted with their visions of
Empire ... that nothing will cure us except some great and painful shock ... You are, at all events, right in trying to bring about
a saner mood by appeals to reason.[114]

When commenting on the nephew's manuscript Lord Hobhouse
recounted how he had 'always thought that in 1868, and again in
1880, the nation was, under Gladstone's mighty impulse, moved to a
higher moral level than it was able to maintain, and it fell back accordingly under the influence of coarser passions when the impulse was
relaxed'. Imperialism, in this sense, was a counterattack against liberal
and moral forces. The uncle further instructed the youth that 'India is
the only real "Empire" we possess ... and with its acquisition Liberalism
had very little to do'.[115]

Although the shared fight against imperialism made Hobhouse
and other younger critics more aware of the profound continuity
between 'Old' and New Liberal radicalism, the fact remained that
anti-imperialists were divided into two loose sub-groups of individual-
ists and collectivists. The first group regarded imperialism and socialism as severe breaches of the liberal principle of *laissez-faire*, while the
latter emphasised that imperialism diverted political attention from
social progress at home. John Morley seems to fit rather ambivalently
into both groups, for while he was a staunch individualist and anti-
collectivist, he also repeatedly used the political catchphrases of collectivist anti-imperialists.

Imperialists, in contrast, were more united in advocating 'social
imperialism', i.e. the combination of imperialism abroad and com-
prehensive social reform at home. This was advocated by Joseph
Chamberlain, Lord Rosebery, and the Fabian Socialists alike.[116] The
Fabian Beatrice Webb even drew a distinction in her diary between
collectivist imperialists and the *laissez-faire* anti-imperialists.[117]
Whereas the individualist anti-imperialists regarded imperialism and
social reform as negative programmes of state action, to social imperialists they both represented positive programmes of state action,
strengthening Britain as well as the empire through the British working classes.[118] As Bernard Semmel has explained, the social imperialist

argument could be based on two premises: one group maintained that the empire was essential for the welfare of the working classes, while the other argued that an elevated condition of the working classes would guarantee 'a healthy and vigorous imperial race' and thus form the basis for imperialism.[119]

The Liberal divisions in regard to imperialism and social reform were manifestations of the general confusion and lack of direction inside the party at the end of the nineteenth century. Dennis Smith has argued that the party 'ultimately failed' in its attempt 'to adapt itself to the new England which was coming into existence'; and it was due to this inability 'to come to terms with a society which was urban, industrial, imperialistic and increasingly democratic' that Liberalism 'ceased to be an effective national force after 1916'.[120] Old Liberals, especially, argued their case too much in mid-Victorian terms to appeal to the public; and the differences between New Liberals and moderate Labour in the early 1900s were only nominal.

PART III

THE CONSTITUTIONAL AND POLITICAL DEBATE ON THE EMPIRE

CHAPTER 7

THE NATURE OF THE
BRITISH EMPIRE

The colonies and India are in opposite extremes. ... [In the colonies] Government and institutions are all ultra-English.[1]

                – J. R. Seeley in 1883

British Empire in India is Empire in the true sense of the term, since Hindostan is governed with imperial sway. So, in their way, are the military dependencies such as Malta and Gibraltar. But the self-governed colonies are not Empire at all.[2]

                – Goldwin Smith in 1894

Imperialists regarded imperialism first and foremost as wide-ranging and unspecified 'empire patriotism' or 'empire pride'. In their view, accordingly, anti-imperialism meant opposing this 'empire patriotism', thus signifying unpatriotic rejection of the British empire. Anti-imperialists, in contrast, defined the concept differently: to them, imperialism formed only one aspect of the British empire. This aspect amounted to militarism, authoritarianism, irrational and emotional jingoism, and anti-constitutionalism. While strongly denouncing this negative aspect, the anti-imperialists generally approved of the self-governing settler empire. Many fierce critics, like William Clarke and Herbert Spencer, even admired it due to their love for the United States, which without British colonisation and emigration would not have come into existence. Thus, if imperialism were to be defined as the imperialists themselves wished to depict it – that is, as overall pride in the empire – it might, indeed, be difficult to find any anti-imperialism: why would someone have opposed the existence of Canada, for instance? Moreover, strictly speaking, what kind of 'imperialism' did Britain's relations with Canada represent? None, the anti-imperialists simply argued, thus drawing a clear division between the 'un-imperialist' settler empire and the 'imperialist' empire of the dependencies.[3] They were against imperialism, not the empire as such. To them, it was all about the *nature* of the British empire: the main question was whether it promoted imperialism or liberal self-government.

These differences in contemporary understandings are important to bear in mind when examining the seemingly utterly complex debate on the British empire in the late-Victorian era. Previous historiography has not always been clear enough about this, for it seems that the imperialists' definition of 'empire patriotism' has been widely accepted without recognising that it was only partly true at the time. This has led to misunderstandings in regard to the nature of both imperialism and anti-imperialism: in the first case when affection for the colonies has been equalled with imperialism; and in the latter when promotion of colonial self-government has been equalled with anti-imperialism.[4] To begin with, many felt affection for the colonies *and* advocated colonial self-government; moreover, these issues were in most cases – at least in the anti-imperialists' opinion – separate from the debate on imperialism *per se*, and often also separate from the debate on Irish home rule.

Goldwin Smith is a good example. He is often considered a leading mid-Victorian anti-imperialist because of his writings in the early 1860s, in which he strongly advocated colonial self-government.[5] Smith, who lived most of his life in Canada, was, indeed, most committed in this stance throughout his life.[6] However, his arguments in favour of colonial self-government and independence would not have made him an anti-imperialist; it was only his fierce and continuous opposition to imperialism and jingoism which did that. Smith himself did not define Britain's relations with the settler empire through 'imperialism', and British imperialism in Africa and Britain's relations with Canada were two separate issues to him. If there was a connection, Smith saw it mainly in the way the Canadians, too, began showing imperialist and jingoist tendencies at the turn of the century; and this he detested as much as the rise of the same sentiments in Britain.[7]

The ambiguous attitudes of the imperialists themselves illustrate further how confused Britons were about the concepts and, most important, how the 'imperialists', too, initially wished to avoid the term 'imperialism' in the context of the British empire. This is true especially in regard to the debate on imperial federation. The debate on federal ideas as a possible solution to future relations between Britain and the colonies began after the rebellion in the Canadas in the late 1830s. Right from the beginning the idea of federalism was defensive in the sense that its supporters regarded it as the way to maintain the unity of the British empire at the time when the colonies gained more and more independence. The adjective 'imperial', referring to the empire, was thus an essential part of the concept; however, it was still considered separately from imperial*ism*. Whereas the latter term was in the late 1870s and early 1880s widely understood as 'continental despotism' – the more positive connotation did not emerge strongly until a little later[8] – imperial federation, meaning a federal British empire, signified colonisation, emigration, and overall closer bonds between Britain and the settler colonies, i.e. 'all the Britains', as one committed protagonist put it.[9]

Had the British empire been comprised only of these 'many Britains', the debate would have been very different indeed. As Frederic Harrison pointed out in 1880, the British empire was 'ten times as vast and fifty times as complex' as 'every empire that ever existed'. It was therefore not even a real empire but only 'an aggregate of dependencies' containing geographical fragments incapable of union, he argued:

> That empire is a vast collection of distant and disparate countries and races, incapable of assimilation with each other or with us, scattered over the planet in every phase of civilisation, with every variation of history; differing in religion, manners, race, and capabilities. ... Duly and rightly to govern, in the high and true sense of the word (that is, wisely to develop the life and energies of

these scattered peoples) would demand the strength, the wealth, the enlightenment, the moral conscience of fifty Englands. Our one England is utterly incapable of this superhuman task.

Although the proper government of this heterogeneous bundle of territories was 'impossible', Harrison continued, it could be garrisoned and occupied; it could be 'held for a few years longer with a hard mechanical pressure, securing external order but repressing all true national life'; with the result of 'further seas of blood, more conquests, more vengeance, ever sliding down the slope of tyranny, cruelty, and panic', thus 'corrupting the true fibre of the nation, and really paralysing it for every duty in Europe and at home'. It was for this very reason that the positivists considered the empire 'an anomaly, a huge excrescence, and abnormal and morbid growth of this fair island and its people'; and as such it was 'very contrary indeed to the glory and gain of England'.[10]

J. R. Seeley's image of the empire as 'the expansion of England' was very different from Harrison's. In his Cambridge lectures in 1883 Seeley summarised the two existing contradictory visions, himself rejecting both:

There are two schools of opinion among us with respect to our Empire, of which schools the one may be called the bombastic and the other the pessimistic. The one is lost in wonder and ecstasy at its immense dimensions, and at the energy and heroism which presumably have gone to the making of it; this school therefore advocates the maintenance of it as a point of honour or sentiment. The other is in the opposite extreme, regards it as founded in aggression and rapacity, as useless and burdensome, a kind of excrescence upon England, as depriving us of the advantages of our insularity and exposing us to wars and quarrels in every part of the globe; this school therefore advocates a policy which may lead at the earliest possible opportunity to the abandonment of it.[11]

Seeley did not regard the possession of a vast territory as evidence of greatness as such, and he certainly did not propagate any 'imperialism'.

He used the term *empire* and the adjective *imperial* relating to that, but *imperialism* was to him, too, something different. Even in his later writings he stuck to the definition that imperialism meant military dictatorship, popular despotism, and rule by an emperor,[12] and as such could not refer to the British empire. Strictly speaking, Seeley argued, imperialism could only follow when 'the army assumes the place of government at once and without resistance'.[13] Nevertheless, the main purpose of his lecture series, also published as a book, was to end any talk of an eventual disintegration of the empire by pointing out that the settler colonies were as integral parts of the United Kingdom as Cornwall or Kent; he detested the expression *possessions*, for it was 'essentially barbaric that one community should be treated as the property of another'.[14] To ponder over their eventual separation from the mother country was thus futile, for the ties of blood, language, and laws were unbreakable and the development into a vast and permanent federalist state of Greater Britain thus inevitable.

Seeley's book *The Expansion of England* was a huge success, selling 80,000 copies in the first two years and remaining in print into the 1950s.[15] Although his purpose was not to encourage the 'bombastic' school any further, Joseph Chamberlain, Cecil Rhodes, Lord Rosebery, W. T. Stead, and many other new 'bombastic' enthusiasts were much inspired by it.[16] They were especially thrilled about Seeley's notion that the settler colonies were in fact integral parts of England and were happy to extend their notion of patriotism accordingly. Lord Rosebery summed up this new revelation in 1885 by stating that 'sane Imperialism ... is nothing but this – a larger patriotism'.[17] This, then, as Deborah Wormell has well pointed out, was quite an apt misreading of Seeley's message. Seeley did not regard 'imperialism' as indicating 'a larger view of the significance of empire'; on the contrary, 'he would undoubtedly have regarded [it] as corrupt use of a precise political scientific term'.[18]

Not surprisingly, Goldwin Smith strongly criticised Seeley's federation scheme. He argued that without British imperial control the cultural and emotional ties between Britain and the colonies would be far stronger.[19] John Morley was of the same opinion.[20] In his view the idea was not only impracticable but also 'puerile and retrograde'.[21] The interests of the several parts of the empire were too various and the problems different, he argued; Britons emigrated rather to the United States than to the British possessions; the colonies were not in the least interested in participating in British wars, nor were they even willing to lower their tariffs.[22] 'Is the time and brainpower of our legislators, and of those of our colonies too, to be diverted perpetually from their own people, to the more showy but less fruitful task of keeping together and managing an artificial Empire?' he asked.[23]

Morley especially criticised Seeley's emphasis on the significance of the empire in English history. Seeley maintained that English historians made 'too much of the mere parliamentary wrangle and the agitations about liberty' in the eighteenth century; in his opinion they should 'perceive that in that century the history of England is not in England but in America and Asia'.[24] Morley, loyal to his own liberal- and constitution-centred conception of Englishness and English history, could not regard the empire and the 'expansion of England' as the central issue. Surely, he argued, the development of free and liberal institutions in England itself was more important: 'patriotism is regard for the wellbeing of the people of a country as well as affection for its flag', he explained.[25]

The Imperial Federation League was founded in July 1884 in order to 'use every constitutional means' and 'the support of men of all political parties' to 'secure by Federation the permanent unity of the Empire'.[26] Duncan Bell has analysed the motives behind the federation movement, concluding that it was mainly galvanised by fear: fear for increasing global competition on the one hand and for domestic disquiet on the other.[27] For a while, the nature and future of the British empire were much debated, and the partition line was not primarily between 'imperialists' and 'anti-imperialists'. Edward Freeman, Goldwin Smith's later successor as Regius professor of modern history at Oxford and not any anti-imperialist, emerged as one of the most vigorous critics of the federation plans.[28] He was much annoyed by the terminological paradox of the whole concept of 'imperial federation', for the two words were the exact opposites of each other. Moreover, pursuing a cause which would make Britain a mere component part of a larger federal state would not be the best way to enhance Britain's greatness and strength, he argued: a truly federal union would mean the end of empire.[29] 'I don't want closer union with the dependent colonies; I want to see them as dependent colonies', Freeman wrote to James Bryce, a member of the Imperial Federation League.[30] The motives to oppose the federation movement could thus be even contradictory, as Smith and Freeman well illustrate: the first advocated full independence for the colonies, while the latter preferred dependent possessions to a federalist union. Most of the League's opponents argued along the lines of Smith and had similarly been campaigning for colonial self-government for decades.[31]

The Boston- and New York-based *North American Review* published in July 1885 William Clarke's bantering account of what he regarded as 'an English imperialist bubble'.[32] Anyone who read English newspapers without being familiar with English affairs might 'be pardoned for imagining that there is a serious movement of great importance' towards an 'Imperial federation between England and her Colonies', Clarke wrote, stating that 'nothing could be farther from the truth'. While two conferences had been held in London in 1884 to discuss the cause, he continued, in both only

> a great deal of vague talk was indulged in as to the delightfulness of a permanent union between England and her Colonies; but not a single practical proposal for the accomplishment of this object was placed before either conference. No two speakers seemed to agree as to methods; the only agreement consisted in inflated rhetoric about the splendour of the Empire.[33]

In Clarke's opinion 'most of those who took part in these deliberations were politicians of a doubtful kind, some of them connected with other very pernicious political movements, while nearly all were animated by what are termed Jingo sentiments'. Neither British nor colonial 'strong political thinkers and leaders' gave any encouragement to the plans, he stressed.[34] Moreover, the paradox of any 'imperial federation' was more than obvious. 'If any kind of federal government or parliament were created, England would of course be related to that government or parliament as any particular State is related to President and Congress at Washington,' Clarke pointed out: 'As a sovereign state, even though small, England would control her own destiny; as a unit in a federal empire, she would be compelled to acquiesce in whatever millions of other people in every part of the world thought was good for her.' Yet, he continued, ironically the imperial enthusiasts argued the exact opposite: that, 'in some inexplicable way', 'this federal empire shall redound to the glory of Great Britain, and give her a prestige she cannot otherwise acquire'. Indeed, he maintained, the real and only purpose was 'to extend and intensify the political power of England at any cost'. A closer union could only mean England's tighter grip on the colonies, taxing them in the name of empire and plunging them into endless imperial wars, he warned.[35]

If the federal idea was interpreted in its strict political sense, the League was in fact advancing colonial independence by promoting them from subject status to equal states alongside the United Kingdom. This interpretation, indeed, generated some support in the colonies;[36] but it is clear that it was not the interpretation of the League promoters, no one of whom was willing to hand any of the British decision-making power over to the colonies. On the contrary, the imperial federation activists presented their scheme particularly as a response to the growing concerns for the dismemberment of the empire through colonial independence. As W. E. Forster, the first president of the Imperial Federation League, summarised it: 'Then why our League? ... For this reason: because in giving self-government to our colonies we have introduced a principle which must eventually shake off from Great Britain, Greater Britain, and divide it into separate States; which must, in short, dissolve the union, unless counteracting measures be taken to preserve it.'[37]

Many found the rhetoric of preventing an eventual imperial decay appealing – among others the not-yet-anti-imperialist J. A. Hobson, a staunch supporter of imperial federation in the 1880s.[38] The same rhetoric, however, was the main reason why the anti-imperialists opposed the federation plans. They valued the settler colonies especially because, in their view, they reflected the traditional English liberal values even better than the mother country at the time. They believed that the Imperial Federation League attempted to destroy exactly that with its seemingly democratic rhetoric of 'blood love'. As William Clarke vividly described, the worst part was that the schemes endangered to tarnish even the colonies with the severe taint of 'imperialism'. John Bright, too, considered the ideas 'impracticable and absurd',[39] and when invited to attend a meeting on imperial federation he declined most decidedly:

> The federation project seems to me to be founded on ignorance alike of history and geography. It is partly or mainly the offspring of the jingo spirit which clamours for a vast and continually widening empire, and seems almost ready to boast that it fights the world outside its own limits. I would recommend all sensible men to let the question rest.[40]

India caused yet another problem in the debate. As Edward Freeman pointed out, this often much valued imperial possession was suddenly neglected altogether.[41] In Seeley's vision the British empire was primarily a natural extension of the nation, 'the expansion of England' or 'Greater Britain'. India, in contrast, was bound to Britain 'only by the tie of conquest' and was thus an anomaly.[42] Far from being 'the brightest jewel in the English diadem' as Disraeli had claimed, Seeley regarded India as a dangerous responsibility which, however, once there, the British had the duty to govern.[43] All the same, British rule in India was, to Seeley, only another 'Asiatic despotism'; 'a good specimen of a bad political system'.[44] Seeley's conceptions were thus similar to those of the anti-imperialists, who insisted on the major difference between the nature of British rule in the conquered territories, which was imperialism, and 'the expansion of England' in the colonies, which was colonisation.

Interestingly, in regard to India Goldwin Smith and J. R. Seeley were of the same opinion. They both defined imperialism in the same negative terms but strongly disagreed as to the position of the settler empire, Smith advocating complete independence for the colonies and Seeley insisting that Canada, for instance, was an integral part of England; British role in India was again something they agreed on. To both Smith and Seeley, British empire in India was 'an Empire in the true sense of the term' and also 'the noblest the world has seen', as even Smith insisted. The determined campaigner for colonial independence and a severe opponent of British military imperialism in Africa, Smith nonetheless maintained that England had 'a real duty' in India, and 'about keeping India there is no question'. This was because the nature of British rule in India had been improving all along and Britain was thus, in his eyes, making amends for its earlier malpractices.[45]

S. R. Mehrotra has pointed out that the exclusion of India in the federation plans was mainly due to the Imperial Federation League's leading motive of preventing the complete independence of the colonies. Unlike them, India was 'securely in hand': India's problems were 'problems of administration and not those demanding a change in her connection with Great Britain'.[46] A federation, it was believed, would make the self-governing colonies more aware of their responsibilities to the empire and persuade them to lower their tariffs to British products and contribute towards the empire's defence liabilities. India, in contrast, was already a free-trade country and maintained a large British army at its own cost; there was no need for persuasion.[47]

Another reason for the neglect of India was that the federation-enthusiasts wanted to galvanise the empire-spirit, and this was more easily done through the settler colonies than a dependency like India. India, with its imperialism and a 'real' empire, was too problematic and 'un-English' compared to the settler empire of 'Greater Britain'. 'It is the Imperial character of the Indian Empire which is its great danger and its great snare. It is not a colony but an empire. It is at best an anomalous thing for a free nation to govern despotically, in a country where her people cannot permanently live,' Frederic Seebohm wrote in 1880;[48] and as already noted, even Seeley concurred. Edward Freeman also stressed that the word 'imperial' referred to the Indian empire, and without India any federation could therefore not be called imperial. Similarly, if the relationship between Britain and India was transformed into a federal union, India would no longer be an 'empire' and the federation could not be 'imperial' – not even to mention the fact that huge India would always outvote the other, much smaller countries in the federation. 'The simple truth is', Freeman thus summed up, 'that the phrase "Imperial Federation" is a contradiction in terms, that what is imperial cannot be federal, and what is federal cannot be imperial.[49]

Irish home rule was supported with an argument very similar to the imperial federation plans: federalism was seen as a powerful alternative for Irish independence. William Gladstone and his supporters in the home rule question were convinced that theirs was a solution that would save the empire from violent dismemberment.[50] Albert Venn Dicey, a constitutional expert, agreed that a federal solution would not be quite as bad as Irish independence, but he strongly opposed the idea nevertheless. A federal system was too alien to British constitutional practice and would even mean a 'constitutional revolution', he argued; for a start, it would necessitate a written constitution. Moreover, any federalism, be that within the empire or within the British Isles, would include a division of sovereignty through 'an elaborate distribution and definition of political powers'.[51]

While the imperialists regarded the empire as the culmination of Britishness, the anti-imperialists stressed the constitution-centred conception of English identity. The first view was strengthened by Seeley's book and the Imperial Federation League; the latter was simultaneously strengthened by A. V. Dicey's *The Law of the Constitution*, published in 1885.[52] As Stefan Collini has summarised, 'Dicey proposed that the distinguishing characteristics of the English constitution were the sovereignty of Parliament, the rule of law, and the ultimate dependence of the conventions of the constitution upon the law of the constitution.'[53] Hence, Dicey 'made the law central to the English people's conception of their own identity',[54] which was exactly the view the anti-imperialists propounded. At the same time, however, Dicey himself was not an anti-imperialist; even less so than Seeley was an imperialist. Dicey opposed both imperial federation and Irish home rule on the ground of opposing the principle of federalism, and without taking any position in regard to imperialism or anti-imperialism in specific. Seeley's logic on the issues was different: he, too, opposed home rule and became an active Liberal Unionist in 1886, which was logical enough in relation to his argument that colonies were integral parts of England; but in contrast to Dicey, he combined his Unionism with strong support for imperial federation. The fact that he opposed

Irish parliamentary self-government but advocated closer union with those areas of the empire which already had separate parliaments illustrates well the defensive and conservative character of the imperial federation movement.

Any stance in the home rule debate cannot be regarded as a decisive indicator of attitudes against or for imperialism. As in the case of the settler colonies, the debate on the position of Ireland was separate. Joseph Cowen and Cecil Rhodes are two examples of staunch imperialists who supported Irish home rule. J. A. Hobson, on the other hand, was an opponent of home rule in the late 1880s, as were John Bright, Goldwin Smith, and Leonard Courtney.[55] While Bright, Smith, and Courtney supported colonial self-government, they considered the Irish situation differently. They did not regard Ireland as a colony; to them, it was primarily part of the United Kingdom. In their eyes the question was therefore not about colonial self-government within the British empire as most of the home rulers conceived it, but about whether the British Isles remained politically united or not. This difference of approach caused a severe break between John Bright and William Gladstone, whose relationship had barely recovered from Bright's strong criticism towards Gladstone's occupation of Egypt in 1882. 'The break in the Liberal party is to be attributed to the unwisdom of its leader', Bright stated to a like-minded colleague. He assured he had 'warm and real' sympathy for the Irish people, but whereas the Gladstonians believed home rule would prevent the eventual separation between Britain and Ireland, Bright was positive it would be 'a successful step' to cause it.[56]

The views on imperialism and the nature of the British empire were thus various and could be as much conflicting as overlapping. If the debate on the British empire is examined as a whole, the settler colonies and Ireland included, there was no clear division line between imperialists and anti-imperialists. In fact, there were three separate entities for debate: the self-governing colonies, Ireland, and imperialism, for which one person could have three separate and even unrelated opinions. Furthermore, the concept of 'imperial federation', like that of 'imperialism', remained highly unspecified. It was referred to in any instance when any scheme favouring closer ties within the empire was propagated, irrespective of whether the plan actually advocated the political principle of federalism; in fact, usually it did not. The union schemes remained imperial more than federal in the sense that Britain was rarely depicted as equal to the others; it was the unquestioned centre of power.

Before Seeley's book and the Imperial Federation League, 'imperialism' was not an ideology attached to the settler colonies, and even afterwards it remained so to the anti-imperialists. Many imperialists, in contrast, began in the mid-1880s to talk about positive imperialism in connection with the settler colonies and negative imperialism in connection with the tropical dependencies and new annexations. Nevertheless, the literal paradox between the terms 'imperial' and 'self-governing' did not disappear and caused severe problems for the Imperial Federation League. The League was utterly incapable of presenting any practical plans along which to proceed, or even of agreeing amongst its members about the ultimate goal. The support remained minimal in Britain and the colonies alike, and the criticisms of Freeman and Smith went unanswered. W. E. Forster and James Bryce, both prominent federationists, were forced to admit that the title of 'Imperial Federation' had been badly chosen. Lord Rosebery, who was the League's president in 1886–92, suggested in 1891 that the name should be changed to National Federation League or Britannic Federation League. No changes were made, however, and the League was dissolved in 1893.[57]

It is noteworthy that still at the turn of the century the Liberal imperialists' conception of the British empire was first and foremost 'white'. To them, it primarily comprised the areas of white settlement, of 'free self-governing communities, bound together, not by force, but by sentiment and affection'; hence their imperialism.[58] The anti-imperialists, in contrast, did not consider that imperialism at all.

John M. Robertson linked imperialism, 'the prevailing fashion of political thought', explicitly with 'an increasing plague of militarism and a fresh florescence of the spurious ethic of patriotism on the lowest planes'. He criticised the idea that there could be 'true' and 'false' imperialism, as some imperialists argued. 'True' imperialism was claimed to generate from the fact that the British empire as such was 'a very fine thing', and should therefore 'be still further developed' into 'a British China as well as a British India'. At the same time, Robertson noted, many politicians 'instinctively' felt that the policy of extension was 'ultimately fatal' but felt 'committed to speaking of the existing empire as a thing wholly glorious'. These 'sane' imperialists, then, tended to hinder further expansion but felt compelled to admire and respect the present empire. This, according to Robertson, was absurd: if the empire really was a good thing, there should not be any reason not to expand that good thing. Thus, the 'sane' imperialist in fact condemned the whole 'theory of imperialism in the lump, while recognising the exigencies of the situation it has thus far created. Empire is one thing, and imperial*ism* another,' he concluded.[59]

In practice this meant that the phrase 'our colonial empire' was used merely in a geographical sense, Robertson stressed, for 'the colonies neither pay tribute to, nor receive laws from, the mother-country'. The sovereign was empress only in India, and it was only 'the convenience of the expression' which had fixed 'the British empire' in use 'for the whole connections and possessions of the United Kingdom', he pointed out. Imperialism, in contrast, aimed for a real empire in its true historical sense, and had always led to the decay and destruction of the imperial societies under military stress. Everywhere it had begun 'in the spirit of injustice; the lust for rule over others on the part of the man who claims freedom for himself; the demand for tribute by the man who hated to pay tribute' – mere common honesty would therefore efficiently exclude the possibility of empire, Robertson argued.[60]

CHAPTER 8

BRITISH ANTI-IMPERIALISTS AND EGYPTIAN AND INDIAN NATIONALISTS

If there could arise in India a nationality-movement similar to
that which we witnessed in Italy, the English Power could not
even make the resistance that was made in Italy by Austria, but
must succumb at once.[1]

– J. R. Seeley in 1883

We ought long ago to have endeavoured to gradually teach the
natives how to govern themselves. But this we have not been
prepared to do, because we know that self-government would
mean that India is no longer to be drained of her resources for
our benefit.[2]

– Henry Labouchere in 1897

The British were strong supporters of anti-imperial nationalisms
throughout the latter half of the nineteenth century. British public opinion was rather unanimously on the side of Italy or Hungary
against the Austrian empire, the Balkans against the Ottoman empire,
or Poland and Finland against the Russian empire. Nationalism within
the British empire caused consequently a major problem: the political will to turn the supporters of nationalism into its suppressors was

lacking, whereas the determination to maintain the unity of the British empire was strong. The most common way to handle the contradiction was denial. It was argued that nationalisms in Ireland, Egypt, or India were not similar to the ones in Italy or Poland: the divisions among the Irish and especially the Indians were much emphasised, and Egyptian nationalism was reduced to a military movement. Nevertheless, Indian nationalism, in particular, found many supporters in Britain.

The nature of Egyptian nationalism was debated for a few years in the early 1880s, especially at the beginning of the British occupation in 1882. Even leading Liberal politicians were not unanimous on the topic. Joseph Chamberlain insisted throughout 1882 that what the Cabinet had dubbed an Egyptian 'revolutionary movement' could in fact 'be the legitimate expression of discontent and of resistance to oppression' which 'ought to be guided and not repressed'.[3] Lord Kimberley, the colonial secretary, agreed that Britain had 'no interest in suppressing any real movement in favour of freer government in Egypt' but stressed that he was 'very incredulous as to the reality of the movement'.[4] Chamberlain continued arguing against the occupation, pointing out that privileged people always said the unprivileged were not fit for representation.[5] 'If Arabi was, as some believe, a real Egyptian patriot animated by real national sentiment and seeking only judicial reforms, we have done a great wrong by throwing our weight into the scale against him', he confided in John Bright, who completely agreed.[6] Later, however, Chamberlain turned into a great admirer of Britain's work in Egypt, which contributed to his image as a notorious example of a 'jingo imperialist' and, as John Morley put it, 'the effective oracle of Imperialist ideals'.[7]

John Morley, who was the editor of the *Fortnightly Review* until November 1882, also considered 'the true nature of the movement' in his July editorial. 'To begin with, it seems impossible to deny that there are natural and spontaneous elements in the movement which it is a great error to overlook or to underrate,' he stated. In his opinion it was 'much more than a mere military clique seeking to overawe the Government'; on the contrary, the evidence seemed to point out 'that the mutinous soldiers really represented a popular sentiment'. Moreover, Morley suspected that Urabi 'had, and has, in him the stuff of which great rulers are made', even though it happened that 'events were too strong for him, and he lost control of his force' after which 'the movement took the shape which is common to military revolutions, and went on its usual course'. His ambiguous conclusion was, then, that there was a 'practicable National party' in Egypt, but it could 'do nothing until their violent and impracticable allies have been reduced to order'.[8]

Seemingly uncertain of whether to support the Egyptian nationalists or British occupation, Morley thus ended up indirectly supporting both by neither denying the existence of a real nationalist movement nor condemning the occupation. This attitude was not rare. Thomas Burt, the trade union leader and Liberal MP, argued that 'the great majority of the people' had 'supported the Government policy in Egypt' only because 'they did not know how far Arabi was accepted as the leader of a real national movement' and 'they had great faith in Mr Gladstone and his colleagues'. Moreover, Burt stressed, even in those circumstances the support had been 'neither unanimous nor enthusiastic'.[9]

Only a handful of critics gave straightforward support to Egyptian nationalism by forthrightly condemning the British occupation. One of them was the Anglo-Indian banker John Seymour Keay, whose book *Spoiling the Egyptians: A Tale of Shame* went quickly through three editions in 1882. Keay declared:

> It is obvious that any action whatever, adverse to the aspirations of the Egyptian people after Constitutional Government, is quite unworthy of Great Britain, which has always been the champion of political liberty and Representative Institutions; and, *à fortiori*, that armed intervention for the purpose of re-establishing the *status quo ante*, which necessarily involved the repression of Representative Government in Egypt, is one of the greatest crimes that could be committed by the British Nation, and must brand it with infamy in the pages of history.[10]

Frederic Harrison, who was struggling with the Anti-Aggression League in the spring 1882, saw sinister economic motives behind the

government's actions and attacked them with all his weight. His interpretation on the causes behind the Egyptian 'revolt' was clear:

> Imagine your own feelings, if you had to send every year some
> forty millions sterling out of the taxes of the country to pay
> Turkish, or Arab, or Chinese bondholders; and then, having
> paid that regularly, that you had to keep a Turkish pasha and
> a Chinese mandarin in London to control your expenditure, so
> that every penny of the Budget had to get the sanction of the
> excellencies, and if Mr. Gladstone or any other Chancellor of the
> Exchequer wished to put on or take off a tax, down would come
> a fleet of ironclads from the Bosphorus into the Thames, and
> train their 80-ton guns right in view of the Tower and Somerset
> House. That is the state of Egypt now.[11]

When the Anti-Aggression League collapsed and Herbert Spencer
retired from active agitation, Harrison joined forces with Wilfrid
Scawen Blunt.[12] Blunt's attention was first attracted by Harrison's writing in the *Pall Mall Gazette* in early June,[13] and he later regretted that
they had not become acquainted earlier. Blunt considered Harrison
'the soundest and most courageous man on foreign policy then in the
Liberal Party, and by far their most vigorous pamphleteer'. He was
sure that if they had only 'met a month or two before' Harrison 'might
have prevented the war, for though not in Parliament, he wielded great
influence'.[14]

Blunt had been working hard on behalf of the Egyptian nationalists
in Britain for several months. He had tried to influence the decision-
making process in the Cabinet by his frequent correspondence with
prime minister Gladstone, Gladstone's private secretary Edward
Hamilton, foreign secretary Lord Granville, and the press. Blunt's
main aim was to convince Gladstone that the movement was really a
national one.[15] He also, an ex-diplomat as he was, asked Gladstone to
authorise him 'to proceed to Cairo on a mission of mediation'.[16]

Undoubtedly, many in Britain thought that the Egyptian Nationalist
Party had largely been enhanced by Blunt himself. In his eagerness to
assist the cause Blunt had sent the 'Programme of the National Party'

to Gladstone and to *The Times* in December 1881, and many found it curious that the party programme had been signed by Blunt. The drawing up of the programme had indeed been Blunt's suggestion, but he stressed that it only consisted 'of what Arabi had told me' and was thus their programme, not his.[17] The programme was published in *The Times* on 1 January 1882, and Blunt considered it was well received. 'Its tone was so studiously moderate, and its reasoning so frank and logical that it seemed impossible the position in Egypt should any longer be misunderstood,' he later stated. However, Blunt calculated that the programme had reached Gladstone 'a fortnight too late' and could therefore not prevent 'the ill-omened Joint Note' of Britain and France at the beginning of January.[18]

Blunt's belief in Gladstone's goodwill towards Egypt had been great all along and was enhanced further at their meeting on 22 March 1882. 'He received me very kindly ... and he was evidently prepared and eager for what I had to say,' Blunt wrote; 'His manner was so encouraging and sympathetic that I spoke easily ... and I could see that every word I said interested and touched him. ... His sympathy was obviously and strongly with the movement,' he testified. Gladstone was, however, suspicious of 'the position of the army and the reason of the prominent part taken by it in public affairs', but Blunt 'assured him that the interference of the soldiers had been greatly exaggerated' and 'the sole reason for the present military preparations was the dread of foreign intervention'.[19] Blunt left from the meeting feeling confident and touched: 'His extreme kindness as he shook hands with me moved me greatly and I was near shedding tears, and went away feeling that he was a good as well as a great man, and wondering only how any one with so good a heart could have arrived at being Prime Minister.'[20]

Throughout the spring of 1882 Blunt was certain that if Gladstone 'knew the truth as to the National aspirations, in an authoritative way, he could not fail to be impressed by it in a sense favourable to them' since the movement was 'very much in accordance with his avowed principles'.[21] Indeed, in the early summer 1882 Blunt believed that his work had borne fruit. 'The first day for weeks I have not thought about Egypt. I consider the whole matter settled now & have played tennis all the afternoon with a light heart,'[22] he wrote in his diary only three days before Harrison's indicting writing appeared in the *Pall Mall Gazette* and the campaign was revived with greater strength. Thus far, Blunt had always regarded the Egyptian question purely as a contradiction between a nationalist movement and a foreign intervention into the affairs of another country. Harrison, on the other hand, had not been interested in Egyptian nationalism per se and did not know the nationalists personally; to him the question was about preventing the 'plot' of the bondholders, as he so clearly pointed out in the *Pall Mall Gazette*. To Blunt, Harrison's article was an eye-opener. Until that day he had believed that British intervention would be prevented by assuring the leading Liberals of the sincere nature of Egyptian nationalism; in June he became more aware of the economic motives behind the issue as well.

'But, alas, there was another Gladstone, the opportunist statesman, who was very different from the first, and whom I was presently to see playing in public "such fantastic tricks before high Heaven as make the angels weep",' Blunt wrote. 'His public life was to a large extent a fraud', he concluded; 'The insincerities of debate were ingrained in him.'[23] In Blunt's eyes, Gladstone, the alleged friend of nationalists, had only one sacred principle: 'that of securing a Parliamentary majority. This was his ultimate reason of all action, his true conscience, to which his nobler aspirations had constantly to be sacrificed.'[24] Blunt assumed that 'some time between the 20th June and the end of the month' Gladstone 'finally hardened his heart against the Egyptians and resolved on military operations – he persuaded himself that it would not be war'.[25] He sadly noted that 'all the jingoism of the Empire, asleep since Disraeli's parliamentary defeat in 1880, was suddenly awake and crying for blood.'[26]

On 28 June 1882 Blunt visited John Bright, whom he found talking 'in a friendly tone, but less sympathetically than Gladstone and less intelligently'. Bright assured Blunt that there would be no hostilities,[27] and Blunt believed he was sincere. 'But the poor man, whose principles were absolutely opposed to warfare, was kept in complete darkness as to what was going on at the Admiralty and the War Office,' Blunt later stated. While many regarded it as a bondholders' war, Blunt was still convinced that the Cabinet had been persuaded to attack by the Foreign Office's theory 'that the mass of the Egyptians were with the Khedive, not with Arabi'.[28] Bright alone disapproved of the bombardment and resigned the Cabinet as a protest. Blunt also received support from Sir Wilfrid Lawson in the House of Commons, but by July they both agreed it was 'hopeless doing anything with the Government'.[29]

Blunt then felt it his duty 'to prepare an "Apologia" of the National movement and of my own connection with it – for this was now being virulently attacked in the press'.[30] He sent proofs of his 'Apologia' to Gladstone and Edward Hamilton before it was published in the September issue of the *Nineteenth Century*. Blunt declared bitterly:

> I have been fighting the battle not only of truth and justice, but also of what I conceived to be distinctly my own country's interest. I could not believe that England had an interest in crushing liberty anywhere or in maintaining evil against good. I could not understand that she could gain anything by joining France in her crusade against the Arabian race and religion, or that in any conceivable circumstance she could profit by a crime. It has been to prevent a crime that I have laboured – alas, in vain![31]

By the publication of this 'Apologia' Blunt's spirits had been much improved by a letter of support from General Gordon. Known as 'Chinese Gordon' at the time and soon to become the hero of all imperialists in the Sudan, Gordon had sent a letter to Blunt from Cape Town on 3rd August, avowing his sympathy with the Egyptian nationalist cause.[32] Blunt wrote triumphantly to Edward Hamilton:

> I have just got a letter from Gordon (Chinese Gordon) in which he expresses his sympathy with Arabi and the Egyptians almost as warmly as I could. I tell you this because Mr. Gladstone said I was the 'one unfortunate exception' among people who knew Egypt. I confess I had rather have Gordon on my side than the whole of the Daily Press.[33]

By the time of Gordon's letter, Blunt's thoughts were beginning to turn into the trial of Urabi and his nationalist colleagues. Frederic Harrison and other positivists soon enlisted for help, although Harrison did not consider himself as much responsible for Urabi's situation as Blunt: whereas Blunt had explicitly encouraged Urabi, Harrison had concentrated on attacking the British government.[34] A. M. Broadley, a Tunis-based British lawyer and a close friend of Blunt's, defended Urabi in the trial with all his energy.[35] Urged by Harrison, John Bright presented a petition to the House of Commons for Urabi's complete freedom, but of no avail.[36] Henry Labouchere, too, emerged as a fierce supporter of Urabi and Egyptian nationalism at this stage.[37]

Urabi was given a death sentence which was commuted to exile in Ceylon. Blunt, however, remained hopeful: in February 1885 he wrote that it was 'generally admitted now in the light of the Soudan rebellion that the Egyptian war was a mistake' and Urabi 'an honest man'.[38] In Blunt's opinion the Mahdi's Islamist movement had the same roots as the Egyptian nationalist movement, both beginning as natural and popular rebellions 'against long misgovernment, and taking later a religious complexion when Christian Europe had intervened in support of the tyrannical ruler against the people'. The significant difference was that 'whereas in Egypt the reformers were enlightened men, representing the humaner and more progressive side of Islam, the Soudanese reformers were reactionary and fanatical'. Thus, the rise of the Mahdi in the Sudan, Blunt argued, provided clear evidence 'that the great, the capital wrong committed by our English Government in 1882 was less the destruction of the hopes of free government in Egypt as a nation, than the treacherous blow its armed intervention struck everywhere at the aspirations of liberal Islam'.[39]

Blunt was very much involved in the campaigns of Indian and Irish nationalists as well. Indeed, after the collapse of Urabi's movement in Egypt he angrily predicted, in his poem *The Wind and the Whirlwind*, that the British empire would eventually fall under the rising nationalisms:

> Thou hast thy foot upon the weak. The weakest
> With his bruised head shall strike thee on the heel.[40]

The following two years Blunt concentrated on advocating the rights of Indian Muslims, after which he began his crusade for Irish home rule.[41] W. T. Stead suggested in 1887 that Blunt should found 'a league of all the fanaticisms', which Blunt found 'a good idea';[42] however, his political activism came to an abrupt end early next year, when his undertakings in Ireland led him to prison for three months. In June 1888 Blunt declared in his diary: 'Here ends the History of my political life.'[43] True to his style, the statement was a bit too theatrical and exaggerated, but nonetheless he largely withdrew to live in Egypt, spending his days gardening and womanising.[44]

Robert D. Osborn, who had a long military career in India behind him, was another anti-imperialist to defend strongly both Egyptian and Indian self-government. Also a member of the Anti-Aggression League in 1882,[45] he wrote fierce articles opposing any British invasion in Egyptian matters before the occupation and arguing for representative government for India.[46] Whether India was 'ready' for it was 'really equivalent to asking if it be wise or possible for a man to make use of his mental capacities', he declared. He ridiculed the British for always blaming other empires of misgovernment but never seeing any fault in their own:

'Able Indian administrators' have succeeded in persuading us that the two hundred millions of human beings who inhabit our Indian Empire are so deficient in mental capacities that to keep them fast bound under the yoke of a military despotism is a most humane and righteous proceeding. Despotisms, we are willing to admit, when they exist in Russia, in Germany, or in Austria, constitute a mode of Government which cannot be condemned too strongly. But in India it is different.[47]

Osborn argued that the 'stories of the mental incompetency of the natives of India and the extraordinary success of British rule' were 'mere legends'.[48] He made comparisons between British and native Indian rule, in favour of the latter: when a native principality was incorporated into British India, 'ruin, utter and complete, fell upon all the upper classes; the stagnation of death upon the lower', Osborn testified.[49]

The connections between Irish nationalism and British anti-imperialism were complex. Most critics of imperialism combined the issues self-evidently, like Blunt; while some others, as was noted in the previous chapter, kept the Irish debate separate from the overall debate on the British empire and imperialism. Moreover, the attitudes were ambiguous on the Irish side as well. Some, like the American Fenian and the editor and proprietor of the *Irish World*, Patrick Ford, saw India 'as an Ireland writ large, a fellow victim of English misgovernment, and a fertile territory for the propagation of the nationalist ideal', as Howard Brasted has put it.[50] Consequently, the *Irish World*, which was a significant channel of American funds to Irish nationalists, was a pioneer in demanding the Irish and Indians to combine 'in a holy crusade' to lay the empire in ruins.[51] Frank Hugh O'Donnell represented a somewhat different approach: he, too, was 'a fervent exponent of imparting Home Rule knowledge to India and of promoting the cause of Indian nationalism', as Brasted has noted;[52] but, and more importantly, it should be noted that he was motivated in this by Irish imperialism. His driving force was anger over the changes in the examination requirements for the Indian civil service in the 1870s, which he considered to favour Cambridge and Oxford graduates at the expense of the Irish. O'Donnell wanted to 'revenge' this to the British and show that they could not get rid of the Irish in regard to Indian matters that easily. He later wrote:

> It was a foul blow. ... As I was an Imperialist as well as a Nationalist I resented the stupidity as well as the injustice of this proceeding. ... If the British Government intended to exclude Irishmen from India, I would teach the British Government that it had undertaken a task beyond its capacities. I resolved to unite all India in a national confederacy of the Indian races and provinces without distinction, to impress upon their racial and religious distinction the seal of a patriotic combination, and to call into being the national co-operation of Indians.[53]

Hence, O'Donnell began working towards a 'Panindian Union', wishing thus to impose Irish, rather than British, values on the empire.[54] His closest ally in this was a wealthy Bengali Hindu, Ganendra Mohun Tagore, who resided in London.[55] O'Donnell had the rather imperialist 'vision of the Eastern continent being led by the Western island' of Ireland or, at least, 'by a Western man'.[56] In 1883 he solemnly declared the foundation of the Constitutional Association of India in Tagore's house in Kensington.[57] 'We had several meetings of the Constitutional Association of India during the twelvemonth that followed,' he later recalled, during which 'Three thousand, six thousand, letters every month carried *my counsels* into every town and townlet, into every court-house and durbar hall of fifty states and provinces.'[58] As if this were not enough, O'Donnell seemed to believe – mistakenly – that he was the real father of the Indian National Congress. 'Within eighteen months the Constitutional Association of India had become the Indian National Congress,' he stated – adding contently that 'But Downing Street had combined with Oxford and Cambridge to eliminate all Irish influence from the future of the Indian Empire!'[59]

Indeed, from the Irish point of view the diversity of imperial influences was even clearer than from the British. The empire provided numerous employment opportunities, not even to mention the emigration; but it also represented the British 'yoke'. Some Irish nationalists saw no contradiction in advocating nationalism in Ireland and imperialism elsewhere: John Redmond even argued that if Ireland was granted home rule it would be more willing to participate in imperial efforts with greater strength.[60] Another Irish MP, Alfred Webb, believed, like O'Donnell, that Ireland's mission was to protect 'weaker peoples' from 'imperial tyranny'[61] – until his trip to India as the president of the Indian National Congress in 1894, when he became convinced of the Indians' capacity to both defend and represent themselves without the Irish as intermediaries.[62]

O'Donnell was not the only one who wished to announce himself the father of Indian nationalism. Blunt, too, stated about his articles in 1884–5 that 'they were indeed, I think, the first complete and fearless apology of Indian home rule which had been published';[63] but he was either consciously overstating his case or simply had not read many other writings than his own. Indeed, by the mid-1880s the debate on the possible development of self-government in India and the Indians' 'fitness' for that was well under way.

Lord Ripon – whom his biographer has somewhat exaggeratingly described as 'by far the most radical of the Liberal Party's spokesmen on India...between 1859 and 1909'[64] – re-established, as the vice-roy of India in 1880–4, the freedom of the press after Lord Lytton's Vernacular Press Act of 1878, advanced education, and, most import-antly, extended local self-government.[65] His reform policies had already caused unrest among the Anglo-Indians, when in February 1883 the Indian government introduced the 'Ilbert Bill', aiming at advancing racial equality by extending the right of qualified Indian magistrates to try Europeans in criminal cases. Ripon did not regard the bill as important as his local self-government schemes, since it introduced no new principles: in theory, eligibility for posts had been determined by fitness for position, irrespective of race or birth, since 1833. However, putting this into practice raised fundamental questions about the nature of British rule in India, and especially of racial equality.[66]

Before anyone had opposed the bill in India, it was strongly attacked in *The Times* by its Calcutta correspondent James Macgregor, who suc-cessfully stirred an extensive propaganda campaign against Ripon's reform policies at large.[67] During the following months all London papers joined *The Times* in its crusade – with only one exception: the *Pall Mall Gazette*, edited by John Morley, supported the bill and denounced the opposition. Later another Liberal paper, *The Daily News*, joined the *Pall Mall Gazette* in support.[68] Ripon was accused of 'the tone of apol-ogy for our presence in India', 'the abandonment of the attitude of a ruler for that of a tutor', and of encouraging 'all who are discontented to believe that they have only to agitate and clamour in order to carry things their own way'.[69] Ripon's supporters in Britain organised a large public meeting in August 1883, presided over by John Bright,[70] for which Ripon was 'greatly gratified' and thanked Bright heartily.[71] He was also strongly encouraged by Sir Arthur Hobhouse, the former legal member of the viceroy's council, and Florence Nightingale, who found Ripon's policy 'wise & steadfast & brave & honest'.[72] Blunt's view was, 'Lord Ripon's appointment to India as Viceroy was the only quite sincere attempt made in foreign policy by Gladstone to carry out in office what he had preached when in opposition.'[73] Henry Cotton, a positivist Indian civil servant, argued, 'the superiority of the natives of the country in administering law and justice to their own people is, indeed, a fact that cannot be seriously disputed', and even that 'the scheme of local self-government adopted by Lord Ripon does not altogether meet the requirements now called for'.[74]

A short-lived British India Committee also worked assiduously in Ripon's support in 1883–4, but 'it was crippled for want of funds, and especially suffered from the lack of a really representative organisation in India', as William Digby, a Committee activist, stated later.[75] Digby had been chosen the first secretary of the National Liberal Club in 1882 and was strongly emerging as an important link between British Liberal radicalism and Indian nationalism.[76] After Ripon's arrival in Britain, Digby organised a dinner in his honour at the National Liberal Club on 25 February 1885. Ripon was most pleased with this gesture, stating relieved: 'I esteem very highly such a proof of their approval from a body so representative of the Liberal Party.'[77]

Digby was furious about the criticism of Lord Ripon, and fiercely supported his policies in his book *India for the Indians – and for England*, which was published in February 1885. Prior to the publication he wrote to Herbert Gladstone: 'In that work I produce (almost entirely from official documents) evidence of the most remarkable character, evidence which if true (as I believe it to be to the very smallest sentence) ought to lead to a re-consideration of our position in India.'[78] In the book Digby reprehended the Anglo-Indians' 'ecstatic admiration of themselves and their doings' which led British statesmen to adopt the same attitude of admiration towards them and to underestimate the Indian character and capabilities.[79] In Digby's opinion British rule in India should be a mere police duty; 'that the British, as they alone can in India, should keep the peace. That done they should stand aside, allowing the people to rule themselves according to their own ideas and experience of what is best.'[80]

In the first instance, the existing Indian states should be made 'secure beyond all doubt', Digby advised in the book. The second step was to begin a process of creating more and more Indian states, 'until the whole Empire shall become a congeries of such States'.[81] Thus, there would not be any 'one Indian nation' which the Congress – and then also Digby – was to champion later; neither was he advocating a democratic representative principle to India, for in this scheme the power belonged to traditional Indian princes and chiefs, notwithstanding the 'partly elected' provincial parliaments. To increase co-operation between various Indian states, Digby urged Britain to activate the Council of Empire – constituting exclusively of Indian princes and high British officials – which had been formally established in 1877 but had remained 'a Paper Council and nothing more'.[82] In all, the system would result in annual savings of £9 million in the Indian budget and everyone would gain, Digby argued.[83] A reviewer in *The Times* stated briefly that Digby's book contained many points which were 'worthy of serious consideration'.[84]

'My suggestions (I believe) are in no degree wild. I recognise all the good England has done in India & is doing at the same time that I show the marked superiority of Native rule under English over-Lordship. The title of my little book, viz. *India for the Indians – and for England*, shows I am no revolutionist in my ideas,' Digby assured Herbert Gladstone, who was not sure whether the secretary of the National Liberal Club should write such a book.[85] Nevertheless, the latter part of the title, – *and for England*, was mere rhetoric, for the book's main message was *India for the Indians*; it did not advocate India for England. Only incidentally, at the end of the book, Digby stated that complete severance between England and India was impossible due to the large imperial debt and vast British investments in India.[86]

Before the formation of the Indian National Congress, the reformers were not certain who the 'representatives' of the Indian people actually were. Digby took the simple way and pointed to the Maharajahs and Nawabs, and the positivist Cotton took much the same stance. Cotton was not willing to democratise the Indian legislatures; instead, he wanted them to reflect the existing society. His scheme was very similar to Digby's: a federation of Indian states, each administered by leading Indians in the caste hierarchy.[87] On the other hand, Lord Ripon placed already in the early 1880s high hopes in the educated middle class, in which he saw genuine potential for progress. The

Indianisation of the civil service and the spread of education at all levels were therefore the most crucial issues to him.[88] Annie Besant had also stated in 1878 her wish to let the supreme power in India gradually pass 'not into the hands of the princes, but into the hands of the Indian people so that a mighty self-governing nation should slowly arise'.[89]

The Ilbert Bill was eventually watered down to please the Anglo-Indian public, and, to some extent, Ripon's local self-government schemes experienced the same fate. The controversy had, however, made it clear to the Indian nationalists and their British friends that formal organisation was necessary. The first direct result was the Indian National Telegraphic Union in 1885, which aimed to undo the monopoly of the 'anti-reformists' in Indian news. The Union made arrangements to send to leading British newspapers a weekly telegram dealing with Indian questions from their point of view, but despite a successful beginning and Lord Ripon's generous contributions, the Union collapsed shortly afterwards in financial difficulties.[90]

The driving force behind the Indian National Telegraphic Union was A. O. Hume, who had resigned from the Indian Civil Service after disagreements with Ripon's predecessor, Lord Lytton. He had stayed in India as a private citizen and contributed immensely to the foundation of the Indian National Congress, of which he became the first president in December 1885. In its programme the Congress called for the Indianisation of the Indian Civil Service, considerable reductions in military expenditure, a parliamentary inquiry into Indian affairs, abolition of the India Council i.e. the council of the secretary of state for India, and Indian representation in the legislative councils of India.[91] In addition, there were several minor demands, both political and economical, in the spirit of equality between the Indians and the British, which contributed to the five main demands.[92] Dadabhai Naoroji spoke eloquently on the need for Indian representation in the legislative councils:

It is not for us to teach the English people how necessary representation is for good government. We have learnt the lesson from them, and knowing from them how great a blessing it is to those nations who enjoy it, and how utterly un-English it is for the English nation to withhold it from us, we can, with confidence and trust, ask them to give us this.

The taxed must have a voice in the taxation that is imposed upon them. We are British subjects, and I say we can demand what we are entitled to expect still at British hands as their greatest and most noble institution and heritage. It is our inheritance also and we should not be kept out of it. Why, if we are to be denied Britain's best institutions, what good is it to India to be under the British sway? It will be simply another Asiatic despotism.

If we are true to ourselves, and perseveringly ask what we desire, the British people are the very people on earth who will give what is right and just.[93]

As explained in a previous chapter, the Indianisation of Indian administration was considered a vital question as much for the sake of economy as equality, and it became naturally a – or even the – central aim of the Indian National Congress. It was, however, an extremely difficult one, since the Indian Civil Service was a significant employer for British youths. In theory its doors were equally open to Indians, but in practice the Indians faced two major obstacles: these were the low age limit for the candidates and the fact that the examinations were held only in England, the trip being very expensive. Organising simultaneous examinations in India were therefore continuously, but unsuccessfully, advocated.[94]

In the days of the East India Company the renewal of its charter every twenty years had brought about a regular and valuable parliamentary inquiry into Indian administration. Since the Crown rule had begun, in 1858, no such inquiry had taken place. Consequently, the nationalists believed that 'the truth' as to Indian affairs 'hardly ever' reached parliament, as N. N. Sen, editor of the Calcutta *Indian Mirror*, put it. Due to the composition of the India Council and Indian legislative councils, Sen argued, 'the truth' was 'always burked' and 'never allowed to rise to the surface'.[95] In addition to the parliamentary inquiry into Indian affairs, the abolition of the India Council was thus considered vital: the Council comprised retired Anglo-Indian officials who were regarded as 'naturally prone ... to hand down to their succesors the British Indian Empire in pretty nearly the same condition in which they found it'. They never confessed the abuses of the system 'which gave them birth', nor were they inclined to reform it;[96] as Lord Ripon put it, the Council was 'the most conservative body now existing in Europe'.[97] Instead of the Council rule, the Congress wished the secretary of state for India to direct the government of India 'on the same principles on which the Secretary of State for the Colonies governs Ceylon and the other Colonies'.[98]

Henry Cotton pointed out already before the foundation of the Indian National Congress that 'internal agitation in Ireland has always been useless; it was only when Irish agitation was supplemented by a powerful phalanx of opinion in England that any concessions were allowed to the sister island. And so it is in the case of India.'[99] A true Indian Political Agency was therefore badly needed in London to undertake vigorous propaganda on behalf of India. For a while this work was under the responsibility of Naoroji, who settled in London in 1886 in search of a parliamentary constituency. This major advocate of the 'drain theory' had spent much time in Britain since the 1850s, and the more he was introduced to the 'British way of thought' and British institutions, the more he became convinced that, as his biographer put it, 'if the British people were true to themselves, true to their inbred sense and traditions of equality, justice, and fair play, they would help India to obtain freedom'.[100]

Naoroji had been in contact with William Digby since 1881, and when he moved to London they soon became close friends. In April 1886 Naoroji found Digby 'depressed' because 'he had not suitable and proper representatives of India' to back up his arguments. Then 'he over and over again repeated that now that I had come, be the result about my object what it may, he will be able to work for India, with more heart and zeal. He was extremely desirous to do all that lay in his power to promote my object,' Naoroji noted happily.[101] When they met again ten days later, the work was well under way. To begin with, Digby strongly recommended Naoroji to change his Parsi headdress to an English top hat: 'better to appear altogether like an Englishman'. He also intended to get Naoroji a ticket to the Conference of the Liberal Association in favour of the Irish Bill and, if aiming to become a Liberal parliamentary candidate, advised him to prepare to speak on behalf of Irish home rule at some point.[102]

Digby thus became the natural ally for Naoroji to turn to in the matter of the Indian Political Agency in London. Naoroji possibly did not know that Digby was already quite a discredited figure in the eyes of the Indian government. His book, *India for the Indians – and for England*, had been closely studied in India as a direct attack against their administration. The government of Madras, where Digby had resided in the 1870s, produced a detailed twenty-page-long memo on the book.[103] They were annoyed by Digby's provocative argument that not only were the Indians capable of governing themselves but also that they did it even better than the British. They regarded Digby as utterly hypocrite, for this 'accuser accepted from the Government he now so gratuitously vilifies the distinction of C.I.E. for services in connection with the famine which, he says, they did nothing to relieve'.[104]

Digby resigned from his post as the secretary of the National Liberal Club in 1887 and founded an Indian and Political General Agency in April 1888. The Agency was to function on a fee-for-service basis, with political associations, Indian native states, or individuals as paying customers.[105] Digby's main aim was to serve the Indian National Congress, and he suggested that all Indian political associations would jointly appoint him as their agent on a yearly fee of £250 plus the expenses.[106] Naoroji's friend W. C. Bonnerjee, who was visiting London, guaranteed personally Digby's expenditure for 1888,[107] and the campaign had a highly promising beginning: 10 000 copies of the report of the 1887 Congress and 'many thousand copies of speeches and pamphlets' were circulated, and a number of public meetings were organised.[108] During the first seven months, about £1700 were spent; the following year's expenditure was estimated at £2500, which Naoroji and A. O. Hume called upon India to provide, unsuccessfully.[109]

In order to provide a broader basis for the movement in Britain and also to make it more appealing to the leading Indian nationalists, a

British Committee of the Indian National Congress was founded in 1889, with Sir William Wedderburn as the president. Hume had first tried to persuade Lord Ripon to assume the Committee's chairmanship, but Ripon declined on the ground that 'it would be at once to destroy all the advantage which my position as an ex V.R. gives me. I must retain an independent position, or I shall lose influence.'[110] Digby's Agency was merged with the Committee, and Digby became the Committee's secretary as well as the editor of its paper *India*, published 1890 onwards. *India* was mainly paid by Indian nationalists and became distributed free to parliamentarians, political clubs, and the British press.

Self-government was a distant goal for the founders of the Congress, but the way for it had to be paved by immediate legislative and administrative reforms. Hume told Naoroji that the efforts were indeed 'directed towards Home Rule for India'.[111] Publicly he stated that 'We, one and all, look forward to a time, say 50, say 70 years hence, when the Government of India will be precisely similar to that of the Dominion of Canada'.[112]

The goal – self-government in 50 to 70 years – was thus moderate indeed and did not satisfy the actual anti-imperialists in Britain who wished to see Britain getting rid of India in their lifetime. Indian nationalists were to some extent offended and confused by their attitude. This clash of opinions is well expressed in the notes written by Naoroji in 1886, after he had been visiting Richard Congreve. Naoroji was amazed at Congreve's views:

He thought the connexion between England and India should be severed; it was injuring England; it was doing harm to the whole English character. The connexion with the Colonies was a weakness. I was of a different opinion that the connexion should continue for the sake of India and that if certain reforms, which were sorely needed by India, were made, the connexion would be a blessing to both.[113]

Herbert Spencer was on the lines of Congreve. He confessed that he had 'not studied Indian affairs to any extent',[114] for they were too alien and forbidding for him. The proper role of India, to Spencer, was to serve as a warning for other non-European peoples. 'The Japanese policy should, I think, be that of *keeping Americans and Europeans as much as possible at arm's length*,' he wrote to his Japanese admirer, for 'In presence of the more powerful races your position is one of chronic danger'. Any closer intercourse would be 'a fatal policy', Spencer cautioned:

> If you wish to see what is likely to happen, study the history of India. Once let one of the more powerful races gain a *point d'appui* and there will inevitably in course of time grow up an aggressive policy which will lead to collisions with the Japanese; these collisions will be represented as attacks by the Japanese which must be avenged; forces will be sent from America or Europe, as the case may be; a portion of territory will be seized and required to be made over as a foreign settlement; and from this there will grow eventually subjugation of the entire Japanese Empire. I believe that you will have great difficulty in avoiding this fate in any case, but you will make the process easy if you allow any privileges to foreigners beyond those which I have indicated.[115]

The staunchest anti-imperialists as well as the staunchest imperialists were not among the active supporters of the Indian National Congress. The Congressmen stressed their loyalty towards the British empire frequently, and, if possible, its British Committee was even more moderate. The reasons for this were obvious: as Anil Seal has well put it, 'Moderation seemed the most persuasive way of bringing the Raj to bargain with them, particularly when it was expressed in the idioms of British politics. More important, the alternatives to moderation threatened to endanger the position which these men already enjoyed.'[116] Hence, A. O. Hume's scheme for the Congress did not emphasise the nationalist fervour; rather, he hoped that it would defuse the fervour by providing a 'safety-valve of great and growing forces'.[117] The Congress and its British Committee sought to point out that if the British repressed the educated natives and their aspirations, it would turn them into a solid opposition against the government; instead, if their ambitions were gratified, they would become the government's staunchest allies. Thus, the Committee was not an anti-imperialist body, and membership in it was generally regarded as a broad statement in support of Indian reform. Wedderburn, the president of the British Committee, has been aptly described as a 'friend of moderates' and 'enemy of extremists',[118] and this was to determine the tone of the Committee for its whole functioning period, 1889–1920.[119]

Due to their not-too-radical tone, the Indian National Congress and its British Committee generated quite wide support among the moderate and reform-minded.[120] Samuel Smith, a Liberal MP and long-time friend of Naoroji's, supported the Indian reforms heartily but felt obliged to add after his criticism that 'If my remarks seem at times to bear hardly upon our administration of India, it is not because I seek to injure it, but to improve it'.[121] The same was true of the radical free-thinker Charles Bradlaugh, another Liberal supporter of the Congress movement. 'I am of the stock of reformers, I am not of the stock of revolutionists', he assured his Indian friends who were visiting Britain: 'I plead ... to divide with you what we have got; but I plead to do it holding our state high, and making it stronger.'[122] Naoroji, wishing to enter the British parliament, was also rather good at balancing between criticism and declarations of loyalty. 'The more you can get Europeans of influence on your side as Presidents taking active part, the less will be the cry that your object was revolutionary and anti-British', he advised his friend in India.[123]

Thus, whereas overtly anti-imperialist criticism would have most probably merely alienated the agitator and his cause, the 'loyal criticism' found supporters. After the Congress of 1889 Digby was able to inform the Indians that the meeting had been noted in nearly every British paper, and mainly in positive tone. He celebrated: 'The Daily News is becoming unmistakably a Congress organ. The investigation which its Editor and one of its leader-writers have made into the movement has thoroughly satisfied them alike as to its bona fide and as to the necessity of the reforms it advocates being granted.'[124] Furthermore, periodical reviews published several articles defending the Congress programme in 1888, and some heavy-weight Indian experts emerged as strong Congress sympathisers: in particular, Sir William Wilson Hunter, the statistical expert; and Sir Richard Garth, a former Conservative MP and subsequent chief justice of Bengal. Garth very much regretted the disparaging tone with which many Englishmen regarded the Indian reform movement. In his opinion the 'evils of despotic rule' were only too clear to face the truth that 'the time has arrived for relaxing, in some degree at least, the tension of that system'.[125]

The relatively wide popularity of the Indian reform movement was mainly due to its undeniable moderation; however, it also implies that British rule in India was commonly accepted as a fact. Even those who were convinced that Britain would be better off without the Indian empire did not think it could be abandoned overnight. They saw that the denial of this would only lead to pessimism and apathy, in which case there would be nothing left to do. Indeed, those who deplored the situation most, like Richard Congreve – whose views were echoed in other positivist writings on India – and Herbert Spencer, did not participate in the debate on Indian reforms at all. Their attitude was similar to that of Richard Cobden, who had declared in 1857 that 'I can't even co-operate with those who seek to "reform" India, for I have no faith in the power of England to govern that country at all permanently'.[126] More hopeful critics, on the other hand, campaigned for imperial reforms which would eventually lead to a peaceful loosening of the ties between Britain and the dependency, giving strong support to the Indian National Congress and its programme.

When writing a biography of Sir William Wedderburn, his colleague from the Indian reform movement wrote:

> There is one statement continually made about British dominion in India that is accepted by imperialists and anti-imperialists alike. It is that the system of British rule is the most remarkable phenomenon in the history of modern government. ... whatever our judgment of its nature, we see it as a unique thing, a highly characteristic product of the British genius. There is, however, a complementary fact that is rarely if ever brought out: namely, that *the corrective movement of political and administrative reform in India is no less characteristic of our people; is, indeed, more essentially*

British than the governing machine itself. It began nearly a century and half ago with Edmund Burke, and it developed in strength throughout the nineteenth century.[127]

The remaining question was, which one was the more typically British: the 'remarkable empire' or this liberal-minded 'corrective movement'.

CHAPTER 9

INDIA, AFRICA, AND IMPERIALISM IN BRITISH PARTY POLITICS

The formulation of the official imperial policy was, of course, under the responsibility of the British parliament. The issue of representative government for India was first raised there in 1880, when David Wedderburn, brother of William Wedderburn, spoke strongly in its favour. At the time only one fellow Liberal most cautiously supported the resolution.[1] From that on, however, the development was to be more rapid than anyone could have anticipated at the time: when Martin Pugh writes about 'the parliamentary India rebels' in the context of the 1930s, he means the die-hard Conservatives who still opposed Indian constitutional reform.[2]

William Digby, as an advanced radical and staunch Gladstonian Liberal, was determined to make Indian reforms part of the Liberal programme, without success. Indian nationalists were not eager to interfere in British party politics, believing that reform would be best accomplished by appealing to both Liberals and Conservatives. Even Naoroji, later Liberal MP, was of this opinion in 1885.[3] Moreover, many moderate Congress supporters in Britain emphasised that Indian reform should not be made an issue in party disputes. Sir W. W. Hunter wrote in 1888: 'The ... danger of the Indian Political Agency in England is that, in its desire to make friends, it may be led into alliances with extreme parliamentary parties. ... this joint question of justice to India and of the stability of our rule in India is not a question for any knot of politicians, but, please God, for the whole British people.'[4] Furthermore, neither Digby nor anyone else managed to get William Gladstone notably interested in India. Florence Nightingale took great pains on the matter but ended up disappointed. A friend of hers who knew both India and Gladstone well wrote to her in early 1885: 'I wish I could hope that you could make some real impression on him; but at his age and at this time, when his hands are so full, what can you expect? He has never given his mind to India, and it is too late now.'[5]

Digby lobbied the Indian reform for the Liberal party since 1881, when he declared that Indian reform was 'a Liberal duty' and requested the National Liberal Federation to take up the Indian issue in earnest. He suggested the Federation to inscribe 'Justice for India' on its banner and appoint a select committee, which would concentrate on Indian issues and advance communication in regard to Indian reforms.[6] The Federation was willing to act and appointed Digby a member of the general committee of the Federation to develop his ideas,[7] but when the party subsequently faced more acute problems in Egypt, the Sudan, and Ireland, enthusiasm for India faded.

Digby's energetic efforts in the National Liberal Club carried him ahead in radical Liberal ranks, securing him parliamentary candidatures for North Paddington in 1885 and South Islington in 1892. He was convinced that the Indian issue would become a success in Liberal politics. At the time of his first election he wrote:

> I remember how keenly my countrymen resisted the stamping out of Polish nationality by the despotic empires of Europe and how warmly they sympathised with the aspirations and the efforts of the Italians to free themselves from the hateful yoke of the Austrians at Venice and of the French at Rome. Consequently, I am sure that the affairs of their fellow-subjects in India and in the Crown Colonies will not be pushed aside as of little concern.

The system of administration now existing in India is as certainly doomed to early overthrow as was Negro slavery in the United States.[8]

In contrast to the majority of Indian nationalists, Digby believed that Indian reform was 'altogether impossible' if it did not come within the range of practical politics. In his opinion it had to be made a party question, and, in particular, it was due to the initiation of Liberals. 'None but Liberals are prepared for the annoyance, vexation, misrepresentation, misunderstanding, which always accompany the initiation of reform – whether for one's own country or for another,' he explained,[9] predicting that, sooner or later, 'special broadly defined Indian reforms will take a regular place in the programmes discussed on Liberal platforms'.[10]

Wilfrid Scawen Blunt, in contrast, wrote to his Conservative friend, Lord Randolph Churchill, that 'if India had to trust solely to the whigs for reform it might wait till Eternity or rather till that crash came which one day will certainly come if the rigidity of the present bureaucratic system is not modified. The whigs are bureaucrats born & bred & will not stir a finger to help us.'[11] A few weeks earlier he had advised his Indian friends 'to agitate continually until they got their rights, as there was no party in England which would do anything for them from any other motive than fear'.[12] Another Conservative supporter of Indian reform, Frederic Pincott, argued that 'Indians are thoroughly Conservative in all their ideas; and hence form the natural allies of the Conservative party'. 'Their loyalty and devotion to constituted authority is proverbial', he maintained, stressing that 'any demands emanating from them' were 'moderate and free from revolutionary taint'.[13]

Nevertheless, the fact remained that the campaigners for Indian reform were mainly radical Liberals. In the 1885 election Blunt was the only Conservative candidate to support the Indian reform; and even he became a Liberal candidate the following year. In addition to his Conservative candidacy in 1885, Blunt contested a seat as a Liberal two times, but failed to get elected.[14] In his electoral address to the constituency of North Camberwell in 1885, Blunt declared he wanted to 'SEE COMPLETE JUSTICE DONE TO IRELAND'.

I would see our Indian Empire maintained and reformed; peace made with the Mahomedan races, and REPARATION DONE TO EGYPT. Above all, I would advocate a return to TRUTH AND PLAIN SPEAKING IN DIPLOMACY, believing that the deceptions and concealments and insincerities of the late Administration have profoundly demoralised the Nation, and threaten us with political decay.[15]

The election of 1885 was thus the first to bring the Indian issue forward on the platform. This was partly due to Blunt, but even more so to Digby and Lalmohan Ghose, an Indian who unsuccessfully contested a Liberal seat in east London in 1885 and 1886,[16] and, most of all, to a three-man delegation from India.[17] At Naoroji's request, the delegation aimed to remain impartial and withdraw from advocating either party per se; the intention was to support some individuals in their campaign and oppose others, the latter being mainly former Anglo-Indian officials like Sir Richard Temple. The delegates were supposed to do this from the Indian point of view only, and not to concern themselves on the candidates' opinions on other issues. However, with the sole exception of Blunt, all their 'friends' were Liberal, and, with no exception, all 'opponents' Conservative.[18]

The delegates' most important aim was to present a moderate and politically neutral appeal for India during the election campaign. The appeal began by acknowledging the benefits of British rule and continued by asking all candidates to require a parliamentary inquiry into Indian affairs. It also called for a decentralised federal government for India, changes in military policy, practical enforcement of equality, and the reform of the legislative councils. In conclusion it urged British voters to elect candidates who would support the parliamentary inquiry into Indian affairs.[19]

The plans for neutrality and moderation came to nothing, since the one who eventually 'took the delegates in tow and guided their fortunes' was William Digby.[20] The Indians' claims of impartiality came to seem somewhat peculiar, when they frequently appeared on Digby's platform pleading for the restoration of Liberal 'Riponism' in Indian policy and rebuking the Conservatives. In the end, the delegates managed to alienate even Blunt to some extent, and Churchill in particular.[21]

Every candidate whom the Indian delegates supported was defeated in the election, while those whom they opposed were all elected.[22] Lord Ripon comforted them by assuring that their friends had not been defeated on any Indian question, but on the Church and Irish questions.[23] Churchill's opinion was that radical Liberals had used the Indians unfairly.[24] In his eyes 'the highly educated native' had become 'a beastly impostor'. He wrote to the viceroy of India: 'Fancy the impudence of those Indian delegates going down to Birmingham to speak against me. They are making great fools of themselves, and their special protégés, Digby and Lalmohan Ghose, have been defeated, I am thankful to say.'[25] Florence Nightingale was not pleased with Digby's behaviour, either. When writing to Wedderburn, she regretted that the Indians 'had fallen so entirely into the hands of Mr Digby, who has lost his election – & is no great loss to our cause – & who used them merely as his Electioneering agents'.[26]

When Naoroji settled in London in April 1886 looking for a parliamentary constituency, Frank Hugh O'Donnell suggested an Irish constituency. His idea was to combine Indian reform with Irish home rule:

> The precise point to which the negotiation was narrowed down was that four natives of India, to be selected by the Indians themselves, men of university attainments and considerable power of oratory, should be elected for Irish constituencies, to be Irish Home Rulers on all Irish questions, and to be members for India, and to be backed by the Irish party, on Indian affairs.[27]

Parnell, however, 'simply could not understand how the proposal could excite interest in Ireland',[28] for the Irish had their own issues and concerns. Naoroji also met another setback, when Richard Congreve, whom he had expected to help him, was equally discouraging. Congreve told him frankly that he did not wish to see Indians in the British parliament, assuring Naoroji that he would attain any object better by working outside: 'The peculiar ways and complications of the ways of

Parliament leave no scope to work in it. Once in, you do not know where you are, or what you can do, and have little chance.'[29] Moreover, when Naoroji was made a Liberal parliamentary candidate for Holborn, another friend, Sir George Birdwood, wrote that while he earnestly desired 'to see a native of India in Parliament', he felt unable to help Naoroji in any way, since he was politically 'all for Chamberlain – and dead against Mr. Gladstone and his supporters'.[30] Major Evans Bell, on the other hand, was eager to help Naoroji in the election campaign, as were John Slagg, W. S. Blunt, and John Bright.[31] W. T. Stead, too, undoubtedly smelling a good story, asked Naoroji to send any material about him and his election campaign to be published in the *Pall Mall Gazette*.[32] William Digby also promoted Naoroji's cause energetically, but this first attempt in 1886 was unsuccessful.

Naoroji's candidature enhanced the Indian nationalist cause among the Liberals, and their overall attitude towards the Indian National Congress was cautiously positive. Herbert Gladstone visited India in 1886–7 and urged every Englishman, especially MPs, to go and see the rise of educated India by themselves. 'There was a combination of earnestness, moderation and ability which should entitle the opinions expressed to a fair and full consideration', he testified.[33] The Grand Old Man himself, when interviewed by Digby in April 1889, assured 'I have always had good will towards the Indian people and have done for them, from time to time, all that has seemed to me possible.' Digby sought to convince Gladstone that 'if ever there was any organisation in the British Empire which deserved the hearty support of all English Liberals, it is this of the Congress', emphasising the constitutional manner the Congress acted.[34] Gladstone was rather suspicious of the 'seditious native press' which, he had heard, contained 'writings of a disloyal character'. Digby assured that he, who was an expert in Indian press, did not know of any such instances; 'but as a matter of fact District officials in India are such irresponsible despots that they resent all comment on their actions however mild, and call that sedition what probably any unprejudiced person would say fair criticism'. Gladstone 'could well believe that'.[35]

The National Liberal Club hosted a banquet in honour of Naoroji in 1889, who had been selected as a Liberal candidate for the second time, now for Central Finsbury. Ironically, it was the front-row anti-imperialist Frederic Harrison who offered the toast for the empire at the banquet. Harrison discussed the different views on empire in his lengthy toast speech, declaring that he himself belonged to neither the 'bombastic' nor the 'pessimistic' school of empire, as depicted by Sir John Seeley. Since the dinner was a celebration on the occasion of an Indian nationalist becoming a parliamentary candidate in Britain, even Harrison spoke eloquently in favour of the 'unity of empire'.[36]

Charles Bradlaugh and William Digby worked closely together on Indian matters in 1888–91. Digby coached Bradlaugh on numerous Indian issues for questions in the Commons and energetically assisted him in preparing an Indian Reform Bill, which Bradlaugh was to introduce in early 1890. When Bradlaugh's 'membership for India' became more famous, dozens of letters poured to him from India, and Bradlaugh forwarded them regularly to Digby to send answers.[37]

Bradlaugh's Indian Reform Bill was based on the formulations of the 1889 Congress. It aimed at introducing representative government in India by reforming the central and provincial legislative councils so that half of the members would be elected and half nominated. The bill was largely formulated, from the Congress demands, by Digby and Bradlaugh, in collaboration with Ripon and Naoroji.[38] Bradlaugh's bill was soon met by an official Indian Councils Bill, which was introduced in February 1890 by the secretary of state for India, Lord Cross.[39] Digby stated that Cross's bill, which rejected the idea of introducing representative government, was 'wholly unsatisfactory to the Indian People', and A. O. Hume condemned it 'worse than nothing – simply an insult to the country'. In the debate in the House of Lords on 6 March, Lords Northbrook, Ripon, and Kimberley all talked strongly in favour of an elective element in the appointment of members for the councils, but, allegedly mainly due to prime minister Salisbury's strong opposition, Lord Cross was not ready to support it.[40]

Digby then launched a massive petition campaign in support of the introduction of the elective principle into the official Councils Reform Bill, with the result of over six hundred petitions from India with 354 000 signatures for reform, while only two petitions with 24 000 signatures were sent against it. Both opposing petitions came from

Indian Muslims.[41] Encouraged by Lord Ripon, Digby also organised a major tour for a Congress delegation in Britain in spring 1890, consisting of eight prominent nationalists.[42] The deputation arrived in early April and began by public meetings in London, which were also attended by Naoroji, Digby, Wedderburn, and W. S. B. McLaren, Liberal MP.[43] At Bradlaugh's request the tour was then begun from his constituency, Northampton, where the meeting was held with 'very good attendance'.[44] From Northampton the deputation proceeded to the biggest towns of Britain, participating even in a debate at the Oxford Union.[45] The tour ended conveniently with a meeting with William Gladstone, to whom the delegates presented their hopes for representative government by the expansion and reconstitution of the councils. Gladstone replied: 'Well, it seems you must be prepared to wait a little longer for the realization of your hopes. You will have to wait a while.'[46]

Lord Ripon and John Morley concluded that as long as the Irish home rule debate was to the fore, any attempt at Indian reform would be left halfway. 'The time is not favourable for concessions to India, there is a flavour of Home Rule about them which, however mild, would frighten such a House of Commons as this', Ripon wrote to Morley.[47] Many concurred, and the decision was postponed until just before the election of 1892. The legislative councils were then reformed and expanded, but the Congress demands were not met. Salisbury accepted only the principle that the councils should be enlarged and their members allowed to ask 'parliamentary questions' and discuss the budget. The introduction of the elective principle was abandoned, and merely a small new quota of non-official members was admitted to the councils.[48]

During the long election campaign which led to Naoroji's seat in parliament in 1892, Digby was, again, his staunchest supporter. Naoroji made Digby his formal 'direct agent' for the campaign in 1891,[49] and their frequent correspondence in 1889–92 reveals that he had full confidence in Digby, who guided him in Liberal circles and political practice. During these years they informed each other of every appointment and contact they had made in Indian matters.[50] Digby's own campaign was unsuccessful,[51] but Sir William Wedderburn gained a seat at a by-election a year later. Together with W. S. Caine, equally a member of the British Committee of the Indian National Congress, Naoroji and Wedderburn soon founded an Indian Parliamentary Committee, consisting of 154 MPs before 1895. The Parliamentary Committee was not committed to the Congress programme even to the extent of the British Committee; it simply pledged to pay attention to Indian interests so that justice would be done.[52] Many of the members belonged primarily to other pressure groups, such as the temperance, anti-opium, and social purity movements, and these domestic interests strongly influenced their priorities in regard to India.[53] There were also some Congress-sympathisers in the Commons who did not join the Indian Committee, like Sir Charles Dilke and Samuel Smith. They thought their work for Indian reform was more effective if they remained outside any organisation;[54] and Smith, especially, had spoken on behalf of India for a long time before the Committee.[55] Dilke had earlier argued that true nationalists in India preferred a reformed government of India to the British parliament, since the latter would always interfere only when 'there is either a British interest involved or some social question on which there exists strong feeling in England itself'. A good example was the repeal of the Indian cotton duties, which was carried out in the name of free trade, but 'in the teeth of an almost unanimous local native opinion'.[56]

According to Margot Morrow, there was not a single Conservative or Unionist member in the Indian Parliamentary Committee in 1893–5, but even 43.2 per cent of Liberal MPs and 38.3 per cent of Irish nationalist MPs were members. However, as Morrow points out, such statistical strength was illusory, since the Committee was not united in its demands for reform, and its membership did not indicate commitment to the Congress proposals.[57] Even as such, its numbers and a few active members managed to cause the secretary of state for India, Lord Kimberley, some anxiety: 'Every day shows there will be extreme difficulty in carrying on the Government of India in the face of constant attempts to interfere', he wrote to the viceroy, Lord Lansdowne.[58] The India Office was, indeed, sensitive to the attempts to publicise Indian issues in parliament and, as Arnold Kaminsky has put it, it 'exerted extraordinary efforts to neutralize such activities'.[59]

In summer 1893 a narrow majority at the House of Commons for-warded a resolution in favour of simultaneous examinations in both India and Britain for the Indian Civil Service candidates, but, facing strong resistance, the idea was soon watered down without proceed-ing further.[60] Another major demand in the Congress agenda was the parliamentary inquiry into Indian affairs. Eventually, a Royal Commission on Indian Expenditure was appointed in 1895. Headed by Lord Welby, a former permanent secretary of the British treasury, it consisted of MPs and Anglo-Indian officials. Naoroji, Wedderburn, W. S. Caine, and Leonard Courtney were among the representatives, and prominent Indian nationalists came to England to give evidence alongside previous viceroys and officials. 'Let India have complete share in the whole Imperial system and then talk of asking her to contribute to Imperial expenses', Naoroji stated.[61] His solution was to give the whole Indian government into Indian hands, with the excep-tion of the viceroy, the governors, and the commander-in-chief, and even those would be gradually replaced by Indians. The Chairman wondered whether this could be possible, since 'the history of India is that people have been continually slaughtering each other'. Naoroji answered briefly: 'What have you done here? What is the history of Europe? We do not want to go back, because we have learnt as you have learnt.'[62]

The Commission heard the evidence for two years, after which it took three more years to produce the report. The final report, sub-mitted in 1900, was a huge disappointment for Indian reformers, for the existing financial relations between Britain and India were not altered to any great extent. Wedderburn, Caine, and Naoroji submit-ted a minority report to express their disagreement, but Naoroji was nonetheless pleased with the publicity which the Indian issue had gained.[63]

On the whole, the Indian reform still remained an issue for the experts throughout the period, and the anti-imperialists did not take much stance on the question of what policies to pursue in practice. Sir Arthur Hobhouse, like Anglo-Indian officials in general, deprecated the parliamentary interference in the government of India in *details*; but at the same time he, like the anti-imperialists in general, strongly encouraged debate on the *principles* according to which a dependency like India should be governed.[64] 'If we cannot decide here upon the broad principles on which our dependencies are to be governed, we are of all men the most miserable', he declared shortly after his return from India in 1877: 'To say that we cannot judge to what ends the Government of India should be directed is a desertion of our position as a governing people, and an abnegation of our right to have any dependencies at all.' Hence, Hobhouse wished 'to see such a body of intelligent opinion in England as will supply a constant check to the spirit of aggrandizement or Imperialism in India'.[65]

Nevertheless, as it has become clear, the principles were not the main problem after all. Racial equality had been declared in India already in 1833 and repeated in 1858; the Indian legislative councils were reformed in 1892; simultaneous examinations for the Indian Civil Service were narrowly approved in the Commons in 1893; and the parliamentary inquiry into Indian expenditure was carried out by 1900. These, indeed, were concessions towards the very main demands of the Indian National Congress; yet, disappointment in British rule increased year by year. What was lacking was the political will to enforce the principles of equality or simultaneous examinations into practice or – in the case of the councils and the parliamentary inquiry – the political courage to carry out truly reforming and democratising changes.

Military operations notwithstanding, the parliamentary debate on India concerned thus mainly long-term structural changes in the administration. African issues, in contrast, were more acute and often demanded immediate attention and swift decisions. The Liberal party, in particular, suffered from major disagreements at the times of imperial crises, of which the British occupation of Egypt in 1882 was the first.[66] As it has been noted earlier, many potential critics were silenced at the time due to their respect for Gladstone. Some, however, like John Bright, felt obliged to follow their personal conscience. Bright found it 'painful to observe how much of the "jingo" or war spirit can be shown by certain members of a Liberal Cabinet',[67] and soon decided to resign. After the bombardment he refused to take any part in the discussion of the matter, since he felt it to be 'of no avail'.[68] When Gladstone privately explained his views on the occupation, Bright found them

> somewhat strange and unexpected. He urged as if all that has been done in the Egyptian case was right, and even persuaded himself that he is fully justified in the interest of Peace. I made little reply, but gave him no expectation that my view coincided with his or had in any degree changed. ... He seems to have the power of convincing himself that what to me seems glaringly wrong is evidently right. ... He even spoke of our being able to justify our conduct in the great day of account.[69]

Richard Congreve had approached John Bright in the past several times when he had found that some specific problem required parliamentary attention.[70] When he in 1884 insisted on Bright to do more in regard to the Egyptian question, Bright merely replied that 'I have done what I can'. He was most unwilling to add to the government's difficulties any further and stressed that it would not help the situation at all if the Liberals would be forced out of office. 'I do not wonder at your grief,' he assured Congreve; 'I participate in it to the full extent. ... I lament & wait with much anxiety, but I cannot move with any hope of much usefulness.'[71]

Wilfrid Scawen Blunt later listed that, as to the Egyptian question, his 'strong helpers' in parliament were Lord Randolph Churchill, Sir Henry Drummond Wolff, Sir John Gorst, Robert Bourke, Sir Wilfrid Lawson, Henry Labouchere, and 'the Irish party'.[72] The first three were prominent members of the radical Conservative 'Fourth Party', which aimed to attack Gladstone's government by claiming that it was disloyal to its own principles of peace, retrenchment, and reform. In the period of 1882 to 1885, Blunt smugly regarded Churchill, Wolff, and Gorst as his 'disciples' in the Egyptian question; he instructed Churchill that, like in the case of India, also in regard to Egypt '& generally for Western Asia', 'the Whigs will never do anything but harm, because they are Whigs & because they hate the Mohammedans – and the Radicals will never do anything at all, because they are Radicals and will undertake no responsibility'.[73] R. F. Foster has pointed out

that Churchill was mainly interested in embracing the Egyptian cause
because he regarded it as 'the key issue upon which Liberalism contradicted himself', next to Ireland. To the whole 'Fourth Party', Blunt was
'something of a figure of fun', as Foster has put it; especially Wolff's
view of him 'wavered between amusement and irritation', and 'Gorst
described him as somebody who had only got the right idea about
Egypt by accident'.[74]

By 1885 Blunt's main associates in parliament were Liberals, and
already in 1884 he collaborated especially with Labouchere and John
Morley, whom he met through Frederic Harrison. Labouchere's personal
platform was his weekly paper *Truth*, published 1877 onwards, which
gained a circulation of 30 000 copies per week in the 1880s.[75] After his
initial ponderings were over,[76] he opposed the government's Egyptian
policy vehemently both in *Truth* and in parliament. Blunt found
Labouchere 'more practical' than himself, and they 'discussed every
detail of the policy to be suggested to Gladstone'.[77] However, Blunt
also noted Morley's view that 'Lawson and Labouchere have ruined the
Egyptian cause by their jokes – people were afraid of seeming to agree
with them'.[78] Neither Labouchere's reputation nor the anti-imperialist
cause at large was, most likely, advanced by Labouchere's outbursts,
declaring that the British 'were without exception, the greatest robbers
and marauders in regard to ... annexations that had ever existed', and
even 'worse than other countries' because they plundered hypocritic-
ally and 'always pretended' that it was 'for other people's good'.[79]

Both Leonard Courtney and John Morley had cautiously accepted
the British intervention in Egypt in 1882, but the subsequent rise of
the Mahdi in the Sudan caused them to change their minds. 'I am a
little disposed', Courtney told his constituents in October 1884, 'to
ask myself whether, if we could begin again, we should go to Egypt at
all'. As his biographer put it: 'Before long he was to reach the definite
conclusion that it had been a mistake, and that Bright's resignation
had been an act of wisdom as well as of courage.'[80] Morley, then, was
soon 'under strong pressure from such associates as Frederic Harrison,
Leonard Courtney, Sir Wilfrid Lawson, and his chairman at Newcastle,
[Robert] Spence Watson' – not to mention Blunt – to launch 'a vigorous public campaign against British involvement in the Sudan', which

he finally did in early 1885.[81] He explained to Chamberlain that he simply could not 'go for an hour' with a policy which aimed at 'smashing the Mahdi': 'war in the Soudan is an affair of political conscience with me,' he wrote, 'I would rather leave the H. of C., and go back to my books again, than have anything to do with such a business.'[82] Hence, as Kate Courtney noted in his diary in February 1885, amidst the 'Great excitement throughout the country and clamour for a forward policy', Courtney and Morley 'almost alone' raised 'their voices against any further bloodshed'.[83]

On 21 February 1885, first Drummond Wolff and then John Morley visited Blunt, asking for material to be used in preparation of speeches for the Commons. 'It is all very well Morley coming forward now as the champion of peace, but it was his defection from Frederic Harrison and me last year that decided the Government to send the expedition. If he had spoken out then as he does now, he would have prevented it,' Blunt noted bitterly.[84] Three weeks later he discussed the issue of negotiating with the Mahdi with Kate and Leonard Courtney. Blunt showed a draft of a letter he was sending to Gladstone, but Courtney 'said it was not definite enough, and urged me to recast it, stating the exact terms which I thought might be accepted as a basis of negotiation'. Blunt found Kate Courtney 'more enthusiastic than he is, and at leaving I urged her to use her influence with him to keep him up to the mark': 'These Parliament people are absurdly pusillanimous, and though Courtney is the boldest of them he is only half-hearted to speak his mind.'[85]

Others were more enthusiastic. Sir Wilfrid Lawson, himself in the Riviera, wrote to Courtney to send 'one line of encouragement in the splendid fight which you and John Morley – almost alone – are making against the madness of the British nation and its rulers'.[86] Frederic Harrison wrote to both Courtney and Morley, urging them to 'form a powerful party' together, through which they could 'ultimately modify the policy of the Ministry'.[87] 'Your speech on the Soudan war has gone all over the country & puts you in the place of leader of a party,' he praised Morley, assuring that it was 'a chance for you that does not come twice to a man'. 'The rank & file of the Liberals are entirely with you,' and 'at least 50' MPs 'will follow you', Harrison argued; and even if Morley and Courtney would stand alone, 'which you do not, your arguments are unanswerable & have already struck dismay in the Jingoes'.[88] Nothing could be accomplished in London, however, and Harrison thus advised them 'to go straight to the country':

> No possible opposition can be constructed inside the House with this rotten end of a Parliament. If Gladstone could be got to go straight to the people, over the heads of the party and official world, he could do what he liked. Three speeches from him in Lancashire, Midlothian and the Midlands would even now destroy the war party altogether, though it might possibly break up his Cabinet. I congratulate you on your splendid opportunity.[89]

The enthusiasm for 'smashing the Mahdi' and the forward policy in the Sudan did not last long. British officials in Egypt pointed out that the reconquest of the Sudan would be a major operation, and in early April 1885 the political attention was turned to the Russian attack in Penjdeh near the Indian north-western border. Once the immediate crisis was avoided, new issues, Ireland in particular, occupied the political arena. The Egyptian question faded into the background, in spite of Blunt's continuous efforts to advocate British evacuation. Sir William Harcourt and John Morley considered many of Blunt's arguments for Egyptian self-government good and noteworthy, but simultaneously acknowledged the complexity of the situation. 'You have sworn off British politics, a wise determination to which I recommend you to adhere,' Harcourt advised Blunt in 1891.[90] Seven months later, when Blunt rightly suspected that Harcourt was soon to be in office again, he wrote to Harcourt asking him to advance 'a strong Native Ministry in Egypt'.[91] In 1893 Blunt wrote actively to his friends in parliament, urging either a decision of the evacuation of Egypt or an official declaration of an Egyptian protectorate, which would be better than the 'temporary occupation' with an uncertain future.[92] When Sir Charles Dilke, too, reminded the government in 1892 that the occupation of Egypt had always been pledged to be temporary, Joseph Chamberlain advised him: 'I think you do go out of your way to offend them when you advocate evacuation of Egypt, and I ask you to consider if this is worthwhile. Be as Radical as you like – be Home Rule if you must – but be a little Jingo if you can.'[93]

The rise of the Roseberian Liberal imperialist group in the 1890s was largely due to their annoyance at 'the excessive degree to which the party had become a party of protest', as H. C. G. Matthew has put it: 'Before the 1880 government, the Little England view had been a harmless ideological luxury; by 1895 it seemed to be becoming the majority opinion within the party.'[94] To those anti-imperialists who were not in party politics, the emergence of ever more powerful Liberal imperialism served as evidence that major changes were needed in the political map in order to reverse the headway of imperialism. Edward Spencer Beesly complained in 1898 that 'the old classification of politicians has ceased to correspond to the more important differences of opinion' between imperialism and anti-imperialism: that one 'really vital and urgent question' which 'dwarfed all others' had 'nothing to do with existing party divisions'. He was convinced that 'the division of parties on these new lines is bound to come, and cannot be long delayed.'[95] The present party classification 'according to old factions' only guaranteed that every Cabinet 'would have its contingent of Jingoes who would insist on a "continuity" of Jingoism', Beesly argued. The only way to end that was to form a new party, led by John Morley; and that party should be 'determined not only to oppose any further expansion of the Empire, but to prepare wisely for its gradual contraction'.[96]

Frederic Harrison wrote to Morley in August 1899 pointing out that there was, again, 'a great opportunity' for him to stand out as a great anti-imperialist leader. He urged Morley to join forces with Harcourt by putting themselves 'at the head of the Peace Movement', which 'would start a new Mid Lothian campaign, & force the official Liberals to join you'. That would be 'a splendid opening for the right hand of the Old Man', Harrison tried to persuade Morley,[97] who was writing the *Life of Gladstone*. Francis Hirst, who was assisting Morley in the project, noted in his diary at about the same time that 'Mr. Morley is beginning to fear that the Transvaal question may cause a worse split in the Liberal Party than Home Rule.'[98]

While nothing came of any ideas to form an anti-imperialist party, the Unionist Leonard Courtney and the Liberal John Morley worked closely together opposing imperialism before the Boer War. Most notably they appeared together on the same platform at the meeting of the Manchester Transvaal Committee on 15 September 1899.[99] 'Lies! Lies! Lies!' declared Courtney, referring to 'the campaign of calumny pouring daily from the Yellow Press to poison the minds of the people against the Boers', as the *Manchester Guardian* reported,[100] while Morley denounced the war 'wrong' from all possible aspects.[101] Harcourt soon wrote to Morley, 'I envy you the honour of having led the Liberal host into action, and rejoice that I am now able to bring up the reserves in your support.'[102] A crisis like the threat of war always revealed the best of the good and the worst of the bad, Harcourt believed: 'The real majority of the Liberal party remain true to their principles, and the feeble and faint-hearted are shown up in their true colours.'[103] Herbert Spencer also expressed his support, when he wrote to Courtney regretting that 'age and ill-health' prevented him from aiding, but rejoicing that 'there are some among us who think the national honour is not being enhanced by putting down the weak'. 'It is sad to see our Government backing those whose avowed policy is "expansion", which, less politely expressed, means aggression, for which there is a still less polite word, readily guessed,' he wrote.[104]

'No two speakers seemed able to agree' on Liberal policy at the National Liberal Club in 1899, maintained the *Annual Register*.[105] The new Liberal leader in the Commons, Sir Henry Campbell-Bannerman, did not consider the issue of imperialism important at first; himself in the middle ground, he thought that 'this Jingo and anti-Jingo business is purely factitious'.[106] However, by supporting John Morley's stance in parliament, he cautiously stepped the line in favour of the 'anti-Jingo' point of view before the Boer War,[107] which stirred the Liberal imperialist group further.

The clashing views on Liberalism and imperialism were discussed in several articles. J. Guinness Rogers noted in December 1899 that, to some, the concept of 'Liberal Imperialism' had 'the ring of a paradox about it'; that, at first glance, many thought that 'the principles of Liberalism' and imperialism were the opposites of each other.[108]

Rogers, who six years earlier had denounced British imperialism in Uganda,[109] insisted now that there was neither controversy in 'Liberal Imperialism' nor were there even any ultimately damaging differences inside the Liberal party on the question.[110] The weakness of the critics became obvious from their lack of practical suggestions, he argued. 'The question as to whether the war was inevitable is purely academic,' he pointed out, criticising especially John Morley and James Bryce. In Rogers's view they both wasted 'time and strength and temper about the worn-out controversies concerning the might-have-beens of the past', while each of them failed to suggest any alternative policy to war.[111]

An anonymous Liberal expressed, in the *Fortnightly Review* of September 1900, his sadness about 'the brink of the dissolution' which the Liberal party had reached.[112] From the writer's opinion, Rosebery, Labouchere, and Campbell-Bannerman – 'the types of Liberal Imperialism, Radical anti-nationalism, and official attitudinism' – were 'equally responsible for the chaotic disrepute of the party'.[113] Nevertheless, he predicted bright future for Liberalism, since it was 'as certain as anything still below the horizon can well be' that within few years 'the nation will feel the inevitable sickness of Imperialism with a swagger'; moreover when this 'reaction from Imperialistic emotions' would set in, the Liberal party would experience a mighty revival.[114] He was convinced that the revival would lead to the extinction of both the 'Little England party' and the 'Liberal Jingo party', and 'the extreme sentiments upon this subject of the party will be compromised'; at present, the writer believed, that 'The antagonistic wings who describe each other as Little Englanders and Liberal Jingoes are led to misunderstanding through exaggeration of terms.'[115]

Another writer, 'A Liberal without Adjectives', also maintained that the party was incoherent due to the 'exaggeration of terms' and equally that a bright future lay ahead of the party despite that. He acknowledged that some Liberals shared Rosebery's imperialist views but was nevertheless convinced that 'such an attitude' could not 'be put in tune with the sentiments of hundreds of thousands of Liberals all over the country, who hate this war, its motive, its outcome of misery, its repulsive reversal of the noble tradition that England must ever shelter and defend, not destroy, liberty, and hate it with a growing intensity'. The writer stated that while Lord Rosebery was a good leader, his views were not in accordance with the majority of the party; most Liberals were closer to Henry Labouchere in their views, but Labouchere was a hopeless prospect for a leader. 'It would be ... absurd to take Mr. Labouchere as the measure of the love of peace and justice, which is the cornerstone of the faith of the great majority of Liberals in the country,' he wrote; Labouchere simply was 'a dead weight on any cause'.[116]

Like John Bright in 1882, John Morley in 1900 was unwilling to disrupt the Liberal party any further with his criticism. Hence, by the spring of 1900 Morley's willingness to act had disappeared. Courtney moved on from opposing the war to work along the lines of his South Africa Conciliation Committee. Morley, in contrast, wanted nothing to do with practical politics once the war had begun. 'I do not feel any call upon me to commit myself at this stage to any view whatever as to future reconstruction. The country has flung itself into a course of brutality, hypocrisy, illusion and wrong,' he answered to Courtney's attempt to activate him. Morley felt that he had already outlined the principle according to which to act, but he had not been listened to; the problems did not therefore concern him anymore. He wrote to Courtney:

> Let them find out their own wickedness and folly – as they will. Why should I waste time in urging them to abstain from that consummation of their crime on which everybody knows that they were bent, and from which they will not at this time be diverted, though one rose from the dead? ... As to preventing the annexation, or prescribing the true policy under the existing and future circumstances, I should only be battering my head against a stone wall.[117]

Courtney's subsequent requests to Morley were equally unsuccessful. Morley merely replied: 'I cannot persuade myself that the moment requires parliamentary action, though I see nothing decisive to be said against it.' He identified himself with Richard Cobden, who had decades earlier declared that 'You might as well reason with mad dogs as

with men when they have begun to spill each other's blood.' Referring
to this, Morley, too, was convinced 'of the utter uselessness of rais-
ing one's voice in opposition to war when it has once begun'.[118] He
repeated the quotation from Cobden two months later in his address
at the Palmerston Club, adding that 'I have regarded speechmaking
to the country in such a temper as our country has lately exhibited as
very much a waste of time and energy. It is impossible to argue the
present situation as if the war had not taken place.'[119]

Sir Wilfrid Lawson, too, found himself rather incapable of participating in politics in 1900.[120] 'The whole spirit of fair play which we
were accustomed to associate with Englishmen seemed to have van-
ished under the War-fever,' he recalled a decade later:

> Ever and anon, when we began to get the better of the Boers
> and news came of these successes, the 'discerning public' devoted
> themselves to frantic antics in the streets, yelling and dancing
> about like Red Indians. This I believe is called 'Patriotism' or
> 'Imperialism'. ... Hunting the friends of peace about the streets,
> breaking up their meetings and smashing their windows, were
> at this period tolerably common occurrences. The Press almost
> openly encouraged these doings, and worse than that – they were
> virtually condoned in the House of Commons itself.[121]

The Boer War was, undoubtedly, a crucial factor in the election of
1900. Conservative and Unionist posters and leaflets explicitly depicted
the Liberals as 'unpatriotic Little-Englanders' and 'pro-Boers'.[122] Many
critics of the war either lost their seats or declined to be even candidates, for the power of the manly and duty-bound imperialist rhetoric
was unquestionable. As the *Daily Mail* triumphantly declared after
the election: 'Little Englandism has fallen because it supposed that the
people of England were selfish ... Imperialism has won because ... it has
been able to appeal to that instinct of unselfishness which leads men
to ... subordinate the petty desire for material comfort to the demands
of duty.'[123]

Leonard Courtney received anonymous abusive mail at least
October 1899 onwards. One postcard, sent from London in March

1900, declared: 'It would be a good job for old England if you and Stead were hung up to a street Lamppost, it is such curses as you two that cause war, by leading other people to think the English are a weak race that do not mean sticking up for their rights; to hell with you, your dirty little England – go & live with the Boers'.[124]

While the denunciations and violence discouraged some, they also served to enhance the status of those who continued the agitation in spite of them. Leonard Hobhouse was much impressed by Courtney, who now 'assumed heroic stature in Hobhouse's eyes as a result of his principled anti-imperialism', as Stefan Collini has put it.[125] William Clarke, too, admired Courtney for his 'independence and honesty'.[126] 'You feel you can trust him, and you feel it instantly. There is no part of that moral fibre which is unsound. There is nothing in that moral fabric which is squeezable, not to say saleable,' he praised. Clarke regarded Courtney as 'a courteous, sincere, earnest inquirer after truth'; 'never in the course of parliamentary history have a series of abler and more earnest speeches been delivered than he has uttered at Westminster' during the war.[127]

Clarke had lost his faith in party politics long since. He had written in desperation in 1885 how the march of European imperialism had become so inevitable that

> the English Cabinet is no longer master of the situation. The Liberal Cabinet comes into office with professions of peace and retrenchment, and its career is one long record of war, conquest, annexation, and huge expenditure. And this not because Mr. Gladstone did not honestly mean to carry out a policy of peace and retrenchment, but because Imperial necessities overruled personal inclinations.[128]

In a way, then, even Clarke, who was perhaps the most consistent anti-imperialist of the period, was of the opinion that anti-imperialist principles and peaceful intentions were not enough after all, when the dominating ideology in the whole Western world was imperialism. Other committed anti-imperialists, like Herbert Spencer, Richard Congreve, or Edward Spencer Beesly, equally rejected party politics;

and those anti-imperialists who were in parliament, like John Morley, disparaged politics for their lack of principles. Those, who befriended the anti-imperial nationalists, like W. S. Blunt and William Digby, and wanted to defend their interests in parliament, never found their way in.

The anti-imperialist point of view to party politics was well summed up by Frederic Harrison, whose faith in Liberal anti-imperialism was nearly as non-existent as his faith in Conservative anti-imperialism.[129] Harrison stressed that Britain's 'foreign crimes' were 'the work of the military and commercial aristocracy of England' and had thus nothing to do with political parties as such. 'A party attack upon an unjust war, even a genuine protest against barbarity, will tell but little in the long run, whilst the governing classes of this nation maintain and defend the system of military empire,' he argued. These governing classes were to be found in every party, and thus the empire was always kept 'above and outside of all discussion'; it was regarded as 'something that makes everything lawful, and for which everything must be suffered, or committed, or risked'. In short, then, Harrison formulated that 'Imperialism is the creed of all who find in the military empire the glory and the strength of England. And they form the bulk of the official and governing classes, under whichever political chief they are sworn to serve.'[130]

CONCLUSIONS

During this period of roughly twenty years, 'imperialism' was understood in three different ways. First, there was the illiberal authoritarian
imperialism, dominant in the debate before 1882; second, the liberal
humanitarian imperialism, i.e. the 'white man's burden'; and third,
imperialism as a general 'empire feeling' and 'empire patriotism'. To
the anti-imperialists, imperialism always amounted to the first aspect;
they denied and disparaged the other two, which in their eyes were
equivalents to trying to paint black white. The critics of imperialism
thus adhered to the mid-Victorian definition, whereas the society at
large evidently sought for more suitable and positive definitions to
transform the overall negative image of 'imperialism' to counteract
both the increasing debate and criticism and the changing world order
with the increasing competition for markets and political power.

In every way, the anti-imperialists preferred England to the empire.
To them, patriotism was love for England, not for the British empire;
especially, it was love for Britain's non-imperialist liberal and industrial traditions. The principled anti-imperialists, like Herbert Spencer
and John Morley, opposed imperialism first and foremost because they
regarded it as the negation of true liberal-minded Englishness. Those
who used primarily economic arguments also maintained that the
good of Britain was not advanced by imperialism; on the contrary,
they argued that the British paid additional taxes to meet the costs
of the empire and, in addition, imperialism arrested the progress of
domestic reform.

Wilfrid Scawen Blunt and William Digby stand out as somewhat
different from the other anti-imperialists in this sense, although they,

too, stressed continuously that Britain was abandoning its lovable 'true self' and becoming into something completely different and despicable. They both approached the issue of imperialism from a non-British point of view, Blunt mainly from the Egyptian or, more broadly, the Muslim one, and Digby from the Indian nationalist one. Theirs was to be the main concern of the twentieth-century debate on imperialism: how to meet the rising nationalisms within the empire, and, in particular, to what extent they should be accepted as legitimate and 'national'. Blunt and Digby were practical propagandists, not profound intellectual thinkers like Spencer, Morley, or Richard Congreve; still they were ahead of their time in their support to Egyptian and Indian nationalism.

None of the late-Victorian anti-imperialists regarded the empire and imperialism as synonymous. Instead, they insisted that, at large, the British 'empire' was really not an empire at all, and imperialism was a new departure in British politics and was due to the Indian influence. Rather than being anti-empire as such, these critics used the term anti-imperialism as synonymous with constitutionalism and 'true patriotism' on the one hand, and anti-militarism, anti-aggression, and anti-jingoism on the other.

In their view the union which was generally understood as the British empire mainly symbolised the expansion of England in the form of emigration to settler colonies, and this was not such a bad thing in itself. What they were opposed to was the new policy of imperialism, which meant annexing already densely populated territories and, because of its authoritarianism, was not compatible with the true greatness of England. Anti-imperialists thought that this imperialism was ruining the position of England as a kingdom as well as its relations with the settler colonies. Thus, when they were defending the empire against imperialism, the empire – as a figure of speech, not to be understood as any 'real' empire – signified the English-speaking settler colonies and imperialism other territories. Not many noted the confusion in this, although some anti-imperialists tried to point out that in fact the settler colonies did not even form an 'empire' like India did. Some took the misconceptions so far that they began to talk about positive imperialism in the connection of the settler colonies and negative imperialism in the connection of the tropical dependencies and new annexations. This confusion of terms was apparent in the concept of the Imperial Federation League as well, and was clearly one of the reasons it collapsed in a decade: the attribute 'imperial' was simply not considered suitable.

In practice anti-imperialism had, of course, plenty of limitations. The fact that the British East India Company had conquered India might have been widely deplored, but not much could be done about it afterwards. In practice, then, anti-imperialism did not necessarily mean advocating active withdrawal but opposition to any further expansion of the empire and preparation for its gradual contraction. There was vigorous debate every time Britain was expanding its territories in Africa, Indian borders, or China, especially because the expansion was nearly always carried out at the risk of war with France or Russia and led to the arms race in the 1890s. It was also argued that if India were ruled according to 'English' rather than 'imperial' traditions imperialism would wither away gradually and naturally: as soon as the Indian government was liberalised and Indianised the days of authoritarian rule and 'martial law' would be over and there would only be a free commonwealth of self-governing nations.

The opinions and attitudes of the anti-imperialists cannot be reduced to a simplistic 'orientalist' theory about western culture. Even at this age of 'high imperialism', their views and actions cannot be explained away by some cultural code of behaviour, even an unconscious one. These individuals all approached the issue of imperialism from their own premises and employed a notably non-racist rhetoric in the process. Rather than regarding non-western cultures as something 'other' and inferior, they repeatedly criticised British imperialism from a very empathetic point of view.

The positivist anti-imperialism was a side product of the positivist belief in a completely different kind of society in future. This positivist future would have excluded both god-centred religions and imperialism; they linked their moral religion of humanity and anti-imperialism closely together. The most committed positivists, like Congreve, opposed not only large empires but also large states. In this sense, the positivist vision of the world order was very local in its nature, consisting of small entities; however, it also was extremely global in its evolutionary scheme for the regeneration of the whole humankind towards positivism. This made the positivists somewhat different from other anti-imperialists, like Blunt and Spencer in particular, who severely questioned whether uniform types of civilisation were any good for the world at all. The gap was far from wide, however, since the positivist world was to be tolerant in the extreme: as Harrison declared, 'In the religion of Humanity there are no distinctions of skin, or race, of sect or creed; all are our brothers and fellow-citizens of the world – children of the same great kith and kin.'[1]

NOTES

Introduction: Multiple Faces of an Imperial Culture

1. Linda Colley, *Britons: Forging the Nation, 1707–1837* (London, 2003).
2. The notion of the British empire as 'a revivified nation-state operating at an international level' had become explicit during the Napoleonic Wars: C. A. Bayly, *Imperial Meridian: The British Empire and the World 1780–1830* (London, 1989), esp. p. 102.
3. On 'the traditional Englishness as the historical incarnation of an ideal English freedom from 1688', see Robert Colls, 'Englishness and the Political Culture', in Robert Colls and Philip Dodd (eds), *Englishness: Politics and Culture 1880–1920* (London, 1986), pp. 29–61.
4. W. S. Blunt's Autograph diaries, 17 January 1902: Blunt Papers, Ms 373–1975, p. 24, FM.
5. Miles Taylor, 'Imperium et Libertas? Rethinking the Radical Critique of Imperialism during the Nineteenth Century', *The Journal of Imperial and Commonwealth History*, 19:1 (1991), pp. 1–23.
6. Ibid., pp. 3–4.
7. Andrew Porter, 'Trusteeship, Anti-Slavery, and Humanitarianism', and idem, 'Religion, Missionary Enthusiasm, and Empire', in idem (ed.), *OHBE*, vol. III (Oxford, 1999), pp. 198–221, 222–46; John Cell, 'The Imperial Conscience', in Peter Marsh (ed.), *The Conscience of the Victorian State* (New York, 1979), pp. 173–213; Greg Cuthbertson, 'Preaching Imperialism: Wesleyan Methodism and the War', in David Omissi and Andrew S. Thompson (eds), *The Impact of the South African War* (Basingstoke and New York, 2002), pp. 157–72.
8. Cell, 'The Imperial Conscience', p. 207.
9. Cuthbertson, 'Preaching Imperialism: Wesleyan Methodism and the War'.
10. H. R. Fox Bourne, *The Aborigines Protection Society: Chapters in History* (London, 1899), p. 27.
11. Ibid., pp. 40–1, 45–6.

12. E. H. H. Green, 'Gentlemanly Capitalism and British Economic Policy, 1880–1914: The Debate over Bimetallism and Protectionism', in Raymond E. Dumett (ed.), *Gentlemanly Capitalism and British Imperialism: The New Debate on Empire* (London and New York, 1999), p. 48.

13. Henry Pelling, *Popular Politics and Society in late Victorian Britain* (2nd edn, London and Basingstoke, 1979 [1968]), ch. 5; Richard Price, *An Imperial War and the British Working Class: Working-Class Attitudes and Reactions to the Boer War 1899–1902* (Studies in Social History, London and Toronto, 1972).

14. Bernard Porter, *The Absent-Minded Imperialists: Empire, Society, and Culture in Britain* (Oxford, 2004). To some extent, P. J. Marshall has also implied the same in his 'Imperial Britain', *The Journal of Imperial and Commonwealth History*, 23:3 (1995), pp. 379–94.

15. Porter, *The Absent-Minded Imperialists*, p. 39.

16. Ibid., ch. 8.

17. See especially John M. MacKenzie, *Propaganda and Empire: The Manipulation of British Public Opinion, 1880–1960* (Manchester, 1984); idem (ed.), *Imperialism and Popular Culture* (Manchester, 1986); idem, 'Empire and Metropolitan Cultures', in Porter (ed.), *OHBE*, III, pp. 270–93.

18. Porter, *The Absent-Minded Imperialists*, p. 192.

19. See also Thomas Metcalf's notion on the two divergent ruling strategies in India, one stressing the similarities between the Indians and the British and another pointing to the 'enduring difference' between them: Thomas R. Metcalf, *Ideologies of the Raj* (The New Cambridge History of India III:4, Cambridge, 2003 [1995]).

20. Porter, *The Absent-Minded Imperialists*, p. 244.

21. Ibid., pp. 244–5.

22. Ibid., p. 247.

23. See Colls, 'Englishness and the Political Culture', pp. 31, 43. Although the stresses were somewhat different in the twentieth century, the appeals to English virtues survived: Nicholas Owen, 'Critics of Empire in Britain', in Judith M. Brown and Wm. Roger Louis (eds), *OHBE*, vol. IV (Oxford, 1999), pp. 188–211.

24. This comes clear in all his writings, but is most obvious in Dadabhai Naoroji, *Poverty and Un-British Rule in India* (London, 1901).

25. Elizabeth Longford, *A Pilgrimage of Passion: The Life of Wilfrid Scawen Blunt* (London, 1979); D. A. Hamer, *John Morley: Liberal Intellectual in Politics* (Oxford, 1968); L. T. Hobhouse and J. L. Hammond, *Lord Hobhouse: A Memoir* (London, 1905); G. P. Gooch, *Life of Lord Courtney* (London, 1920); Martha S. Vogeler, *Frederic Harrison: The Vocations of a Positivist* (New York and Oxford,

1984); R. J. Hind, *Henry Labouchere and the Empire 1880–1905* (University of London Historical Studies XXXI, London, 1972); Algar Labouchere Thorold, *The Life of Henry Labouchere* (London, 1913); A. G. Gardiner, *The Life of Sir William Harcourt* (2 vols, London, 1923); F. W. Hirst, *Early Life & Letters of John Morley* (2 vols, London, 1927); P. J. Cain, *Hobson and Imperialism: Radicalism, New Liberalism, and Finance 1887–1938* (Oxford, 2002); David Long, *Towards a New Liberal Internationalism: The International Theory of J. A. Hobson* (LSE Monographs in International Studies, Cambridge, 1996).

26. A. J. P. Taylor, *The Trouble Makers: Dissent over Foreign Policy 1782–1939* (London, 1957); A. P. Thornton, *The Imperial Idea and its Enemies: A Study in British Power* (London, 1966).

27. Bernard Porter, *Critics of Empire: British Radical Attitudes to Colonialism in Africa 1895–1914* (London, 1968), p. 88. A second edition, with a new introduction, was published in 2008 with a new title *Critics of Empire: British Radicals and the Imperial Challenge*.

28. Ibid., p. 90.

29. Ibid., p. 91.

30. Paul Ward, *Red Flag and Union Jack: Englishness, Patriotism and the British Left, 1881–1924* (Royal Historical Society Studies in History, New Series, Woodbridge, 1998).

31. John W. Auld, 'The Liberal Pro-Boers', *Journal of British Studies*, 14 (1975), p. 79. Italics added.

32. J. P. Parry, 'The Impact of Napoleon III on British Politics, 1851–1880', *Transactions of the Royal Historical Society*, 6th series, 11 (2001), pp. 147–75; see also Richard Koebner and Helmut Dan Schmidt, *Imperialism: The Story and Significance of a Political Word, 1840–1960* (Cambridge, 1965), pp. 1–195; C. C. Eldridge, *England's Mission: The Imperial Idea in the Age of Gladstone and Disraeli 1868–1880* (London, 1973).

33. Parry, 'The Impact of Napoleon III on British Politics', p. 163.

34. Ibid., p. 168.

35. Ibid., pp. 173–4.

36. See especially C. A. Bodelsen, *Studies in Mid-Victorian Imperialism* (Copenhagen, 1924); R. L. Schuyler, 'The Climax of Anti-Imperialism in England' and 'The Rise of Anti-Imperialism in England', *Political Science Quarterly*, 36 (1921), pp. 537–60 and 37 (1922), pp. 440–71; Rita Hinden, *Empire and after* (London, 1949).

37. On this debate see Ronald Robinson and John Gallagher, 'The Imperialism of Free Trade', *Economic History Review*, 2nd series, 6 (1953), pp. 1–15; idem, with Alice Denny, *Africa and the Victorians: The Official Mind of Imperialism* (2nd edn, London and Basingstoke, 1981 [1961]); Wm. Roger Louis (ed.),

Imperialism: The Robinson and Gallagher Controversy (New Viewpoints, New York and London, 1976); Ged Martin, '"Anti-Imperialism" in the Mid-Nineteenth Century and the Nature of the British Empire, 1820–70', in Ronald Hyam and Ged Martin, *Reappraisals in British Imperial History* (Cambridge Commonwealth Series, London, 1975), pp. 88–120; B. A. Knox, 'Reconsidering Mid-Victorian Imperialism', *The Journal of Imperial and Commonwealth History*, 1 (1973), pp. 155–72; C. C. Eldridge, 'Mid-Victorian imperialism reconsidered', *Trivium*, 15 (1980), pp. 63–72.

38. R. A. Macfie, *A Glance at the Position & Prospects of the Empire: An Address Delivered by request of the Musselburgh Young Men's Association, on 19th January, 1872* (London, 1872), p. 32.

39. Parry, 'The Impact of Napoleon III on British Politics', pp. 168–9.

40. Richard Williams, *The Contentious Crown: Public Discussion of the British Monarchy in the Reign of Queen Victoria* (Aldershot, 1997), ch. 6, esp. pp. 153–5, 166–79.

41. On the debate as well as the general context, see C. C. Eldridge, *Disraeli and the Rise of a New Imperialism* (The Past in Perspective, Cardiff, 1996); Koebner and Schmidt, *Imperialism*, chs 5–6; J. P. Parry, 'Disraeli and England', *The Historical Journal*, 43 (2000), pp. 699–728; P. J. Durrans, 'A Two-Edged Sword: The Liberal Attack on Disraelian Imperialism', *The Journal of Imperial and Commonwealth History*, 10:3 (1982), pp. 262–84; idem, 'Beaconsfieldism', in C. C. Eldridge (ed.), *Empire, Politics and Popular Culture: Essays in Eighteenth and Nineteenth Century British History* (Lampeter, 1989 [*Trivium*, vol. 24]), pp. 58–75; Ann Pottinger Saab, *Reluctant Icon: Gladstone, Bulgaria, and the Working Classes, 1856–1878* (Harvard Historical Studies 109, Cambridge, Mass., 1991); Hugh Cunningham, 'Jingoism in 1877–78', *Victorian Studies*, 14 (1971), pp. 429–53.

42. John Morley, *The Life of Richard Cobden*, vol. II (Jubilee edn, London, 1896 [1879]), p. 205.

43. John Bright's diary, 9 March 1876: *The Diaries of John Bright*, edited by R. A. J. Walling (London, 1930), p. 377.

44. Parry, 'The Impact of Napoleon III on British Politics', p. 171.

45. Ibid., pp. 172–3.

46. Anthony S. Wohl, '"Dizzi-Ben-Dizzi": Disraeli as Alien', *Journal of British Studies*, 34 (1995), pp. 375–411.

47. Edward Dicey, 'Our Route to India', *NC*, 1 (June, 1877), pp. 665–85; idem, 'Mr. Gladstone and Our Empire', *NC*, 2 (September, 1877), pp. 292–308.

48. William Ewart Gladstone, 'England's Mission', *NC*, 4 (September, 1878), p. 569.

49. Robert Lowe, 'Imperialism', *FR*, 24 (October, 1878), pp. 458, 459.

50. Ibid., p. 459.
51. Ibid., p. 462.
52. Ibid., pp. 460–1.
53. Ibid., p. 465.
54. James Winter, *Robert Lowe* (Toronto, 1976), pp. 307–8.
55. This imperialistic rhetoric of patriotism was especially employed by the Conservatives at election time: see Paul Readman, 'The Conservative Party, Patriotism, and British Politics: The Case of the General Election of 1900', *Journal of British Studies*, 40 (2001), pp. 107–45.
56. This rhetoric was very characteristic of the time. Georgios Varouxakis has examined the patriotic and cosmopolitan thought of nine prominent late-Victorian intellectuals, and argues that they all equalled 'true' patriotism with moral commitment to humanity and maintained that the term 'patriotism' was being misused by many contemporaries: Georgios Varouxakis, ' "Patriotism", "Cosmopolitanism" and "Humanity" in Victorian Political Thought', *European Journal of Political Theory*, 5 (2006), pp. 100–18.
57. Free Briton, *Mr. Chamberlain against England: A Record of His Proceedings* (London, n.d.), pp. 8–9.
58. Ibid., p. 10.
59. On public moralists, see Stefan Collini, *Public Moralists: Political Thought and Intellectual Life in Britain 1850–1930* (Oxford, 1991), esp. pp. 2–3; and on the importance of character, ibid., ch. 3.
60. Ibid., ch. 2.
61. Quoted in Hobhouse and Hammond, *Lord Hobhouse*, p. 219.
62. Collini, *Public Moralists*, pp. 65–6.
63. G. M. Young, *Portrait of an Age* (2nd edn, London, 1952 [1936]), p. vi.
64. Peter J. Cain and Mark Harrison (eds), *Imperialism: Critical Concepts in Historical Studies* (3 vols, London and New York, 2001), contain numerous articles discussing the concept of imperialism from the late nineteenth to the late twentieth century, illustrating how the meaning has changed over time.
65. J. Lawson Walton, 'Imperialism', *CR*, 75 (March, 1899), pp. 306–7.
66. Lowe, 'Imperialism', pp. 453–65. Lowe had lived in Australia in the 1840s and been actively involved in politics there.
67. Taylor, 'Imperium et Libertas?', p. 13.
68. Like in Andrew S. Thompson, *Imperial Britain: The Empire in British Politics, c. 1880–1932* (Harlow, 2000).
69. Hirst, *Early Life & Letters of John Morley*, II, p. 200.
70. See especially Herbert Spencer, *Facts and Comments* (London, 1902).
71. Deborah Wormell, *Sir John Seeley and the Uses of History* (Cambridge, 1980), pp. 149–50.

72. Frederic Harrison, *Autobiographic Memoirs*, vol. I (London, 1911), p. 181.

73. Evans Bell, *A Letter to H. M. Durand, Esq., C.S.I., of the Bengal Civil Service, Barrister-at-Law* (London, 1884), p. v.

74. J. M. Robertson, *Wrecking the Empire* (London, 1901).

75. Free Briton, *Mr. Chamberlain against England*, pp. 9–10.

76. Sir William Harcourt in West Monmouthshire, 31 May 1899: quoted in Gardiner, *The Life of Sir William Harcourt*, II, pp. 496–7.

77. H. M. Hyndman, *The Transvaal War and the Degradation of England* (Reprinted from *Justice*, London, 1899), preface, dated 14 October 1899.

78. Francis W. Hirst, Gilbert Murray, and John L. Hammond, *Liberalism and the Empire: Three Essays*: reprinted in Peter Cain (ed.), *The Empire and Its Critics, 1899–1939: Classics of Imperialism*, vol. I (London 1998 [1900]), pp. xv–xvi.

79. W. S. Blunt's Autograph diaries, 29 March 1898: Blunt Papers, Ms 359–1975, pp. 4–5, FM.

80. Henry Crompton and Richard Congreve, 'Imperialism' (Serial No. 4 of 'The Religion of Humanity, or Human Catholicism: The Western Republic'), in Richard Congreve, *Essays: Political, Social, and Religious*, vol. II (London, 1892 [1879]), p. 105. Italics added.

81. Ibid., p. 106.

82. Crompton and Congreve, 'Imperialism', p. 107.

83. Ibid., p. 109.

84. This question has been explored in Edwin Berkeley Tompkins, *Anti-Imperialism in the United States: The Great Debate, 1890–1920* (Philadelphia, 1970); Gerald E. Markowitz (ed.), *American Anti-Imperialism 1895–1901* (The Garland Library of War and Peace, New York and London, 1976); Steven C. Call, 'Protesting against Modern War: A Comparison of Issues Raised by Anti-Imperialists and Pro-Boers', *War in History*, 3 (1996), pp. 66–84; R. Craig Brown, 'Goldwin Smith and Anti-imperialism', *The Canadian Historical Review*, 43 (1962), pp. 93–105.

85. Tompkins, *Anti-Imperialism in the United States*, p. 2; Call, 'Protesting Against Modern War'.

86. Tompkins, *Anti-Imperialism in the United States*, pp. 66, 148; Brown, 'Goldwin Smith and Anti-Imperialism', p. 95.

87. Tompkins, *Anti-Imperialism in the United States*, pp. 237–8. Not surprisingly, American anti-imperialists were quick to publish their own satirical versions of Kipling's poem: ibid., pp. 239–42.

88. Gerald E. Markowitz, 'Preface', in idem (ed.), *American Anti-Imperialism*, pp. 12–13.

89. Hamer, *John Morley*, p. 290, for example.

90. Hyndman, *The Transvaal War and the Degradation of England*, preface.

91. Wilfrid Scawen Blunt, *Gordon at Khartoum: Being a Personal Narrative of Events, in Continuation of "A Secret History of the English Occupation of Egypt"* (London, 1911), p. 28.

92. Vogeler, *Frederic Harrison*, pp. 192–3; Tim Gray, 'Herbert Spencer's Liberalism – From Social Statics to Social Dynamics', in Richard Bellamy (ed.), *Victorian Liberalism: Nineteenth-century political thought and practice* (London and New York, 1990), p. 114.

93. William Clarke, 'The Rt. Hon. Leonard Courtney: A Character Sketch', *The Young Man* (August, 1900): reprinted in Herbert Burrows and John A. Hobson (eds), *William Clarke: A Collection of His Writings, with a Biographical Sketch* (London, 1908), p. 272.

Chapter 1   The Costs and Gains of the Empire

1. Adam Smith, *An Inquiry into the Nature and Causes of the Wealth of Nations* (2 vols, London, 1776), esp. vol. II, ch. 7 'Of Colonies'.

2. The ideas of Adam Smith and his followers in the context of the British empire have been well examined in Bernard Semmel, *The Rise of Free Trade Imperialism: Classical Political Economy, the Empire of Free Trade, and Imperialism, 1750–1850* (Cambridge, 1970); Donald Winch, *Classical Political Economy and Colonies* (Cambridge, Mass., 1965), ch. 2; Bernard Semmel, *The Liberal Ideal and the Demons of Empire: Theories of Imperialism from Adam Smith to Lenin* (Baltimore and London, 1993), ch. 2; Oliver MacDonagh, 'The Anti-Imperialism of Free Trade', *Economic History Review*, 2nd series, 14 (1962), pp. 489–501.

3. See especially Richard Cobden, 'How Wars Are Got up in India: The Origin of the Burmese War', in *The Political Writings of Richard Cobden*, vol. II (London and New York, 1867 [1853]), pp. 23–106; James L. Sturgis, *John Bright and the Empire* (University of London Historical Studies XXVI, London, 1969); also Goldwin Smith, *The Empire: A Series of Letters, Published in 'The Daily News', 1862, 1863* (Oxford and London, 1863).

4. F. W. Hirst, *Early Life & Letters of John Morley*, vol. II (London, 1927), chs 9–10; D. A. Hamer, *John Morley: Liberal Intellectual in Politics* (Oxford, 1968).

5. See for instance his second Midlothian speech in Dalkeith, 26 November 1879: in W. E. Gladstone, *Political Speeches in Scotland, November and December 1879, by the Right Hon. W. E. Gladstone, M.P.* (London, 1879) [reprinted with an introduction as *Midlothian Speeches 1879* (The Victorian Library, Leicester, 1971)], pp. 64–5.

6. Anthony Howe, *Free Trade and Liberal England 1846–1946* (Oxford, 1997), p. 186.
7. On the Cobden Club, see ibid., pp. 116–52.
8. Ibid., p. 216.
9. Sir David Wedderburn, *British Colonial Policy* (London, 1881), p. 17.
10. Sir George Campbell, *The British Empire* (London, 1887), p. 1.
11. Ibid., p. 2.
12. See especially P. J. Cain and A. G. Hopkins, *British Imperialism, 1688–2000* (2nd edn, Harlow, 2002 [1993]); Raymond E. Dumett (ed.), *Gentlemanly Capitalism and British Imperialism: The New Debate on Empire* (London and New York, 1999); on the strategic considerations see especially the classic Ronald Robinson and John Gallagher, with Alice Denny, *Africa and the Victorians: The Official Mind of Imperialism* (2nd edn, London and Basingstoke, 1981 [1961]).
13. Lance E. Davis and Robert A. Huttenback, *Mammon and the Pursuit of Empire: The Political Economy of British Imperialism, 1860–1912* (Interdisciplinary perspectives on modern history, Cambridge, 1986); see also Michael Edelstein, *Overseas Investment in the Age of High Imperialism: The United Kingdom, 1850–1914* (London, 1982); Patrick K. O'Brien, 'The Costs and Benefits of British Imperialism 1846–1914', *Past and Present*, No. 120 (1988), pp. 163–200; Paul Kennedy, 'Debate: The Costs and Benefits of British Imperialism 1846–1914', *Past and Present*, No. 125 (1989), pp. 186–92; Avner Offer, 'Costs and Benefits, Prosperity and Security, 1870–1914', in Andrew Porter (ed.), *OHBE*, vol. III (Oxford, 1999), pp. 690–711.
14. Davis and Huttenback, *Mammon and the Pursuit of Empire*, p. 315.
15. Ibid., pp. 250, 317.
16. Ibid., pp. 191, 306.
17. Ibid., p. 304.
18. Ibid., chs 4 and 6.
19. Kennedy, 'Debate: The Costs and Benefits of British Imperialism', p. 187.
20. Offer, 'Costs and Benefits, Prosperity and Security'; see also Mario Tiberi, *The Accounts of the British Empire: Capital Flows from 1799 to 1914*, translated from Italian by Judith Turnbull (Aldershot, 2005).
21. O'Brien, 'The Costs and Benefits of British Imperialism', p. 199.
22. Annie Besant, *Egypt* (London, 1882), p. 1.
23. 'John Bright at Glasgow', quoted in *The Times*, 23 March 1883.
24. John Bright to Goldwin Smith, 7 January 1883: quoted in Goldwin Smith, *A Selection from Goldwin Smith's Correspondence: Comprising Letters Chiefly to and from his English Friends, Written between the Years 1846 and 1910*, collected by Arnold Haultain (London, 1913), pp. 141–2.

25. Cain and Hopkins, *British Imperialism*, p. 316.

26. John Morley, 'Egyptian Policy: A Retrospect', *FR*, 32 (July, 1882), p. 119. This was also the view of Leonard Courtney: G. P. Gooch, *Life of Lord Courtney* (London, 1920), p. 172.

27. *Pall Mall Gazette*, 7 June 1882: quoted in M. E. Chamberlain, 'British Public Opinion and the Invasion of Egypt, 1882', *Trivium*, 16 (1981), p. 5; see also the reprint of Harrison's writings in 1882 in Frederic Harrison, *National & Social Problems* (London, 1908), pp. 195–210.

28. Frederic Harrison in 1882: reprinted in ibid., pp. 199–200.

29. Campbell, *The British Empire*, p. 177.

30. A. J. Wilson, 'The Eleventh Plague of Egypt', *FR*, 32 (November, 1882), pp. 656–7. For well-articulated critical writings against the occupation of Egypt at the same time see also J. Seymour Keay, *Spoiling the Egyptians: A Tale of Shame, Told from the Blue Books* (3rd edn, revised and enlarged, London, 1882); M. G. Mulhall, 'Egyptian Finance', *CR*, 42 (October, 1882), pp. 525–35; J. Seymour Keay, ' "Spoiling the Egyptians": A Rejoinder', *CR*, 42 (November, 1882), pp. 764–85; and a counter-argument provided by Sheldon Amos, ' "Spoiling the Egyptians": Revised Version', *CR*, 42 (October, 1882), pp. 509–24.

31. Wilson, 'The Eleventh Plague of Egypt', p. 665.

32. Ibid., p. 667.

33. A. G. Hopkins, 'The Victorians and Africa: A Reconsideration of the Occupation of Egypt, 1882', *Journal of African History*, 27 (1986), p. 365.

34. Wilfrid Scawen Blunt, 'Lord Cromer and the Khedive', *NC*, 33 (April, 1893), pp. 571–85; idem, 'The Khedive and Lord Cromer', *NC*, 35 (February, 1894), pp. 177–88.

35. R. J. Hind, *Henry Labouchere and the Empire 1880–1905* (University of London Historical Studies XXXI, London, 1972), pp. 147–50.

36. Ibid., p. 153.

37. Ibid., pp. 156, 176–80.

38. Cain and Hopkins, *British Imperialism*, p. 314.

39. Hirst, *Early Life & Letters of John Morley*, II, pp. 214–20; Gooch, *Life of Lord Courtney*, pp. 173, 176–7.

40. Wemyss Reid, ' "The Burden of Egypt", II: Our Promise to Withdraw', *NC*, 39 (April, 1896), p. 562.

41. F. Reginald Statham, 'How to get out of the South African Difficulty', *FR*, 29 (March, 1881), pp. 285–301; also Alfred Aylward, 'Africa and the Empire', *FR*, 31 (April, 1882), pp. 505–17. Later the same view was most strongly advocated by John Merriman, in 'Some South African Questions', *FR*, 47 (March, 1890), pp. 297–309.

42. *Truth*, 19 April 1883, p. 537: quoted in Hind, *Henry Labouchere and the Empire*, p. 194.

43. George Baden-Powell, 'English Money in South Africa', *CR*, 48 (October, 1885), p. 503.

44. Campbell, *The British Empire*, pp. 142–3.

45. J. Pope Hennessy, 'The African Bubble', *NC*, 28 (July, 1890), pp. 1–4.

46. H. H. Johnston, 'The Value of Africa: A Reply to Sir John Pope Hennessy', *NC*, 28 (August, 1890), pp. 170–1.

47. J. Pope Hennessy, 'Is Central Africa Worth Having? I' *NC*, 28 (September, 1890), pp. 478–87; Edward Dicey, 'Is Central Africa Worth Having? II', *NC*, 28 (September, 1890), pp. 488–500.

48. Ibid., p. 488.

49. Sir William Harcourt to John Morley, 23 September 1892: quoted in A. G. Gardiner, *The Life of Sir William Harcourt*, vol. II (London, 1923), p. 193.

50. Sir William Harcourt to William Gladstone, 20 September 1892: quoted in ibid., p. 192.

51. Charles W. Dilke, 'The Uganda Problem', *FR*, 53 (February, 1893), p. 145.

52. Ibid., p. 146.

53. Ibid., p. 147.

54. Ibid., p. 148.

55. Sir William Harcourt to Lord Rosebery, 27 September 1892: quoted in Gardiner, *Life of Harcourt*, II, pp. 196–7.

56. Davis and Huttenback have calculated that the cost of the Ugandan railway was almost £9 million between 1896 and 1914, while Robert Kubicek has stated that the British taxpayer met a bill of £5.5 million: Davis and Huttenback, *Mammon and the Pursuit of Empire*, p. 305; Robert Kubicek, 'British Expansion, Empire, and Technological Change', in Porter (ed.), *OHBE*, III, p. 258.

57. Dilke, 'The Uganda Problem', p. 153.

58. Joseph Thomson, 'Downing Street *versus* Chartered Companies in Africa', *FR*, 46 (August, 1889), pp. 173–85; A. B. Kemball, 'Correspondence: The Imperial British East Africa Company', *FR*, 54 (November, 1893), pp. 707–12; Lorne, 'Chartered Companies', *NC*, 39 (March, 1896), pp. 375–80.

59. Harcourt Journal, 31 October 1892: quoted in Gardiner, *Life of Harcourt*, II, p. 199.

60. Francis Comyn, 'The Seamy Side of British Guiana', *NC*, 39 (March, 1896), pp. 390–8; H. D. Traill, '"The Burden of Egypt", I: The Difficulties of Withdrawal', *NC*, 39 (April, 1896), p. 555; Edward Spencer Beesly, 'Fashoda', *PR*, 6 (November, 1898), pp. 181–4.

61. Wilfrid Scawen Blunt, 'The Truth of the Dongola Adventure', *NC*, 39 (May, 1896), pp. 741, 744.

62. Goldwin Smith to J. X. Merriman, 22 September 1896: quoted in Smith, *A Selection from Goldwin Smith's Correspondence*, p. 296.

63. O'Brien, 'The Costs and Benefits of British Imperialism', pp. 175–86; Davis and Huttenback, *Mammon and the Pursuit of Empire*, ch. 3, esp. pp. 109–10. 'Foreign' here refers to the countries outside the formal British empire, i.e. all European countries, the United States, and Latin America as the most important ones.

64. O'Brien, 'The Costs and Benefits of British Imperialism', pp. 173–4; Davis and Huttenback, *Mammon and the Pursuit of Empire*, p. 75. Furthermore, almost all British finance which went to the empire in this period went to Canada, the dependent empire (India and Africa) ranking last among the overseas recipients: ibid., pp. 43–51, 71–2.

65. O'Brien, 'The Costs and Benefits of British Imperialism', pp. 180–1.

66. Davis and Huttenback, *Mammon and the Pursuit of Empire*, pp. 107–10.

67. Richard Congreve, 'India', in idem, *Essays: Political, Social, and Religious* (London, 1874 [1857]), p. 85.

68. Edward Spencer Beesly, 'Wei-Hai-Wei', *PR*, 6 (May, 1898), pp. 85–8; John Atkinson Hobson, 'Free Trade and Foreign Policy', *CR*, 74 (August, 1898), pp. 167–80; also R. S. Gundry, 'China: Spheres of Interest, and the Open Door', *FR*, 66 (July, 1899), pp. 37–52; and an earlier example from a Congrevian positivist, J. H. Bridges, 'Is Our Cause in China Just?', *FR*, 18 (November, 1875), pp. 642–63.

69. Farrer, 'Does Trade Follow the Flag?', *CR*, 74 (December, 1898), pp. 810–11.

70. Ibid., pp. 817–19.

71. Ibid., pp. 827–31.

72. Masham, 'Does Trade Follow the Flag? A Reply', *CR*, 75 (February, 1899), p. 218.

73. Ibid., p. 220.

74. William Clarke, 'The Social Future of England', *CR* (January, 1899): reprinted in Herbert Burrows and John A. Hobson (eds), *William Clarke: A Collection of His Writings, with a Biographical Sketch* (London, 1908), p. 48.

75. John M. Robertson, *Patriotism and Empire*: reprinted in Peter Cain (ed.), *The Empire and its Critics, 1899–1939: Classics of Imperialism*, vol. I (London, 1998 [1899]), p. 174.

76. Ibid., p. 175.

77. Ibid., p. 179.

78. Ibid., pp. 180–1.

79. Ibid., pp. 182–3.

80. P. J. Cain , *Hobson and Imperialism: Radicalism, New Liberalism, and Finance 1887–1938* (Oxford, 2002), pp. 5–7; John M. Robertson, *The Fallacy of Saving: A Study in Economics* (London, 1892).

81. This was prevalent in J. A. Hobson, 'Capitalism and Imperialism in South Africa', *CR*, 77 (January, 1900), pp. 1–17; see also Peter J. Cain, 'British Radicalism, the South African Crisis, and the Origins of the Theory of Financial Imperialism', in David Omissi and Andrew S. Thompson (eds), *The Impact of the South African War* (Basingstoke and New York, 2002), p. 183.

82. Hobson, 'Free Trade and Foreign Policy', p. 167.

83. Ibid., pp. 177–8.

84. Ibid., p. 179.

85. Ibid.

86. Hobson, 'Capitalism and Imperialism in South Africa', p. 5; idem, *The War in South Africa: Its Causes and Effects* (2nd edn, London, 1900), pp. 189–97.

87. Ibid., pp. 206–40.

88. H. M. Hyndman, *The Transvaal War and the Degradation of England* (Reprinted from *Justice*, London, 1899); also H. C. Thomson, *The Supreme Problem in South Africa: Capital and Labour, With Suggestions for the Basis of an Enduring Peace* (Reprinted from the *Investors' Review*, London, n.d.).

89. Frederic Harrison, 'Mr J. A. Hobson on the Transvaal', *PR*, 8 (April, 1900), pp. 69–73.

90. Cain, 'British Radicalism, the South African Crisis, and the Origins of the Theory of Financial Imperialism', p. 179.

91. Iain R. Smith, *The Origins of the South African War, 1899–1902* (Origins of Modern Wars, London and New York, 1996). This is also the view endorsed by Cain and Hopkins, see especially P. J. Cain and A. G. Hopkins, 'Afterword: The Theory and Practice of British Imperialism', in Dumett (ed.), *Gentlemanly Capitalism and British Imperialism*, p. 210.

Chapter 2   Anti-Aggression and Anti-War Movements

1. William Clarke, 'The Curse of Militarism', *The Young Man* (May, 1901): reprinted in Herbert Burrows and John A. Hobson (eds), *William Clarke: A Collection of His Writings, with a Biographical Sketch* (London, 1908), p. 122.

2. Herbert Spencer, *Political Institutions: Being Part V of the Principles of Sociology (The Concluding Portion of Vol. II)*: reprinted in *Herbert Spencer: Collected Writings*, vol. VIII (London, 1996 [1882]), chs 17–18.

3. This is the title Spencer used in the brief section about the League in his memoirs: Herbert Spencer, *An Autobiography*, vol. II (London, 1904), ch. 60.

4. Ibid., p. 375.

5. Ibid., pp. 375–6.

6. Herbert Spencer to John Bright, 2 July 1881: quoted in David Duncan, *The Life and Letters of Herbert Spencer*: reprinted in *Herbert Spencer: Collected Writings*, vol. II (London, 1996 [1908]), p. 221.

7. John Bright to Herbert Spencer, 9 July 1881: Herbert Spencer Papers, Ms 791/152, SHL.

8. Spencer, *Autobiography*, II, p. 376.

9. On the concepts see Paul Laity, 'The British Peace Movement and the War', in David Omissi and Andrew S. Thompson (eds), *The Impact of the South African War* (Basingstoke and New York, 2002), p. 140; Paul Laity, *The British Peace Movement 1870–1914* (Oxford Historical Monographs, Oxford, 2001), pp. 6–8; see also ibid., pp. 95–6 on the Peace Society and the Anti-Aggression League.

10. On the context see R. Shannon, *Gladstone and the Bulgarian Agitation* (London, 1963); Ann Pottinger Saab, *Reluctant Icon: Gladstone, Bulgaria, and the Working Classes, 1856–1878* (Harvard Historical Studies 109, Cambridge, Mass., 1991).

11. Frederic Harrison, *Autobiographic Memoirs*, vol. II (London, 1911), pp. 119–20.

12. Frederic Harrison, 'Martial Law in Kabul', *FR*, 26 (December, 1879), pp. 767–84; idem, 'Martial Law in Kabul, Part II', *FR*, 27 (March, 1880), pp. 435–59.

13. Frederic Harrison, *National & Social Problems* (London, 1908), p. 163.

14. L. T. Hobhouse and J. L. Hammond, *Lord Hobhouse: A Memoir* (London, 1905), pp. 137–8.

15. Harrison, *Autobiographic Memoirs*, II, p. 121.

16. Martha S. Vogeler, *Frederic Harrison: The Vocations of a Positivist* (New York and Oxford, 1984), p. 138.

17. Note written by Lord Hobhouse: quoted in Hobhouse and Hammond, *Lord Hobhouse*, p. 138.

18. Spencer, *Autobiography*, II, p. 376; Hobhouse and Hammond, *Lord Hobhouse*, p. 138.

19. Spencer, *Autobiography*, II, p. 377.

20. Harrison, *Autobiographic Memoirs*, II, p. 123; idem, *National & Social Problems*, p. 184.

21. Frederic Harrison's speech at the Anti-Aggression Conference in February 1882, in *Anti-Aggression League Pamphlets, No. 1* (March, 1882): reprinted in Harrison, *National & Social Problems*, pp. 184–5.

22. Herbert Spencer's diary, 22 February 1882: quoted in Duncan, *The Life and Letters of Herbert Spencer*, p. 221.

23. Herbert Spencer to Dr Cazelles, 23 February 1882: quoted in ibid., p. 222.

24. Herbert Spencer in 1882: quoted in ibid., p. 223.

25. Herbert Spencer to John Bright, 24 June 1882: quoted in ibid., p. 224.

26. This is reprinted in Harrison, *National & Social Problems*, pp. 187–94.

27. Frederic Harrison's address to Labour Associations on 26 June 1882, in ibid., p. 189.

28. Harrison, *Autobiographic Memoirs*, II, pp. 122–3.

29. W. S. Blunt's diary entry 26 June 1882: quoted in Wilfrid Scawen Blunt, *Secret History of the English Occupation of Egypt: Being a Personal Narrative of Events* (London, 1907), p. 358.

30. Harrison, *Autobiographic Memoirs*, II, p. 123; idem, *National & Social Problems*, p. 184.

31. Spencer, *Autobiography*, II, p. 377.

32. Ibid., p. 378.

33. Sir Wilfrid Lawson, *A Memoir*, edited by George W. E. Russell (London, 1909), p. 134.

34. Ibid., p. 132.

35. Ibid., p. 138, see also pp. 141–2.

36. Lawson quoted in Anthony Howe, *Free Trade and Liberal England 1846–1946* (Oxford, 1997), p. 186n.

37. Increased Armaments Protest Committee, *Empire, Trade, and Armaments: An Exposure* (London, 1896), back of the front cover.

38. The other members of the executive committee were The Rev. W. Copeland Bowie, F. Leatham Bright, W. P. Byles, F. G. Cash, The Rev. Dr Clifford, Dr W. Evans Darby, A. E. Fletcher, The Rev. Geo. Giddins, J. F. Green, Walter Jerrold, C. E. Maurice, Fenwick Miller, T. P. Newman, Sydney Olivier, Eliza Orme, S. S. Tayler, W. M. J. Williams: Increased Armaments Protest Committee, *Empire, Trade, and Armaments: An Exposure*, back of the front cover.

39. According to Paul Laity the publication was written by Perris: Laity, *The British Peace Movement 1870–1914*, p. 133.

40. Increased Armaments Protest Committee, *Empire, Trade, and Armaments: An Exposure*, p. 1.

41. Ibid.

42. Ibid., pp. 5–12. The larger context of the arms race in the 1890s has been explored in Laity, *The British Peace Movement 1870–1914*, ch. 5.

43. Increased Armaments Protest Committee, *Empire, Trade, and Armaments: An Exposure*, pp. 12–24.

44. Ibid., p. 12.
45. Ibid., pp. 15–19.
46. Lawson, *A Memoir*, p. 138.
47. Sir Wilfrid Lawson, 'Wei-Hai-Wei', Easter 1898: printed in Sir Wilfrid Lawson and F. Carruthers Gould, *Cartoons in Rhyme and Line* (London, 1905), p. 62. See also Sir Wilfrid Lawson, 'The Partition of China', 29 December 1897: printed in ibid., p. 90.
48. Laity, *The British Peace Movement 1870–1914*, passim; Howard Evans, *Sir Randal Cremer: His Life and Work* (London, 1909); Lewis Appleton, *Memoirs of Henry Richard, the Apostle of Peace* (London, 1889); Charles S. Miall, *Henry Richard, M.P.: A Biography* (London, 1889).
49. Laity, 'The British Peace Movement and the War', p. 138.
50. H. R. Fox Bourne, *The Aborigines Protection Society: Chapters in History* (London, 1899), p. 41.
51. Laity, *The British Peace Movement 1870–1914*, p. 94. Clark was also vice-chairman of the International Arbitration and Peace Association's Committee in 1881–90: ibid., p. 95.
52. Sir Wilfrid Lawson in a public peace meeting in Liverpool, 15 March 1881: quoted in ibid., p. 94.
53. G. P. Gooch, *Life of Lord Courtney* (London, 1920), pp. 140–57. On the concept of 'pro-Boer' and its increasing use towards the end of the century see Arthur Davey, *The British Pro-Boers 1877–1902* (Cape Town, 1978), p. 9; on the various 'pro-Boer' organisations, see ibid., ch. 5.
54. Laity, 'The British Peace Movement and the War', pp. 142–4, 147–8; John W. Auld, 'The Liberal Pro-Boers', *Journal of British Studies*, 14 (1975), pp. 84–5.
55. Gooch, *Life of Lord Courtney*, chs 17–18; Harrison, *Autobiographic Memoirs*, II, p. 129; Vogeler, *Frederic Harrison*, p. 236; Stephen Koss, *The Pro-Boers: The Anatomy of an Antiwar Movement* (Studies in Imperialism, Chicago and London, 1973), p. 81. On the active 'pro-Boers' in 1899–1902 see Davey, *The British Pro-Boers*, pp. 11–12.
56. South Africa Conciliation Committee, 'The Committee's Manifesto as Issued to the Public Press on 15th January, 1900', SACC Pamphlet No. 15: reprinted in Koss (ed.), *The Pro-Boers*, p. 82.
57. South Africa Conciliation Committee, 'The Treatment of the Natives in South Africa', SACC Pamphlet No. 41: reprinted in Koss (ed.), *The Pro-Boers*, p. 88.
58. Harrison, *Autobiographic Memoirs*, II, p. 129.
59. Auld, 'The Liberal Pro-Boers', pp. 85–6.
60. Frederic Whyte, *Life of W. T. Stead* (2 vols, London, 1925); Raymond L. Schults, *Crusader in Babylon: W. T. Stead and the Pall Mall Gazette* (Lincoln,

1972); J. O. Baylen, 'W. T. Stead as publisher and editor of the *Review of Reviews*', *Victorian Periodicals Review*, 12 (1979), pp. 70–84.

61. On Stead's aggressive campaign, see his weekly magazine *War against War in South Africa* (30 issues between October 1899 – August 1900); W. T. Stead, *How Not to Make Peace: Evidence as to Homestead Burning Collected and Examined* (Stop-the-War Committee, London, 1900); F. W. Reitz, *A Century of Wrong*, with preface by W. T. Stead (London, 1900); Laity, 'The British Peace Movement and the War', p. 150; Koss, *The Pro-Boers*, p. 81. On the Hague Conferences and the South African War see Laity, *The British Peace Movement 1870–1914*, ch. 6.

62. W. S. Blunt's Autograph diaries, 28 January 1900: Blunt Papers, Ms 366–1975, pp. 27–8, FM.

63. Wilfrid Scawen Blunt, *My Diaries: Being a Personal Narrative of Events 1888–1914,* vol. II (London, 1919), pp. 402–3.

64. *Manchester Guardian*, 15 February 1900: quoted in Auld, 'The Liberal Pro-Boers', p. 86; Davey, *The British Pro-Boers*, pp. 87–8.

65. Auld, 'The Liberal Pro-Boers', p. 87. On Liberal imperialists see H. C. G. Matthew, *The Liberal Imperialists: The Ideas and Politics of a Post-Gladstonian Élite* (Oxford Historical Monographs, London, 1973).

66. Laity, 'The British Peace Movement and the War', p. 148. Hammond was the editor of the *Speaker* at the time and he transformed the paper into an anti-expansionist organ under his editorship: Peter Clarke, *Liberals and Social Democrats* (Modern Revivals in History, Aldershot, 1993 [1978]), pp. 76–7.

67. Laity, 'The British Peace Movement and the War', p. 148.

68. Clarke, 'The Curse of Militarism', pp. 118–19.

Chapter 3   India and the Drain Theory

1. Lord George Hamilton when secretary of state for India: quoted in Bipan Chandra, *The Rise and Growth of Economic Nationalism in India: Economic Policies of Indian National Leadership, 1880–1905* (New Delhi, 1966), p. 1.

2. [J. A. Hobson] *pseud.* Nemo, 'Ethics of Empire', *The Progressive Review*, 2 (August, 1897), p. 459.

3. F. Seebohm, 'Imperialism and Socialism', *NC*, 7 (April, 1880), p. 734.

4. Frederic Harrison, 'Empire and Humanity', *FR*, 27 (February, 1880), p. 297.

5. Ibid., pp. 298–9.

6. Ibid., p. 299.

7. James Geddes, *The Logic of Indian Deficit* (London, 1871), p. vi.

8. Ibid. Geddes's radical ideas were presented in India as well: James Geddes, 'Our Commercial Exploitation of the Indian People – I, II, and III', *Calcutta*

Review, 55 (1872), pp. 340–81, 56 (1873), pp. 139–70, 352–82. See also Geraldine Hancock Forbes, 'The English Positivists and India', *Bengal Past and Present*, 93 (1974), pp. 79–81.

9. Geddes, *The Logic of Indian Deficit*, p. v. The pamphlet led to Geddes's examination before the East India Finance Committee: Geddes, *The Logic of Indian Deficit* (2nd edn, London, 1872 [1871]), preface.

10. William Digby, *British Rule in India: Has It Been, Is It Still, a Good Rule for the Indian People?* (London, 1891), pp. 7–11.

11. William Digby, *Indian Problems for English Consideration, a Letter to the Council of the National Liberal Federation* (Birmingham, 1881), pp. 30–42; idem, *India for the Indians – and for England* (London, 1885), pp. 23–44, 62–82; see also his *British Rule in India* and *'Prosperous' British India: A Revelation from Official Records* (London, 1901).

12. William Digby, *The Famine Campaign in Southern India (Madras and Bombay Presidencies and Province of Mysore) 1876–1878* (2 vols, London, 1878); Edward C. Moulton, 'William Digby', in Joseph O. Baylen and Norbert J. Gossman (eds), *Biographical Dictionary of Modern British Radicals*, vol. 3: 1870–1914 (New York and London, 1988), p. 269.

13. John Bright's diary, 20 November 1879: *The Diaries of John Bright*, edited by R. A. J. Walling (London, 1930), p. 431.

14. On Digby's campaigning see Mira Matikkala, 'William Digby and the British Radical Debate on India from the 1880s to the 1890s' (unpublished MPhil dissertation, University of Cambridge, 2004); also idem, 'William Digby and the Indian question', *Journal of Liberal History*, issue 58 (2008), pp. 12–20.

15. Martin Gilbert, 'Famine in India: Sir Antony MacDonnell and a Policy Revolution in 1902', in Donovan Williams and E. Daniel Potts (eds), *Essays in Indian History: In Honour of Cuthbert Collin Davies* (London, 1973), pp. 152–4.

16. Sir Richard Temple in *Famine Commission of 1880, Select Evidence*, question 71: quoted in ibid., p. 155.

17. Government of India, Department of Revenue and Agriculture, *Reply to J. Caird*: quoted in ibid.

18. Lord Northbrook to Lord Ripon, 7 September 1881: quoted in ibid., p. 156. Northbrook and Ripon both became later supporters of the Indian National Congress.

19. Gilbert, 'Famine in India', p. 156.

20. Arthur Hobhouse, 'Some Reflections on the Afghan Imbroglio', *FR*, 28 (September, 1880), pp. 396–7.

21. W. S. Blunt's diary entry of 5 August 1880, in 'Alms to Oblivion: Gods & False Gods', ch. 5 'Angelina': Blunt Papers, Ms 327–1975, p. 4, FM. On the

friendships see also Martha S. Vogeler, *Frederic Harrison: The Vocations of a Positivist* (New York and Oxford, 1984), pp. 136–9.

22. William Gladstone in Glasgow, 5 December 1879: *Political Speeches in Scotland, November and December 1879, by the Right Hon. W. E. Gladstone, M.P.* (London, 1879) [reprinted with an introduction as *Midlothian Speeches 1879* (The Victorian Library, Leicester, 1971)], p. 202.

23. R. J. Hind, *Henry Labouchere and the Empire 1880–1905* (University of London Historical Studies XXXI, London, 1972), p. 200.

24. Ibid.

25. Lance E. Davis and Robert A. Huttenback, *Mammon and the Pursuit of Empire: The Political Economy of British Imperialism, 1860–1912* (Interdisciplinary perspectives on modern history, Cambridge, 1986), p. 155.

26. Lord Kimberley to Lord Ripon, 11 January 1883: quoted in ibid., p. 156.

27. Ibid., pp. 14–15.

28. B. R. Tomlinson, *The Economy of Modern India, 1860–1970* (The New Cambridge History of India III:3, Cambridge, 1993), p. 13.

29. H. M. Hyndman, *The Indian Famine and the Crisis in India* (London, 1877); idem, 'The Bankruptcy of India', *NC*, 4 (October 1878), pp. 585–608 and 5 (March, 1879), pp. 443–62; idem, 'Bleeding to Death', *NC*, 8 (July, 1880), pp. 157–76.

30. Dadabhai Naoroji, *Poverty of India* (London, 1878), p. 38.

31. For a discussion on the drain theory in more detail see S. Ambirajan, 'Dadabhai Naoroji: the First Economist of Modern India', *Research in the History of Economic Thought and Methodology*, 16 (1998), pp. 155–78. See also B. N. Ganguli, *Dadabhai Naoroji and the Drain Theory* (London, 1965); Tomlinson, *The Economy of Modern India*, pp. 13–14.

32. Digby, *Indian Problems for English Consideration*, p. 46.

33. Ibid., p. 47.

34. J. Seymour Keay, 'The Spoliation of India', *NC*, 14 (July, 1883), pp. 1–22 and (August, 1883), 356; idem, 'The Spoliation of India II', *NC*, 15 (April, 1884), pp. 559–82; idem, 'The Spoliation of India III', *NC*, 15 (May, 1884), pp. 721–40.

35. Sir Charles Trevelyan in his evidence before the Parliamentary Committee on Indian Finance in 1873: quoted in Keay, 'The Spoliation of India', p. 4.

36. Ibid., p. 19.

37. Florence Nightingale, 'Our Indian Stewardship', *NC*, 14 (August, 1883), pp. 329–38; S. K. Ratcliffe, *Sir William Wedderburn and the Indian Reform Movement* (London, 1923), pp. 39–40, 120–1; Sir Edward Cook, *The Life of Florence Nightingale*, vol. II (London, 1913), p. 453.

38. Wilfrid Scawen Blunt, *Ideas About India* (London, 1885), p. 3.

39. Ibid., pp. 15–16.

40. Ibid., pp. 25, 36.

41. Samuel Smith, *My Life-Work* (London, 1902), p. 178.

42. Ibid., pp. 196–7; Samuel Smith, 'India Revisited', *CR*, 49 (June, 1886), pp. 794–819 and 'India Revisited. II', *CR*, 50 (July, 1886), pp. 60–79; idem, *India Revisited: Its Social and Political Problems* (London, 1886).

43. Smith, 'India Revisited', p. 795.

44. Sir M. E. Grant Duff, 'India: A Reply to Mr. Samuel Smith, M.P. I', *CR*, 51 (January, 1887), pp. 8–31 and 'India: A Reply to Mr. Samuel Smith, M.P. II', *CR*, 51 (February, 1887), pp. 181–95. Grant Duff's articles were not, of course, the first official defence: see especially the long list of reasons given in favour of British rule in India in Sir Richard Temple, *India in 1880* (London, 1880), pp. 496–8; also The Government of India, *Statement Exhibiting the Moral and Material Progress and Condition of India* (published regularly since 1859).

45. Dadabhai Naoroji to D. E. Wacha, 28 February 1887: quoted in Dadabhai Naoroji, *Correspondence, Vol. II: Part I. Correspondence with D. E. Wacha, 4.11.1884 to 23.3.1895,* edited with an introduction and notes by R. P. Patwardhan (Bombay, 1977), p. 11.

46. Dadabhai Naoroji, 'Sir M. E. Grant Duff's Views about India. – I', *CR*, 52 (August, 1887), pp. 221–35 and 'Sir M. E. Grant Duff's Views about India. – II', *CR*, 52 (November, 1887), pp. 694–711.

47. Eugene F. Irschick, *Dialogue and History: Constructing South India, 1795–1895* (Berkeley, 1994), pp. 166–9.

48. Dadabhai Naoroji to A. O. Hume, December 1887: quoted in R. P. Masani, *Dadabhai Naoroji: The Grand Old Man of India* (London, 1939), p. 292.

49. *Kesari*, 31 January 1888: quoted in Chandra, *The Rise and Growth of Economic Nationalism in India*, p. 497; see also ibid., pp. 551–2.

50. Gilbert, 'Famine in India', pp. 157–9.

51. Sir C. Aitchison, *Lord Lawrence* (Rulers of India series, Oxford, 1892); Gilbert, 'Famine in India', p. 159.

52. H. S. Maine minute, *Parliamentary Papers* 1878/9, LX, pp. 338–40: quoted in Clive Dewey, 'The End of the Imperialism of Free Trade: The Eclipse of the Lancashire Lobby and the Concession of Fiscal Autonomy to India', in Clive Dewey and A. G. Hopkins (eds), *The Imperial Impact: Studies in the Economic History of Africa and India* (Commonwealth Papers 21, University of London, Institute of Commonwealth Studies, London, 1978), p. 64.

53. For instance, Lord George Hamilton to a Lancashire deputation, 12 December 1895, *Parliamentary Papers* 1896 LX, pp. 404–5: quoted in ibid., pp. 64–5.

54. Ibid., p. 65.

55. Chandra, *The Rise and Growth of Economic Nationalism in India*, pp. 88–9, 217–70.

56. See for instance Digby, *India for the Indians – and for England*, pp. 91–4.

57. Blunt, *Ideas about India*, pp. 170–1.

58. Peter Harnetty, *Imperialism and Free Trade: Lancashire and India in the Mid-Nineteenth Century* (Manchester, 1972). On Wedderburn: Edward Moulton, 'William Wedderburn and Early Indian Nationalism, 1870–1917', in Kenneth Ballhatchet and David Taylor (eds), *Changing South Asia: Politics and Government* (London, 1984), p. 49; Anthony Howe, *Free Trade and Liberal England 1846–1946* (Oxford, 1997), p. 141n.

59. Henry Fawcett, *Free Trade and Protection* (London, 1878), pp. 170–2; idem, *Indian Finance: Three Essays, Republished from the 'Nineteenth Century'* (London, 1880). On Fawcett's Indian campaign see John Wood, 'Henry Fawcett and the British Empire', *The Indian Economic and Social History Review*, 16 (1979), pp. 395–414 and Sumanta Niyogi, 'The Defence of Colony's Interests in Parliament: Henry Fawcett and the Indian Cotton Duties', *Quarterly Review of Historical Studies*, 18 (1979), pp. 230–4.

60. Lawrence Goldman, 'Introduction: "An Advanced Liberal": Henry Fawcett, 1833–1884', in idem (ed.), *The Blind Victorian: Henry Fawcett and British Liberalism* (Cambridge, 1989), p. 32. See also Phyllis Deane, 'Henry Fawcett: The Plain Man's Political Economist', in ibid., pp. 93–110.

61. John Bright at the meeting gathered to express support to Lord Ripon's Indian policy: *The Times*, 2 August 1883.

62. 'Mr. Bright at Birmingham', *The Times*, 23 November 1885.

63. 'Mr. Bright on the Indian Civil Service', *The Times*, 9 July 1887.

64. Dewey, 'The End of the Imperialism of Free Trade', pp. 35, 40.

65. Ira Klein, 'English Free Traders and Indian Tariffs, 1874–96', *Modern Asian Studies*, 5 (1971), pp. 266–7.

66. See P. Harnetty, 'The Indian Cotton Duties Controversy, 1894–1896', *English Historical Review*, 77 (1962), pp. 684–702; Klein, 'English Free Traders and Indian Tariffs', pp. 251–71; P. F. Clarke, *Lancashire and the New Liberalism* (Cambridge, 1971), pp. 79–80, 85–7.

67. Dewey, 'The End of the Imperialism of Free Trade', p. 36.

68. Ibid., p. 39. For the debate on the opium trade see S. Maccoby, *English Radicalism 1886–1914* (London, 1953), pp. 432–6; Hunt Janin, *The India–China Opium Trade in the Nineteenth Century* (Jefferson and London, 1999), pp. 178–83.

69. Richard Congreve, 'The Opium Trade and the Indian Revenue' (Serial No. 5 of 'The Religion of Humanity, or Human Catholicism: The Western

Republic'), in idem, *Essays: Political, Social, and Religious*, vol. II (London, 1892 [1880]), pp. 115–16.

70. James Geddes to Richard Congreve, 8 January 1879: quoted in ibid., p. 116.

71. James Geddes to Richard Congreve, 9–10 June, 1879: quoted in ibid., p. 117.

72. Ibid., pp. 117–18.

73. W. S. Blunt to a friend in the late 1870s: quoted in Wilfrid Scawen Blunt, *Secret History of the English Occupation of Egypt: Being a Personal Narrative of Events* (London, 1907), p. 62.

74. W. S. Blunt to Harry Brand in the late 1870s: quoted in ibid., pp. 62–3.

75. Sir John Strachey and Richard Strachey, *The Finances and Public Works of India from 1869 to 1881* (London, 1882), p. 429.

76. William Digby's notes of an interview with Lord Ripon, 10 November 1888: Ripon Papers, Add. Mss 43636, ff. 155–6, BL; 'The Man of the Month. Mr. W. Digby, C.I.E.', *Greater Britain*, No. 4 (February, 1891), p. 311.

77. Geddes, *The Logic of Indian Deficit*, p. vii.

78. Strachey and Strachey, *The Finances and Public Works of India*, p. 83.

79. Davis and Huttenback, *Mammon and the Pursuit of Empire*, p. 307.

80. Published in *India*, No. 16 (16 January 1891). See also subsequent issues of *India*, esp. No. 18 (6 March 1891).

81. 'The Man of the Month. Mr. W. Digby, C.I.E.', *Greater Britain*, No. 4 (February, 1891), pp. 310–11.

82. Ibid., p. 311.

83. Ibid.

84. *Greater Britain*, No. 5 (March, 1891), pp. 340–4; Digby, *British Rule in India*.

85. Ibid., p. 7.

86. Ibid., p. 12.

87. J. B. Pennington, 'The Evils of the Salt Monopoly in India, and the Agitation against Opium, Ganja and Alcohol', *The Imperial and Asiatic Quarterly Review*, 6 (October, 1893), p. 315; [W. T. Stead], 'Indian Salt-Tax and Cholera', *Review of Reviews*, 8 (December, 1893), p. 634.

88. Sir Auckland Colvin, 'The Perilous Growth of Indian State Expenditure', *NC*, 36 (October, 1894), pp. 645–63 and 'Indian Frontiers and Indian Finance', *NC*, 38 (November, 1895), pp. 870–88.

89. Sir George Chesney, *Indian Polity: A View of the System of Administration in India* (3rd edn, London, 1894 [1868]), pp. 394–5.

90. Ibid., p. 397.

91. Ibid., p. 398.

92. Premansukumar Bandyopadhyay, *Indian Famine and Agrarian Problems: A Policy Study on the Administration of Lord George Hamilton, Secretary of State for*

India 1895–1903 (Calcutta, 1987), pp. 16–18, 21. The attacks on Hamilton were somewhat unfair since he was in fact kept back by the viceroy, Lord Elgin: ibid., pp. 18–22.

93. William Digby to Lord Hamilton, 4 January 1897: published in *The Times*, 7 January 1897.

94. India Office to William Digby, 6 January 1897: published in *The Times*, 7 January 1897.

95. Bandyopadhyay, *Indian Famine and Agrarian Problems*, p. 53.

96. The debates on 15 February, 23 March, and 3 April 1900: *Hansard's Parliamentary Debates*, 4th ser., vol. LXXIX p. 89, vol. LXXXI pp. 176–7, 1080–131.

97. Lord Hamilton to Lord Curzon, 5 April 1900: quoted in Bandyopadhyay, *Indian Famine and Agrarian Problems*, pp. 73–4.

98. Lord Curzon to Lord Hamilton, 23 April 1900: quoted in ibid., p. 74.

99. Ibid., pp. 76–8.

100. See the very extensive debate in the Commons on 26 July 1900: *Hansard's Parliamentary Debates*, 4th ser., vol. LXXXVI, pp. 1345–438.

101. *The Daily News* and *The Manchester Guardian*, 27 July 1900; *The Times*, 28 July 1900: quoted in Bandyopadhyay, *Indian Famine and Agrarian Problems*, pp. 79–80.

102. Ibid., p. 226.

103. J. L. Hammond, 'Colonial and Foreign Policy', in Francis W. Hirst, Gilbert Murray, and John L. Hammond, *Liberalism and the Empire: Three Essays*: reprinted in Peter Cain (ed.), *The Empire and Its Critics, 1899–1939: Classics of Imperialism*, vol. II (London 1998 [1900]), pp. 209–10.

104. W. S. Blunt's Autograph diaries, 5 February 1900: Blunt Papers, Ms 366–1975, pp. 32–3, FM.

105. W. S. Blunt's Autograph diaries, 1 August 1900: Blunt Papers, Ms 367–1975, pp. 57–8, FM.

106. See J. N. Gupta, *Life and Work of Romesh Chunder Dutt C.I.E.* (London, 1911), esp. pp. 282–6; Romesh Dutt, *Open Letters to Lord Curzon on Famines and Land Assessments in India* (London, 1900); idem, *Indian Famines: Their Causes and Prevention* (London, 1901).

107. Ibid., pp. 4–13.

108. Ibid., p. 15.

109. Dadabhai Naoroji, *Poverty and Un-British Rule in India* (London, 1901); Digby, *'Prosperous' British India*.

110. Ibid., p. 25. By 'pousta' Digby referred to 'a preparation of opium, the effect of which was in a few months to destroy all the bodily and mental powers of the wretch who was drugged with it, and to turn him into a helpless

idiot', which he had adopted from Lord Macaulay: 'The Man of the Month.
Mr. W. Digby, C.I.E.', *Greater Britain*, No. 4 (February, 1891), p. 311.

111. Digby, *'Prosperous' British India*, p. 43.

112. Ibid., p. 202. Digby referred to Thomas Inwood Pollard, *The Indian Tribute and the Loss by Exchange; an Essay on the Depreciation of Indian Commodities in England* (Calcutta, 1884).

113. Sir George Campbell, *The British Empire* (London, 1887), p. 70.

114. Digby, *'Prosperous' British India*, pp. 231–2.

115. Although Digby did also argue that cheap Indian labour caused distress to the British farmer, too: ibid., p. 201.

116. Tomlinson, *The Economy of Modern India*, pp. 11–12, 22–3.

117. Neil Charlesworth, *British Rule and the Indian Economy 1800–1914* (Studies in Economic and Social History, London and Basingstoke, 1982), pp. 68–70.

Chapter 4   Patriotism, 'Loyalty', and Morality

1. Sir Wilfrid Lawson, 'Kruger's Bible', June 1900: printed in Sir Wilfrid Lawson and F. Carruthers Gould, *Cartoons in Rhyme and Line* (London, 1905), p. 44.

2. Bernard Semmel, *The Liberal Ideal and the Demons of Empire: Theories of Imperialism from Adam Smith to Lenin* (Baltimore and London, 1993), p. 50; see also ibid., pp. 43–53.

3. Ibid., pp. 50–1.

4. Hugh Cunningham, 'The Conservative Party and Patriotism', in Robert Colls and Philip Dodd (eds), *Englishness: Politics and Culture 1880–1920* (London, 1986), p. 295.

5. Ibid., p. 299.

6. *Pall Mall Gazette*, 21 June 1887: quoted in Richard Williams, *The Contentious Crown: Public Discussion of the British Monarchy in the Reign of Queen Victoria* (Aldershot, 1997), p. 177.

7. Herbert Spencer, *The Study of Sociology*: reprinted in *Herbert Spencer: Collected Writings*, vol. VI (London, 1996 [1873]), ch. 9.

8. Ibid., p. 204.

9. Ibid., p. 205.

10. Ibid., p. 206.

11. Ibid., pp. 216–17.

12. Robert Lowe, 'Imperialism', *FR*, 24 (October, 1878), p. 461.

13. Annie Besant, *The Story of Afghanistan; Or, Why the Tory Government Gags the Indian Press: A Plea for the Weak Against the Strong* (London, 1879), pp. 3–4.

14. Idem, *Egypt* (London, 1882), p. 16.

15. W. S. Blunt's diary entry 27 June 1882: quoted in Wilfrid Scawen Blunt, *Secret History of the English Occupation of Egypt: Being a Personal Narrative of Events* (London, 1907), pp. 358–9.

16. John Viscount Morley, *Recollections*, vol. II (London, 1917), p. 80.

17. Sneh Mahajan, *British Foreign Policy 1874–1914: The Role of India* (Routledge Studies in Modern European History, London and New York, 2002), pp. vii–viii.

18. Charles Marvin, 'A Short, Plain Policy for Afghanistan', *CR*, 48 (September, 1885), pp. 343–51. For other writings with similar warnings, see Arminius Vambéry, 'Will Russia Conquer India?' *NC*, 17 (January and February, 1885), pp. 25–42, 297–311; Charles Marvin, *Russia's Power of Attracting India* (London, 1885); Major W. Sedgwick, *India for Sale: Kashmir Sold* (Calcutta, 1886); Robert N. Cust, 'Would India Gain by the Extinction of European Government?' *Asiatic Quarterly Review*, 9 (April, 1890), pp. 257–75; Captain Younghusband, 'The Invasion of India by Russia', *NC*, 33 (May, 1893), pp. 727–48; George N. Curzon, 'India between Two Fires', *NC*, 34 (August, 1893), pp. 177–86.

19. E. Ashmead Bartlett, *Shall England Keep India?* (London, 1886) p. 2: Lord Curzon's copy with his notes is in Lord Curzon Collection, Mss Eur. F111/53, OIOC.

20. The Maharajah Duleep Singh to *The Times*, 28 August and 6 September 1882, published in *The Times* of 31 August and 8 September 1882; *The Times*, leading article 31 August 1882; Michael Alexander and Sushila Anand, *Queen Victoria's Maharajah: Duleep Singh 1838–93* (London, 2001 [1980]), chs 7–10.

21. Evans Bell, *The Annexation of the Punjaub, and the Maharajah Duleep Singh* (London, 1882). Bell had formerly served in India but had lost his appointment after advocating the claims of a dispossessed Indian ruling family. Subsequently he had made several attacks against the Indian Civil Service, always defending native rulers.

22. Copy of a letter from Sir Henry Ponsonby to Lord Kimberley, 20 December 1883: Ripon Papers, Add. Mss 43524, ff. 124–5, BL.

23. Lord Kimberley to Lord Ripon, 1 August 1884: Ripon Papers, Add. Mss 43525, f. 137, BL.

24. Copy of a letter from Maharajah Duleep Singh to Sir Henry Ponsonby, 18 July 1884: Ripon Papers, Add. Mss 43525, ff. 139–140, BL.

25. Lord Kimberley to Lord Ripon, 27 December 1883: Ripon Papers, Add. Mss 43524, ff. 120–1, BL.

26. Alexander and Anand, *Queen Victoria's Maharajah*, chs 11–16.

27. John Morley's address to the General Committee of the Liberal Association in Newcastle, 1 April 1885: quoted in F. W. Hirst, *Early Life & Letters of John Morley*, vol. II (London, 1927), p. 221.

28. Henry Labouchere in the House of Commons, 22 September 1886: *Hansard's Parliamentary Debates*, 3rd ser., vol. CCCIX, p. 1339.

29. G. P. Gooch, *Life of Lord Courtney* (London, 1920), pp. 354–5.

30. Leonard Courtney's letter to the editor, *The Times*, 19 October 1896.

31. John M. Robertson, *Patriotism and Empire*: reprinted in Peter Cain (ed.), *The Empire and Its Critics, 1899–1939: Classics of Imperialism*, vol. I (London, 1998 [1899]), pp. 200–1.

32. Peter the Hermit, *The Brigands in Egypt: Solution of the International Crisis: Letters to an Englishman, by Peter the Hermit* (Translated from the French, London, 1882), p. 26.

33. See John Edwin McGee, *A Crusade for Humanity: The History of Organised Positivism in England* (London, 1931). For a study on the significance of positivism to the British intellectual life in the mid-Victorian era and to Frederic Harrison and John Morley in particular, see Christopher Kent, *Brains and Numbers: Elitism, Comtism, and Democracy in Mid-Victorian England* (Toronto, 1978), esp. chs 7–9. T. R. Wright, *The Religion of Humanity: The Impact of Comtean Positivism on Victorian Britain* (Cambridge, 1986) is yet another good study on positivism although neither Wright nor Kent discussed the issue of anti-imperialism as such.

34. See especially Richard Congreve, 'India', in idem, *Essays: Political, Social, and Religious* (London, 1874 [1857]), pp. 67–106; Henry Crompton and Richard Congreve, 'Imperialism' (Serial No. 4 of 'The Religion of Humanity, or Human Catholicism: The Western Republic'), in Richard Congreve, *Essays: Political, Social, and Religious*, vol. II (London, 1892 [1879]), pp. 105–11; Richard Congreve et al., *International Policy: Essays on the Foreign Relations of England* (2nd edn, London 1884 [1866]); and the periodical *Positivist Review*, passim, published from 1893 onwards.

35. Auguste Comte, *Cours de philosophie positive* (6 vols, Paris, 1830–42); idem, *Système de politique positive* (4 vols, Paris, 1851–4); idem, *Catéchisme positiviste* (Paris, 1852); McGee, *A Crusade for Humanity*, ch. 1.

36. Ibid., p. 10.

37. Ibid., p. 12.

38. Ibid., pp. 37–8.

39. Richard Congreve's letter to a friend, 19 August 1881: quoted in Geraldine Hancock Forbes, 'The English Positivists and India', *Bengal Past and Present*, 93 (1974), p. 75.

40. Congreve, 'India', pp. 92–3.

41. Crompton and Congreve, 'Imperialism', pp. 110–11.

42. Ibid., p. 110.

43. Richard Congreve, 'The Government and Uganda', in idem, *Essays: Political, Social, and Religious and Historical Lectures*, vol. III (London, 1900 [1892]), pp. 1–2.

44. Frederic Harrison, *Autobiographic Memoirs*, vol. I (London, 1911), pp. 313–14; idem, *Martial Law in Kabul (Reprinted from the FR, with additions)* (London, 1880).

45. Ibid., p. 3.

46. Frederic Harrison, 'Empire and Humanity', *FR*, 27 (February, 1880), pp. 288–308; idem, *National & Social Problems* (London, 1908), ch. 11.

47. Ibid., p. 244.

48. Harrison, 'Empire and Humanity', p. 290.

49. Ibid., p. 295.

50. Ibid., p. 299.

51. Harrison, *National & Social Problems*, p. 225; idem, 'The Boer War (December 1899)': quoted in ibid., ch. 9.

52. Ibid., pp. 227–8.

53. Letters from Herbert Spencer to Frederic Harrison: Harrison Collection, 1/107, BLPES; Harrison, *Autobiographic Memoirs*, II, p. 113; Sydney Eisen, 'Frederic Harrison and Herbert Spencer: embattled unbelievers', *Victorian Studies*, 12 (1968), pp. 33–56.

54. Richard Congreve to Herbert Spencer, 9 July 1884: quoted in David Duncan, *The Life and Letters of Herbert Spencer*: reprinted in *Herbert Spencer: Collected Writings*, vol. II (London, 1996 [1908]), p. 256.

55. Herbert Spencer to Frederic Harrison, 28 April 1901: Harrison Collection, 1/107, BLPES.

56. Harrison, *Autobiographic Memoirs*, II, p. 99.

57. The correspondence between Frederic Harrison and John Morley: Harrison Collection, 1/52–94, BLPES.

58. Frederic Harrison to Goldwin Smith, 27 January 1900: quoted in Goldwin Smith, *A Selection from Goldwin Smith's Correspondence: Comprising Letters Chiefly to and from His English Friends, Written between the Years 1846 and 1910*, collected by Arnold Haultain (London, 1913), p. 340.

59. Goldwin Smith to Frederic Harrison, 9 December 1900: Harrison Collection, 1/106, BLPES.

60. J. H. Bridges, 'Imperialism and Patriotism', *PR*, 6 (April, 1898), pp. 67–9.

61. John Henry Bridges to Fanny Torlesse, 1899: quoted in Susan Liveing, *A Nineteenth-Century Teacher: John Henry Bridges, M.B., F.R.C.P.* (London, 1926), p. 244.

62. Edward Spencer Beesly, 'Fashoda', *PR*, 6 (November, 1898), p. 181.

63. Ibid., p. 182.

64. Ibid., p. 183.

65. Edward Spencer Beesly, 'The Indian Millstone', *PR*, 2 (June, 1894), p. 100.

66. The London Positivist Society, 'The Russian Approach to India' (1885): quoted in ibid., p. 99.

67. Edward Spencer Beesly, 'Wei-Hai-Wei', *PR*, 6 (May, 1898), p. 85.

68. Idem, 'Jingoes and Imperialists', *PR*, 7 (March, 1899), p. 55.

69. Ibid., pp. 57–8.

70. For an analysis of this rhetoric see Paul Readman, 'The Conservative Party, Patriotism, and British Politics: The Case of the General Election of 1900', *Journal of British Studies*, 40 (2001), pp. 107–45.

71. Ibid., pp. 120–3.

72. William Clarke, 'The Genesis of Jingoism', *Progressive Review*, 2 (February, 1897): reprinted in Herbert Burrows and John A. Hobson (eds), *William Clarke: A Collection of His Writings, with a Biographical Sketch* (London, 1908), p. 108.

73. Ibid., p. 111.

74. Ibid., p. 113.

75. William Clarke, 'Bismarck', *CR*, 75 (January, 1899): reprinted in Burrows and Hobson (eds), *William Clarke*, pp. 218–19.

76. Lord George Hamilton, *Parliamentary Reminiscences and Reflections, 1868 to 1885* (London, 1917), pp. 329–30. On Hamilton's hatred towards the Manchester School see ibid., pp. 318–31.

77. J. Lawson Walton, 'Imperialism', *CR*, 75 (March, 1899), pp. 305–6.

78. Ibid., pp. 306–7, 309. On another rather similar contemporary view of the development of the 'imperial spirit' see J. H. Muirhead, 'What Imperialism Means', *FR*, 68 (August, 1900), pp. 177–87.

79. R. Wallace, 'The Seamy Side of "Imperialism"', *CR*, 75 (June, 1899), p. 785. The writer was most likely Robert Wallace, a Liberal MP, who died suddenly the same month; but it may also have been Dr Russell Wallace.

80. Ibid., p. 786.

81. Ibid., p. 791.

82. Ibid., p. 792.

83. Ibid., pp. 792–3.

84. Ibid., p. 799.

85. Lord Rosebery's speech in the City Liberal Club, 5 May 1899: quoted in A. G. Gardiner, *The Life of Sir William Harcourt*, vol. II (London, 1923), p. 495.

86. Sir William Harcourt's speech in West Monmouthshire, 31 May 1899: quoted in ibid., pp. 496–7.

87. Ibid., p. 597.
88. Ibid., pp. 597–8. Italics added.
89. John St. Loe Strachey, *The Adventure of Living: A Subjective Autobiography* (London, 1922), pp. 13, 298.
90. Ibid., pp. 299, 309.
91. Ibid., p. 301.
92. J. M. Robertson, *Wrecking the Empire* (London, 1901).
93. Strachey, *The Adventure of Living*, p. 301.

Chapter 5   Progress and Civilisation – or Degradation and Re-barbarisation

1. Annie Besant, *The Story of Afghanistan; Or, Why the Tory Government Gags the Indian Press: A Plea for the Weak against the Strong* (London, 1879), p. 16.
2. Sir Richard Temple, *India in 1880* (London, 1880), pp. 496, 498.
3. James Fitzjames Stephen, *Liberty, Equality, Fraternity* (London, 1873); K. J. M. Smith, *James Fitzjames Stephen: Portrait of a Victorian Rationalist* (Cambridge, 1988), chs 6–7.
4. He wrote several articles on this for the *Nineteenth Century* in this period.
5. John Cell, 'The Imperial Conscience', in Peter Marsh (ed.), *The Conscience of the Victorian State* (New York, 1979), pp. 173–213; D. W. Bebbington, *The Nonconformist Conscience: Chapel and Politics, 1870–1914* (London, 1982), pp. 106–26. The ideals of the Oxford Idealists paved the way for the moral duty-bound conception of imperialism: see Eric Stokes, *The Political Ideas of English Imperialism: An Inaugural Lecture Given in the University College of Rhodesia and Nyasaland* (London, 1960).
6. Paul Cocks, 'The Rhetoric of Science and the Critique of Imperialism in British Social Anthropology, c. 1870–1940', *History and Anthropology*, 9 (1995), pp. 93–119.
7. Like in A. H. Sayce, 'Upper Egypt under English Rule', *CR*, 45 (April, 1884), pp. 504–12; V. Lovett Cameron, 'Our Duty in the Soudan', *CR*, 47 (April, 1885), pp. 573–8; John Lubbock, 'England and the Soudan', *CR*, 47 (April, 1885), pp. 562–72.
8. George Baden-Powell, 'English Money in South Africa', *CR*, 48 (October, 1885), p. 508.
9. Ibid., p. 507.
10. Henry Birchenough, 'The Future of Egypt, II: The Niger and the Nile, a Warning', *NC*, 44 (December, 1898), p. 901.
11. Lord George Hamilton, *Parliamentary Reminiscences and Reflections, 1886–1906* (London, 1922), p. 278. He referred to the murders and outrages which

were directed against British officials in India in 1897: ibid., pp. 275–7. These opinions parallel interestingly with contemporary objections to the education of women: see Susan Kingsley Kent, *Sex and Suffrage in Britain, 1860–1914* (Princeton, 1987).

12. Hamilton, *Parliamentary Reminiscences and Reflections, 1886–1906*, pp. 278–9.

13. Richard Cobden to Mr Gilpin, 28 March 1858: quoted in John Morley, *The Life of Richard Cobden*, vol. II (Jubilee edn, London, 1896), p. 217.

14. Herbert Spencer, *Social Statics: or, the Conditions Essential to Human Happiness Specified, and the First of Them Developed*: reprinted in *Herbert Spencer: Collected Writings*, vol. III (London, 1996 [1851]), ch. 27.

15. Ibid., p. 358.

16. Ibid., p. 359.

17. Ibid., p. 363.

18. Ibid., p. 364.

19. Ibid., pp. 366–7.

20. Ibid., p. 371.

21. Herbert Spencer to F. W. Chesson, 18 November 1880: quoted in David Duncan, *The Life and Letters of Herbert Spencer*: reprinted in *Herbert Spencer: Collected Writings*, vol. II (London, 1996 [1908]), pp. 219–20.

22. Herbert Spencer to Algernon Charles Swinburne, 8 March 1881: quoted in ibid., p. 220.

23. Edward Dicey, 'Is Central Africa Worth Having? II', *NC*, 28 (September, 1890), pp. 488–500.

24. Alfred Aylward, 'Africa and the Empire', *FR*, 31 (April, 1882), p. 510.

25. Ibid., pp. 510–11.

26. Wilfrid Scawen Blunt, *Gordon at Khartoum: Being a Personal Narrative of Events, in Continuation of "A Secret History of the English Occupation of Egypt"* (London, 1911), p. 96.

27. Ibid., p. 98.

28. Charles W. Dilke, 'The Uganda Problem', *FR*, 53 (February, 1893), p. 155.

29. Henry M. Stanley, *In Darkest Africa or, The Quest, Rescue, and Retreat of Emin, Governor of Equatoria* (2 vols, London, 1890); see also Iain R. Smith, *The Emin Pasha Relief Expedition, 1886–1890* (Oxford, 1972).

30. R. Bosworth Smith, 'Englishmen in Africa', *CR*, 59 (January, 1891), pp. 69–70.

31. Ibid., p. 73.

32. Ibid., pp. 71–2.

33. Ibid., p. 74.

34. Ibid., p. 75.

35. Grant Allen, 'Democracy and Diamonds', *CR*, 59 (May, 1891), p. 667.

36. Ibid., pp. 669–70.

37. Ibid., p. 671.

38. Ibid., p. 675.

39. Ibid., p. 677.

40. The correspondence between Herbert Spencer and Grant Allen: Herbert Spencer Papers, Mss 791, SHL.

41. Richard Le Gallienne, 'Grant Allen', *FR*, 66 (December, 1899), pp. 1005–25.

42. Richard Congreve, 'The Government and Uganda', in idem, *Essays: Political, Social, and Religious and Historical Lectures*, vol. III (London, 1900 [1892]), pp. 1–2.

43. Edward Spencer Beesly, 'Fashoda', *PR*, 6 (November, 1898), p. 182; idem, 'Jingoes and Imperialists', *PR*, 7 (March, 1899), p. 57.

44. Beesly, 'Fashoda', p. 183.

45. Elisabeth Lecky, 'A Warning to Imperialists', *NC*, 40 (July, 1896), p. 19.

46. See especially Annie Besant, *The Transvaal* (London, 1881).

47. Kate Courtney to Brooke Lambert, 16 November 1900: quoted in John W. Auld, 'The Liberal Pro-Boers', *Journal of British Studies*, 14 (1975), p. 94.

48. H. M. Hyndman, *The Transvaal War and the Degradation of England* (Reprinted from *Justice*, London, 1899), p. 7.

49. Ibid., pp. 8, 13–14.

50. W. S. Blunt to Lord Ripon, 9 January 1884: Ripon Papers, Add. Mss 43634, f. 118, BL.

51. W. S. Blunt to Henry Primrose, 9 January 1884: Ripon Papers, Add. Mss 43634, f. 116, BL.

52. W. S. Blunt to Lord Ripon, 9 January 1884: Ripon Papers, Add. Mss 43634, ff. 119–120, BL.

53. W. S. Blunt to Lord Ripon, 21 January 1884: Ripon Papers, Add. Mss 43634, ff. 133–4, BL.

54. W. S. Blunt to Henry Primrose, 6 March 1884: Ripon Papers, Add. Mss 43634, ff. 167–8, BL; W. S. Blunt to Lord Ripon, 6 March 1884: Ripon Papers, Add. Mss 43634, ff. 169–170, BL.

55. W. S. Blunt's Autograph diaries, 4 November 1894: Blunt Papers, Ms 342–1975, pp. 38–40, FM.

56. John M. Robertson, 'Charles Bradlaugh: An Account of His Parliamentary Struggle, Politics and Teachings', in Hypatia Bradlaugh Bonner, *Charles Bradlaugh: A Record of His Life and Work*, vol. II (London, 1895), pp. 198–9.

57. See especially Nancy Fix Anderson, ' "Mother Besant" and Indian National Politics', *The Journal of Imperial and Commonwealth History*, 30:3 (2002), pp. 27–54; idem, 'Bridging Cross-Cultural Feminisms: Annie Besant and Women's Rights in England and India, 1874–1933', *Women's History Review*, 3

(1994), pp. 563–80; Mark Bevir, 'In Opposition to the Raj: Annie Besant and the Dialectic of Empire', *History of Political Thought*, 19 (1998), pp. 61–77.

58. Anderson, '"Mother Besant" and Indian National Politics', pp. 28–9.

59. Annie Besant in *India – Present and Future: An Interview with Mrs. Annie Besant, from 'The New Age'* (1896), pp. 14–17: quoted in Anderson, 'Bridging Cross-Cultural Feminisms', p. 567.

60. Annie Besant, *Theosophy and Imperialism* (London, 1902), p. 13: quoted in ibid.', p. 568.

61. Ibid., pp. 573–5.

62. See Bernard Porter, *The Absent-Minded Imperialists: Empire, Society, and Culture in Britain* (Oxford, 2004).

63. W. E. H. Lecky, *The Empire, Its Value and Its Growth: An Inaugural Address Delivered at the Imperial Institute, Nov. 20, 1893, under the Presidency of H.R.H. the Prince of Wales* (London, 1893), pp. 3–4.

64. Ibid., pp. 5–6.

65. Ibid., p. 11.

66. Ibid., pp. 12–14.

67. Ibid., p. 14.

68. Ibid., pp. 19–20.

69. Ibid., p. 25.

70. Benjamin Kidd, *Social Evolution: With Appendix Containing Reply to Criticisms* (3rd edn, London, 1898 [1894]); idem, *The Control of the Tropics* (New York and London, 1898); D. P. Crook, *Benjamin Kidd: Portrait of a Social Darwinist* (Cambridge, 1984). *Social Evolution* was published in the United States in 1894, in Germany and Sweden in 1895, in France in 1896, in Russia in 1897, and in Italy in 1898.

71. Crook, *Benjamin Kidd*, pp. 3–4, 67–8.

72. Ibid., p. 68.

73. Kidd, *Social Evolution*, p. 138.

74. Ibid., pp. 151–9.

75. Ibid., pp. 160–5.

76. Ibid., p. 168.

77. Ibid., pp. 322–7.

78. Kidd, *The Control of the Tropics*, pp. 59–60.

79. H. F. Wyatt, 'The Ethics of Empire', *NC*, 41 (April, 1897), p. 529; also W. S. Lilly, 'The Burden of Empire', *FR*, 68 (October, 1900), pp. 533–43.

80. Crook, *Benjamin Kidd*, pp. 86, 104–6, 145.

81. William Clarke to Benjamin Kidd, 10 December 1895: quoted in ibid., p. 106.

82. Besant, *The Story of Afghanistan*, p. 14.

83. Ibid., p. 15.

84. Frederic Harrison, 'Empire and Humanity', *FR*, 27 (February, 1880), p. 298.

85. Ibid., p. 299.

86. Martha S. Vogeler, *Frederic Harrison: The Vocations of a Positivist* (New York and Oxford, 1984), p. 237.

87. Goldwin Smith to W. E. Gladstone, 23 November 1878: quoted in Goldwin Smith, *A Selection from Goldwin Smith's Correspondence: Comprising Letters Chiefly to and from His English Friends, Written between the Years 1846 and 1910*, collected by Arnold Haultain (London, 1913), p. 71.

88. Goldwin Smith to J. X. Merriman, 1 December 1899: quoted in ibid., p. 333.

89. Goldwin Smith to J. X. Merriman, 25 January 1900: quoted in ibid., p. 339.

90. See Tim Gray, 'Herbert Spencer's liberalism – from social statics to social dynamics', in Richard Bellamy (ed.), *Victorian Liberalism: Nineteenth-Century Political Thought and Practice* (London and New York, 1990), pp. 118–25; Herbert Spencer, *The Principles of Biology* (2 vols, London, 1864, 1867); David Wiltshire, *The Social and Political Thought of Herbert Spencer* (Oxford Historical Monographs, Oxford, 1978), pp. 255–6.

91. Duncan, *The Life and Letters of Herbert Spencer*, p. 222.

92. Gray, 'Herbert Spencer's Liberalism', p. 115.

93. Wiltshire, *The Social and Political Thought of Herbert Spencer*, pp. 243–6.

94. Herbert Spencer to Moncure D. Conway, 15 August 1900: quoted in Duncan, *The Life and Letters of Herbert Spencer*, p. 450.

95. Herbert Spencer, *Facts and Comments* (London, 1902): see especially the sections 'Patriotism' on pp. 88–91 and 'Imperialism and Slavery', pp. 112–21. The book generated great interest in the Continent, too: Duncan, *The Life and Letters of Herbert Spencer*, p. 461.

96. Spencer, *Facts and Comments*, pp. 112–15.

97. Lord Hobhouse to his cousin Sir Charles Hobhouse, 14 April 1902: quoted in L. T. Hobhouse and J. L. Hammond, *Lord Hobhouse: A Memoir* (London, 1905), pp. 222–3.

98. Herbert Spencer to James Sully, 10 December 1899: quoted in Duncan, *The Life and Letters of Herbert Spencer*, pp. 421–2.

99. Herbert Spencer to W. S. Blunt, 1 October 1898: quoted in ibid., pp. 410–11. *The Wind and the Whirlwind* is printed in Wilfrid Scawen Blunt, *The Poetical Works of Wilfrid Scawen Blunt: A Complete Edition*, vol. II (London, 1914), pp. 221–35.

100. Herbert Spencer to W. S. Blunt, 23 June 1899: quoted in Duncan, *The Life and Letters of Herbert Spencer*, p. 412.

101. W. S. Blunt, 'Satan Absolved: A Victorian Mystery' (1899), in idem, *The Poetical Works of Wilfrid Scawen Blunt*, II, p. 285. The whole poem is a 38-page-long politico-poetical narrative.

102. Herbert Spencer to W. S. Blunt, 28 October 1899: quoted in Duncan, *The Life and Letters of Herbert Spencer*, p. 413.

103. W. S. Blunt's Autograph diaries, 31 December 1895: Blunt Papers, Ms 348–1975, p. 48, FM.

104. W. S. Blunt's Autograph diaries, 5 January 1896: Blunt Papers, Ms 349–1975, p. 1, FM.

105. Herbert Spencer to W. S. Blunt, 6 October 1898: Blunt Papers, Ms 1136–1977, FM.

106. W. S. Blunt's Autograph diaries, 22 December 1900: Blunt Papers, Ms 369–1975, pp. 20–1, FM.

107. Wilfrid Scawen Blunt, *The Shame of the Nineteenth Century, a Letter Addressed to the 'Times'* (n.p., 1900), pp. 1–2.

108. Ibid., pp. 2–4.

109. Ibid., pp. 4–5.

110. Ibid., p. 6.

111. Ibid., p. 7.

112. Beesly, 'Jingoes and Imperialists', p. 56.

113. Ibid., p. 57.

114. Sir Wilfrid Lawson, 'Cock-a-doodle-doo', 24 October 1900: printed in Sir Wilfrid Lawson and F. Carruthers Gould, *Cartoons in Rhyme and Line* (London, 1905), p. 47.

115. David Blitz, 'Russell and the Boer War: From Imperialist to Anti-Imperialist', *Russell: the Journal of Bertrand Russell Studies*, 19 (2000), pp. 117–42.

116. Bertrand Russell to Louis Couturat, 18 December 1899: quoted in ibid., p. 125. The letters quoted have been translated from French to English by David Blitz.

117. Louis Couturat to Bertrand Russell, 24 December 1899: quoted in ibid., p. 126.

118. Bertrand Russell to Louis Couturat, 24 March 1900: quoted in ibid., pp. 126–7.

119. Louis Couturat to Bertrand Russell, 6 April 1900: quoted in ibid., pp. 127–8.

120. Herbert Spencer, 'The Ethics of Kant', *FR*, 44 (July, 1888), pp. 142–56.

121. Louis Couturat to Bertrand Russell, 6 April 1900: quoted in Blitz, 'Russell and the Boer War', p. 129.

122. Bertrand Russell to Louis Couturat, 5 May 1900: quoted in ibid., p. 130.

123. Bertrand Russell to Louis Couturat, 25 June 1902: quoted in ibid., p. 133.

Chapter 6   Old and New Liberal Anti-Imperialism

1. [J. A. Hobson] *pseud.* Nemo, 'Ethics of Empire', *The Progressive Review*, 2 (August, 1897), p. 461.

2. John M. Robertson, *Patriotism and Empire*: reprinted in Peter Cain (ed.), *The Empire and Its Critics, 1899–1939: Classics of Imperialism*, vol. I (London, 1998 [1899]), p. 141.

3. F. W. Hirst, *Early Life & Letters of John Morley*, vol. II (London, 1927), p. 210; John Morley, *Liberal Principles and Imperialism: A Speech by the Right Hon. John Morley, M.P., at Oxford, June 9, 1900* (National Reform Union Pamphlets, Manchester, 1900), p. 6.

4. F. Seebohm, 'Imperialism and Socialism', *NC*, 7 (April, 1880), p. 726.

5. Ibid., p. 727.

6. Ibid., p. 728.

7. Ibid., pp. 729–31.

8. For a comparison in his own words, see for instance David Duncan, *The Life and Letters of Herbert Spencer*: reprinted in *Herbert Spencer: Collected Writings*, vol. II (London, 1996 [1908]), p. 422.

9. Herbert Spencer to J. E. Cairnes, 21 March 1873: quoted in ibid., p. 61.

10. Herbert Spencer to W. C. Croft, December 1881: quoted in ibid., p. 224.

11. Herbert Spencer, 'The Coming Slavery', *CR*, 45 (April, 1884), p. 474; also idem, *The Man* versus *the State* (London, 1884); idem, 'From Freedom to Bondage', in idem, *Essays: Scientific, Political, & Speculative*, vol. III (London, 1891), pp. 445–70.

12. Herbert Spencer to A. M. Scott, 26 July 1900: quoted in Duncan, *The Life and Letters of Herbert Spencer*, p. 449. Spencer regarded the late-Victorian 'regression to socialism', like the simultaneous 'regression to imperialism', as natural retrogression in 'the rhythm of motion' in between periods of progress: M. W. Taylor, *Men versus the State: Herbert Spencer and Late Victorian Individualism* (Oxford Historical Monographs, Oxford, 1992), pp. 182–3.

13. Goldwin Smith, *Essays on Questions of the Day: Political and Social* (2nd edn, London, 1894 [1893]), pp. v–vi.

14. Ibid., pp. 142–3.

15. L. T. Hobhouse and J. L. Hammond, *Lord Hobhouse: A Memoir* (London, 1905), ch. 7.

16. Ibid., p. 221.

17. Ibid., p. 224.

18. Lord Hobhouse to A. G. Symonds, 30 September 1900: quoted in ibid., p. 221.

19. Lord Hobhouse to A. G. Symonds, 17 March 1902: quoted in ibid., p. 223. He referred, of course, to the Anti-Aggression League.

20. D. A. Hamer, *John Morley: Liberal Intellectual in Politics* (Oxford, 1968), p. 60; John Morley, *Edmund Burke: A Historical Study* (London, 1867).

21. Hamer, *John Morley*, pp. 347–8.

22. For a comparison of Burke's and Mill's thought in this sense see Uday Singh Mehta, *Liberalism and Empire: A Study in Nineteenth-Century British Liberal Thought* (Chicago and London, 1999).

23. John Morley to James Bryce, 26 September 1900: quoted in Hamer, *John Morley*, p. 325.

24. John Morley, 'A Political Epilogue', *FR*, 24 (September 1878), pp. 329–31.

25. Hamer, *John Morley*, p. 137; John Morley, 'Irish Revolution and English Liberalism', *NC*, 12 (November, 1882), pp. 647–61.

26. *The Times*, 2 April 1885: quoted in Hamer, *John Morley*, p. 162.

27. *The Times*, 20 and 26 October, 12 November 1885: quoted in ibid., pp. 162–3.

28. *The Times*, 20 January and 26 May 1899: quoted in ibid., p. 316.

29. Ibid., pp. 307–15.

30. Ibid., pp. 289–91.

31. John Morley to Andrew Carnegie, 21 October 1894: quoted in ibid., p. 295.

32. John Morley to Lord Spencer, 25 September 1900: quoted in ibid.

33. A. G. Gardiner, *The Life of Sir William Harcourt*, vol. II (London, 1923), pp. 329–30, 466–9.

34. Hamer, *John Morley*, pp. 320–1, 329.

35. Ibid., p. 322.

36. Ibid., pp. 322–3; Morley, *Liberal Principles and Imperialism*, p. 5.

37. *The Times*, 11 June 1900: quoted in Hamer, *John Morley*, p. 323; also published in Morley, *Liberal Principles and Imperialism*, p. 15.

38. John Morley to Frederic Harrison, 23 December 1900, and to Sir William Harcourt, 6 November 1899: quoted in Hamer, *John Morley*, p. 331.

39. Francis W. Hirst, *In the Golden Days* (London, 1947), ch. 6; Wilfrid Scawen Blunt, *My Diaries: Being a Personal Narrative of Events, 1888–1914*, vol. I, (London, 1919), pp. 397–9; Hamer, *John Morley*, pp. 333–7.

40. Ibid., pp. 339–40.

41. H. M. Hyndman to W. S. Blunt, 9 July 1884: Blunt Papers, Ms 249–1975, FM.

42. Sir Wilfrid Lawson, 'Learn to Think Imperially', 19 January 1904: printed in Sir Wilfrid Lawson and F. Carruthers Gould, *Cartoons in Rhyme and Line* (London, 1905), p. 24.

43. J. Guinness Rogers, 'Shall Uganda Be Retained?', *NC*, 33 (February, 1893), p. 220.

44. Ibid., p. 234.

45. Charles F. G. Masterman, 'Realities at Home', in idem et al., *The Heart of the Empire: Discussions of Problems of Modern City Life in England, with an Essay on Imperialism* (London, 1901), p. 1.

46. G. P. Gooch, 'Imperialism', in ibid., p. 308.

47. William Clarke, 'The Limits of Collectivism', *CR*, 63 (February, 1893): reprinted in Herbert Burrows and John A. Hobson (eds), *William Clarke: A Collection of His Writings, with a Biographical Sketch* (London, 1908), p. 30; see also William Clarke, 'Political Defects of the Old Radicalism', *Political Science Quarterly*, 14 (March, 1899): reprinted in ibid., pp. 59–75.

48. Herbert Burrows, 'Biographical Sketch: His Later Years', in ibid., pp. xv–xvi.

49. Ibid., p. xix. 'The Cities of the Plain' refer, of course, to the Genesis's tale of Sodom and Gomorrah, which were destroyed because of the sins of their inhabitants.

50. 'The Rainbow Circle: 1st Session, Nov. 1894 – June 1895', in Michael Freeden (ed.), *Minutes of the Rainbow Circle, 1894–1924* (Camden Fourth Series vol. 38, London, 1989), p. 17. On New Liberals see H. V. Emy, *Liberals, Radicals and Social Politics 1892–1914* (Cambridge, 1973); Peter Clarke, *Liberals and Social Democrats* (Modern Revivals in History, Aldershot, 1993 [1978]), esp. ch. 3 on imperialism; Bernard Porter, *Critics of Empire: British Radical Attitudes to Colonialism in Africa 1895–1914* (London, 1968), ch. 6; the story of the Rainbow Circle also in Clarke, *Liberals and Social Democrats*, pp. 54–61.

51. 'The Rainbow Circle: 1st Session', in Freeden (ed.), *Minutes of the Rainbow Circle*, pp. 17–26.

52. William Clarke to Ramsay MacDonald, 2 February 1896: quoted in Peter Weiler, 'William Clarke: The Making and Unmaking of a Fabian Socialist', *The Journal of British Studies*, 14 (1974), p. 101.

53. Ibid., pp. 101–2.

54. William Clarke to Henry Demarest Lloyd, 7 May 1897: quoted in ibid., p. 104.

55. William Clarke to Sidney Webb, 21 November 1899: quoted in ibid., p. 107.

56. William Clarke, 'The Present Mood of England', *New England Magazine*, 16 (August, 1897), p. 693: quoted in ibid., p. 106.

57. The session contained papers from both imperialists and anti-imperialists: speakers were J. M. Robertson, William Clarke, Douglas Morrison, Herbert Samuel, C. P. Trevelyan, W. P. Reeves, H. R. Fox Bourne, and

J. A. Hobson: 'The Rainbow Circle: 6th Session 1899–1900', in Freeden (ed.), *Minutes of the Rainbow Circle*, pp. 69–79.

58. The Minute of the Rainbow Circle, 4 October 1899: No. 47 in ibid., p. 70.

59. William Clarke's address on 'Imperialism & Democracy', in the Minute of the Rainbow Circle, 1 November 1899: No. 48 in ibid., p. 71.

60. Ibid., pp. 71–2.

61. The Minute of the Rainbow Circle, 1 November 1899: No. 48 in ibid., p. 72.

62. The Minute of the Rainbow Circle, 6 December 1899: No. 49 in ibid., pp. 72–3.

63. Herbert Samuel's address on 'Imperialism in relation to Social Reform', in the Minute of the Rainbow Circle, 17 January 1900: No. 50 in ibid., pp. 73–4.

64. The Minute of the Rainbow Circle, 17 January 1900: No. 50 in ibid., p. 74.

65. J. A. Hobson's address on imperialism, in the Minute of the Rainbow Circle, 30 May 1900: No. 54 in ibid., p. 79.

66. William Clarke, 'Bismarck', *CR*, 75 (January, 1899): reprinted in Burrows and Hobson (eds), *William Clarke: A Collection of His Writings*, p. 220.

67. William Clarke, 'The Rt. Hon. Leonard Courtney: A Character Sketch', *The Young Man* (August, 1900): reprinted in ibid., p. 275. One cannot help but note the accurateness of this prophesy in regard to the Soviet Union.

68. Burrows, 'Biographical Sketch', p. xxiii.

69. Clarke, *Liberals and Social Democrats*, p. 72.

70. Jim Herrick, 'The Politician', in G. A. Wells (ed.), *J. M. Robertson (1856–1933), Liberal, Rationalist, and Scholar: An Assessment by Several Hands* (London, 1987), pp. 32–3.

71. Robertson, *Patriotism and Empire*, pp. 170–1.

72. Ibid., pp. 172–3.

73. Ibid., p. 187.

74. Ibid., p. 188.

75. Ibid., pp. 189–90.

76. Ibid., p. 204.

77. Ibid., p. 203.

78. J. L. Hammond, 'Colonial and Foreign Policy', in Francis W. Hirst, Gilbert Murray, and John L. Hammond, *Liberalism and the Empire: Three Essays*: reprinted in Peter Cain (ed.), *The Empire and its Critics, 1899–1939: Classics of Imperialism*, vol. II (London 1998 [1900]), p. 211.

79. Hirst, Murray, and Hammond, *Liberalism and the Empire*, p. xii.

80. Ibid., p. xiii.

81. I. D. MacKillop, *The British Ethical Societies* (Cambridge, 1986), p. 158.

82. P. J. Cain , *Hobson and Imperialism: Radicalism, New Liberalism, and Finance 1887–1938* (Oxford, 2002), p. 81.

83. Porter, *Critics of Empire*, pp. 161–3.

84. MacKillop, *The British Ethical Societies*, pp. 158–62. For a very brief summary of the debate in the *Ethical World* in 1898–1900 see ibid., p. 191.

85. Cain , *Hobson and Imperialism*, p. 53.

86. Ibid., p. 66.

87. Ibid., pp. 63–4.

88. J. A. Hobson, 'Mr. Kidd's "Social Evolution" ', *American Journal of Sociology*, 1 (November, 1895), pp. 299–312; Cain, *Hobson and Imperialism*, p. 59.

89. [J. A. Hobson] *pseud.* Nemo, 'Ethics of Empire', *The Progressive Review*, 2 (August, 1897), pp. 448–62.

90. Cain , *Hobson and Imperialism*, pp. 65–6.

91. Ibid., p. 75.

92. [Hobson] Nemo, 'Ethics of Empire', pp. 449–450.

93. Ibid., pp. 451–2.

94. Ibid., p. 454.

95. Ibid., p. 456.

96. See J. A. Hobson, 'Herbert Spencer', *South Place Magazine*, 9 (January, 1904), pp. 49–55; Michael Freeden, 'Hobson's evolving conceptions of human nature', in idem (ed.), *Reappraising J. A. Hobson: Humanism and Welfare* (London, 1990), pp. 58–9.

97. John Atkinson Hobson, 'Free Trade and Foreign Policy', *CR*, 74 (August, 1898), p. 168.

98. See Cain , *Hobson and Imperialism*, ch. 5, esp. p. 126.

99. Freeden, 'Hobson's evolving conceptions of human nature', pp. 60–2; Gustave Le Bon, *Les Lois psychologiques de l'evolution des peuples* (Paris, 1894), translated in English as *The Psychology of Peoples* (London, 1899); idem, *La psychologie des foules* (Paris, 1895), translated in English as *The Crowd: A Study of the Popular Mind* (London, 1896).

100. J. A. Hobson, *The Psychology of Jingoism* (London, 1901), p. 17.

101. Ibid., p. 20.

102. Ibid., p. 33.

103. Ibid., p. 70.

104. Ibid., pp. 107–39.

105. Ibid., p. 131.

106. *Ethical World*, 8 July 1899: quoted in MacKillop, *The British Ethical Societies*, p. 1.

107. Clarke, *Liberals and Social Democrats*, p. 66.

108. Ibid., pp. 68–9. They all shared a firm belief in free trade.

109. Stefan Collini, *Liberalism and Sociology: L. T. Hobhouse and Political Argument in England 1880–1914* (Cambridge, 1979), pp. 54, 77.

110. Ibid., p. 81.

111. Ibid., pp. 83–6.

112. Lord Hobhouse to Leonard Hobhouse, 2 October 1904: quoted in Hobhouse and Hammond, *Lord Hobhouse*, p. 241.

113. L. T. Hobhouse, *Democracy and Reaction*, edited with an introduction and notes by P. F. Clarke (Society & the Victorians, Brighton, 1972 [1904]).

114. Lord Hobhouse to Leonard Hobhouse, 2 October 1904: quoted in Hobhouse and Hammond, *Lord Hobhouse*, p. 242.

115. Lord Hobhouse to Leonard Hobhouse, autumn 1904: quoted in ibid., p. 243.

116. Bernard Semmel, *Imperialism and Social Reform: English Social-Imperial Thought 1895–1914* (Studies in Society 5, London, 1960), esp. ch. 2; G. R. Searle, *The Quest for National Efficiency: A Study in British Politics and Political Thought, 1899–1914* (Oxford, 1971); H. C. G. Matthew, *The Liberal Imperialists: The Ideas and Politics of a Post-Gladstonian Élite* (Oxford Historical Monographs, London, 1973), esp. chs 3, 5, 7; George Bernard Shaw (ed.), *Fabianism and the Empire: a Manifesto by the Fabian Society* (London, 1900).

117. Beatrice Webb, *Our Partnership* (London, 1948), pp. 104–5.

118. Semmel, *Imperialism and Social Reform*, p. 235.

119. Ibid., p. 234.

120. Dennis Smith, 'Englishness and the Liberal Inheritance after 1886', in Robert Colls and Philip Dodd (eds), *Englishness: Politics and Culture 1880–1920* (London, 1986), p. 255.

Chapter 7   The Nature of the British Empire

1. J. R. Seeley, *The Expansion of England: Two Courses of Lectures* (London, 1883), p. 176.

2. Goldwin Smith, *Essays on Questions of the Day: Political and Social* (2nd edn, London, 1894 [1893]), p. 141.

3. Of course, a self-governing settler colony like Canada could be equally imperialistic in its own policies, but that represented Canadian imperialism, not British imperialism towards Canada.

4. The classic example is of course C. A. Bodelsen, *Studies in Mid-Victorian Imperialism* (Copenhagen, 1924); see also Oliver MacDonagh, 'The Anti-Imperialism of Free Trade', *Economic History Review*, 2nd series, 14 (1962), pp. 489–501; Ged Martin, ' "Anti-imperialism" in the mid-nineteenth century and the nature of the British empire, 1820–70', in Ronald Hyam and Ged Martin, *Reappraisals in British Imperial History* (Cambridge Commonwealth Series, London, 1975), pp. 88–120; Andrew S. Thompson, *Imperial Britain: The Empire in British Politics, c. 1880–1932* (Harlow, 2000).

5. Goldwin Smith, *The Empire: A Series of Letters, Published in 'The Daily News',
   1862, 1863* (Oxford and London, 1863). A major exception is R. Craig
   Brown, 'Goldwin Smith and Anti-Imperialism', *Canadian Historical Review*,
   43 (1962), pp. 93–105, which examines Smith's opposition to imperialism at
   the end of the century, not his campaign for colonial self-government.

6. See Smith, *Essays on Questions of the Day*.

7. Brown, 'Goldwin Smith and Anti-imperialism'.

8. See Richard Koebner and Helmut Dan Schmidt, *Imperialism: The Story and
   Significance of a Political Word, 1840–1960* (Cambridge, 1965), pp. 1–195;
   also J. P. Parry, 'The Impact of Napoleon III on British Politics, 1851–1880',
   Transactions of the Royal Historical Society, 6th series, 11 (2001), pp. 147–75.

9. James Stanley Little, *A World Empire: Being an Essay upon Imperial Federation*
   (London, 1879), p. 5.

10. Frederic Harrison, 'Empire and Humanity', *FR*, 27 (February, 1880),
    pp. 296–7.

11. Seeley, *The Expansion of England*, pp. 293–4.

12. Idem, *Introduction to Political Science: Two Series of Lectures* (London, 1896),
    pp. 318–19; idem, *A Short History of Napoleon the First* (London, 1886),
    p. 278; Deborah Wormell, *Sir John Seeley and the Uses of History* (Cambridge,
    1980), pp. 149–50.

13. Seeley, *A Short History of Napoleon the First*, p. 243.

14. Seeley, *The Expansion of England*, pp. 63–6.

15. Wormell, *Sir John Seeley and the Uses of History*, pp. 154–5.

16. Ibid., p. 155.

17. Quoted, without source, in Robert Rhodes James, *Rosebery: A Biography of
    Archibald Philip, Fifth Earl of Rosebery* (London, 1963), p. 158; also Wormell,
    Sir John Seeley and the Uses of History, p. 156.

18. Ibid., p. 150.

19. Goldwin Smith, 'The Expansion of England', *CR*, 45 (April, 1884), pp. 524–40.

20. John Morley, 'The Expansion of England', *Macmillan's Magazine*, 49 (February,
    1884): reprinted in idem, *Critical Miscellanies*, vol. III (London, 1886), pp.
    291–335.

21. Ibid., p. 335.

22. Ibid., pp. 305–16.

23. Ibid., p. 321.

24. Seeley, *The Expansion of England*, p. 9; Morley, 'The Expansion of England',
    p. 294.

25. Ibid., p. 306.

26. Howard LeRoy Malchow, *Agitators and Promoters in the Age of Gladstone and
    Disraeli: A Biographical Dictionary of the Leaders of British Pressure Groups*

Founded between 1865 and 1886 (Garland Reference Library of Social Science, vol. 176, New York and London, 1983), p. xvii, see also p. 241.

27. Duncan S. A. Bell, 'The Debate about Federation in Empire Political Thought, 1860–1900' (unpublished PhD thesis, University of Cambridge, 2004).

28. Edward A. Freeman, 'Imperial Federation', *Macmillan's Magazine*, 51 (April, 1885), pp. 430–45; idem, *Greater Greece and Greater Britain, and, George Washington the Expander of England: Two Lectures* (London, 1886); M. D. Burgess, 'Imperial Federation: Edward Freeman and the Intellectual Debate on the Consolidation of the British Empire in the Late Nineteenth century', *Trivium*, 13 (1978), pp. 77–94; Wormell, *Sir John Seeley and the Uses of History*, pp. 98, 168–9.

29. Freeman, 'Imperial Federation', passim; Burgess, 'Imperial Federation: Edward Freeman and the intellectual debate', pp. 82–4.

30. Edward Freeman to James Bryce, 16 January 1887: quoted in ibid., p. 88.

31. Lord Norton, Lord Bury and Henry Thring are good examples: see their articles in the *NC* in 1884–6.

32. William Clarke, 'An English Imperialist Bubble', *North American Review* (July, 1885): reprinted in Herbert Burrows and John A. Hobson (eds), *William Clarke: A Collection of His Writings, with a Biographical Sketch* (London, 1908), pp. 76–89. He repeated much of his earlier contentions, see William Clarke, 'The Future of the Canadian Dominion', *CR*, 38 (November, 1880): reprinted in ibid., pp. 129–58.

33. Clarke, 'An English Imperialist Bubble', p. 76.

34. Ibid., pp. 76–7.

35. Ibid., pp. 80–5.

36. See for instance John Merriman, 'The Closer Union of the Empire', *NC*, 21 (April, 1887), esp. pp. 510–11. Merriman was a member of the Cape Legislative Assembly and a close friend of Goldwin Smith's; he consistently opposed British imperialism in South Africa.

37. Forster, 'Imperial Federation', p. 201.

38. P. J. Cain, *Hobson and Imperialism: Radicalism, New Liberalism, and Finance 1887–1938* (Oxford, 2002), p. 54.

39. John Bright to John Morton, an Australian delegate who agreed with Bright, 7 February 1887: quoted in John Bright, *The Public Letters of the Right Hon. John Bright*, edited by H. J. Leech (2nd edn, London, 1895 [1885]), p. 228.

40. John Bright to the president of the Manchester Statistical Society, 12 January 1887: quoted in ibid., p. 227.

41. Freeman, 'Imperial Federation', p. 444; Burgess, 'Imperial Federation: Edward Freeman and the intellectual debate', pp. 85–6.

42. Seeley, *The Expansion of England*, p. 11.

43. Ibid., pp. 183–96.

44. Ibid., p. 236.

45. Smith, *Essays on Questions of the Day*, p. 144.

46. S. R. Mehrotra, 'Imperial Federation and India, 1868–1917', *Journal of Commonwealth Political Studies*, 1 (1961), p. 29.

47. Ibid., pp. 30, 32.

48. F. Seebohm, 'Imperialism and Socialism', *NC*, 7 (April, 1880), pp. 735–6.

49. Freeman, *Greater Greece and Greater Britain*, p. 106: quoted in Mehrotra, 'Imperial Federation and India', p. 31; see also Freeman, 'Imperial Federation', p. 430.

50. See J. L. Hammond, *Gladstone and the Irish Nation* (London, 1964 [1938]).

51. A. V. Dicey, 'Home Rule from an English Point of View', *CR*, 42 (July, 1882), pp. 85, 73.

52. Idem, *Lectures Introductory to the Study of the Law of the Constitution* (London, 1885); Stefan Collini, *Public Moralists: Political Thought and Intellectual Life in Britain 1850–1930* (Oxford, 1991), pp. 287–301.

53. Ibid., p. 291.

54. Ibid., p. 299.

55. Cain, *Hobson and Imperialism*, p. 54; James L. Sturgis, *John Bright and the Empire* (University of London Historical Studies XXVI, London, 1969), ch. 7; Smith, *Essays on Questions of the Day*, pp. 283–330; Leonard Courtney, 'Ireland', *CR* (April, 1886), pp. 457–70; G. P. Gooch, *Life of Lord Courtney* (London, 1920), ch. 12.

56. John Bright to a Liberal Unionist in Birmingham, 9 February 1887: quoted in Bright, *Public Letters*, p. 139.

57. Burgess, 'Imperial Federation: Edward Freeman and the Intellectual Debate', pp. 91–2. The ultimate decisive issue in 1893 was the division over imperial tariffs: E. H. H. Green, *The Crisis of Conservatism: The Politics, Economics and Ideology of the British Conservative Party, 1880–1914* (London and New York, 1995), p. 40; idem, 'Gentlemanly Capitalism and British Economic Policy, 1880–1914: The Debate over Bimetallism and Protectionism', in Raymond E. Dumett (ed.), *Gentlemanly Capitalism and British Imperialism: The New Debate on Empire* (London and New York, 1999), pp. 47–8.

58. H. C. G. Matthew, *The Liberal Imperialists: The Ideas and Politics of a Post-Gladstonian Élite* (Oxford Historical Monographs, London, 1973), pp. 152, 161–2. The quotation is from Edward Grey in *The Times*, 27 September 1900: quoted in ibid., p. 162. See also J. Compton Rickett, 'Liberalism and Empire', *CR*, 74 (August, 1898), pp. 290–6.

59. John M. Robertson, *Patriotism and Empire*: reprinted in Peter Cain (ed.), *The Empire and Its Critics, 1899–1939: Classics of Imperialism*, vol. I (London, 1998 [1899]), pp. 142–5.

60. Ibid., pp. 145–50.

Chapter 8   British Anti-Imperialists and Egyptian and Indian Nationalists

1. J. R. Seeley, *The Expansion of England: Two Courses of Lectures* (London, 1883), p. 227.

2. Henry Labouchere in *Truth*, 23 September 1897, p. 762: quoted in R. J. Hind, *Henry Labouchere and the Empire 1880–1905* (University of London Historical Studies XXXI, London, 1972), p. 16.

3. Joseph Chamberlain in January 1882: quoted in M. E. Chamberlain, 'Sir Charles Dilke and the British Intervention in Egypt, 1882: Decision Making in a Nineteenth-Century Cabinet, *British Journal of International Studies*, 2 (1976), p. 240.

4. Minute by Lord Kimberley, 28 June 1882: quoted in ibid., p. 241.

5. Ibid.

6. Joseph Chamberlain to John Bright, 31 December 1882: quoted in ibid., p. 242.

7. John Viscount Morley, *Recollections*, vol. II (London, 1917), p. 89.

8. Idem, 'Egyptian Policy: A Retrospect', *FR*, 32 (July, 1882), pp. 109–12.

9. Thomas Burt, 'Working Men and War', *FR*, 32 (December, 1882), pp. 726–7.

10. J. Seymour Keay, *Spoiling the Egyptians: A Tale of Shame, Told from the Blue Books* (3rd edn, revised and enlarged, London, 1882), preface.

11. Frederic Harrison in 1882: reprinted in Frederic Harrison, *National & Social Problems* (London, 1908), pp. 197–8.

12. See Martha S. Vogeler, *Frederic Harrison: The Vocations of a Positivist* (New York and Oxford, 1984), pp. 188–9.

13. Frederic Harrison, 'Money, Sir, Money', *Pall Mall Gazette*, 7 June 1882.

14. Wilfrid Scawen Blunt, *Secret History of the English Occupation of Egypt: Being a Personal Narrative of Events* (London, 1907), pp. 321–2.

15. Especially W. S. Blunt to William Gladstone, 20 February 1882; also Blunt to Earl Granville, 20 March 1882; translations of letters from Egyptian nationals to W. S. Blunt and William Gladstone; Blunt to Gladstone, 9 and 13 May 1882: all in Blunt, *Egypt: Letters to the Right Hon. W. E. Gladstone, M.P. and Others*, in Blunt Papers, PM 43–2004, FM.

16. W. S. Blunt to William Gladstone, 13 May 1882: ibid.

17. Blunt, *Secret History of the English Occupation of Egypt*, p. 173. The programme is printed in ibid., appendix 5 on pp. 556–9. Blunt later maintained that the publication of the programme in *The Times* simultaneously was Sir William Gregory's idea: ibid., p. 174.

18. Ibid., pp. 180–1.

19. Ibid., p. 235.

20. Ibid., p. 237.

21. Ibid., p. 173.

22. W. S. Blunt's diary entry 4 June 1882, in 'Alms to Oblivion', ch. 7 'The Wind and the Whirlwind': Blunt Papers, Ms 326–1975, pp. 10–11, FM.

23. Blunt, *Secret History of the English Occupation of Egypt*, p. 238.

24. Ibid., p. 239.

25. Ibid., p. 347.

26. Ibid., p. 348.

27. Ibid., p. 359; also in John Bright's diary, 29 June 1882: *The Diaries of John Bright*, edited by R. A. J. Walling (London, 1930), p. 484.

28. Blunt, *Secret History of the English Occupation of Egypt*, p. 360.

29. W. S. Blunt's diary entries on 5 and 13 July, in ibid., pp. 364, 369.

30. Ibid., p. 426.

31. Wilfrid Scawen Blunt, 'The Egyptian Revolution: A Personal Narrative', *NC*, 12 (September, 1882), p. 346.

32. General Gordon to W. S. Blunt, 3 August 1882: printed in Blunt, *Secret History of the English Occupation of Egypt*, pp. 427–8.

33. W. S. Blunt to Edward Hamilton, 17 September 1882: Blunt Papers, PM 47–2004, FM. More on Gordon and anti-imperialists, see Mira Matikkala, 'Anti-Imperialism, Englishness and Empire in Late-Victorian Britain' (unpublished PhD thesis, University of Cambridge, 2006), pp. 223–4.

34. Vogeler, *Frederic Harrison*, p. 190.

35. A. M. Broadley, *How We Defended Arábi and His Friends: A Story of Egypt and the Egyptians* (London, 1884).

36. John Bright to Frederic Harrison, 3 April 1883: Harrison Collection, 1/22, BLPES; Vogeler, *Frederic Harrison*, p. 190.

37. Hind, *Henry Labouchere and the Empire*, ch. 5; Algar Labouchere Thorold, *The Life of Henry Labouchere* (London, 1913), ch. 9.

38. W. S. Blunt's diary entry on 19 February 1885, in Wilfrid Scawen Blunt, *Gordon at Khartoum: Being a Personal Narrative of Events, in Continuation of 'A Secret History of the English Occupation of Egypt'* (London, 1911), pp. 378–9.

39. Ibid., p. 79. See also William H. Gregory, 'Egypt and the Soudan: On the Other Side of the Hill', *NC*, (March, 1885), pp. 424–36.

40. Wilfrid Scawen Blunt, 'The Wind and the Whirlwind' (1883), in idem, *The Poetical Works of Wilfrid Scawen Blunt: A Complete Edition*, vol. II (London, 1914), p. 233.

41. Wilfrid Scawen Blunt, *Ideas about India* (London, 1885); idem, *India Under Ripon: A Private Diary* (London, 1909); idem, *The Land War in Ireland: Being a Personal Narrative of Events, in Continuation of 'A Secret History of the English Occupation of Egypt'* (London, 1912).

42. W. S. Blunt's Autograph diaries, 28 March 1887: Blunt Papers, Ms 337–1975, p. 87, FM.

43. W. S. Blunt's Autograph diaries, 26 June 1888: Blunt Papers, Ms 340–1975, p. 31, FM.

44. See Wilfrid Scawen Blunt, *My Diaries, Being a Personal Narrative of Events 1888–1914* (2 vols, London, 1919).

45. Herbert Spencer, *An Autobiography*, vol. II (London, 1904), p. 376.

46. Robert D. Osborn, 'The Value of Egypt to Great Britain', *CR*, 41 (January, 1882), pp. 27–36; idem, 'Representative Government for India', *CR*, 42 (December, 1882), pp. 931–53.

47. Ibid., p. 931.

48. Ibid., p. 932.

49. Ibid., p. 940.

50. H. V. Brasted, 'The Irish Connection: The Irish Outlook on Indian Nationalism 1870–1906', in Kenneth Ballhatchet and David Taylor (eds), *Changing South Asia: Politics and Government* (London, 1984), p. 68.

51. *Irish World*, 23 April 1881, quoted in ibid; see also ibid., p. 71.

52. Brasted, 'The Irish Connection', p. 69; see also idem, 'Indian Nationalist Development and the Influence of Irish Home Rule, 1870–1886', *Modern Asian Studies*, 1 (1980), pp. 37–63.

53. F. Hugh O'Donnell, *A History of the Irish Parliamentary Party*, vol. II (Kennikat Series in Irish History and Culture, New York and London, 1970 [1910]), pp. 425–6.

54. See his account on this in ibid., pp. 423–45. O'Donnell was certain that the British could not rule India without the Irish, whom he regarded as important mediators between the Indians and the British.

55. Ibid., pp. 426–7.

56. Ibid., p. 429.

57. Ibid., p. 442.

58. Ibid., p. 444. Italics added.

59. Ibid., pp. 444–5.

60. John E. Redmond, 'Home Rule – Its Real Meaning: Lecture delivered in Melbourne, July 1883', in idem, *Historical and Political Addresses 1883–97* (Dublin, 1898), p. 182.

61. Alfred Webb to the editor of *Freeman's Journal*, 26 December 1885: quoted in Brasted, 'The Irish Connection', p. 71.

62. Ibid., pp. 71–2.

63. Blunt, *Ideas about India*, p. vii.

64. Anthony Denholm, *Lord Ripon 1827–1909: A Political Biography* (London, 1982), p. 139.

65. Ibid., pp. 149–52; S. Gopal, *The Viceroyalty of Lord Ripon 1880–1884* (Oxford Historical Series: British Series, London, 1953), passim; Lucien Wolf, *Life of the First Marquess of Ripon*, vol. II (London, 1921), chs 14–21.

66. Denholm, *Lord Ripon*, pp. 154–5. On European racism in India, the administration of justice from the 1820s to the mid-1880s, and the emergence of Indian nationalism, see Nemai Sadhan Bose, *Racism, Struggle for Equality and Indian Nationalism* (Calcutta, 1981).

67. *The Times*, 5 February 1883; Edwin Hirschmann, *'White Mutiny': The Ilbert Bill Crisis in India and Genesis of the Indian National Congress* (New Delhi, 1980); Chandrika Kaul, 'England and India: the Ilbert Bill, 1883: a case study of the Metropolitan Press', *Indian Economic and Social History Review*, 30 (1993), pp. 413–36; Sir James Fitzjames Stephen, *Letters on the Ilbert Bill: Reprinted from the "Times"* (London, 1883); *The Ilbert Bill: A Collection of Letters, Speeches, Memorials, Articles, etc. Stating the Objections to the Bill* (London, 1883).

68. Hirschmann, *'White Mutiny'*, pp. 49, 104, 193.

69. *The Times*, 10 April 1883.

70. *Lord Ripon and the People of India: Proceedings of the Public Meeting Held in Willis's Rooms, London, on Wednesday, August 1st, 1883* (London, 1883).

71. Lord Ripon to John Bright, 27 August 1883: Bright Papers, Add. Mss 43389, ff. 349–52, BL.

72. Sir Arthur Hobhouse, 'Native Indian Judges: Mr. Ilbert's Bill', *CR*, 43 (June, 1883), pp. 795–812; L. T. Hobhouse and J. L. Hammond, *Lord Hobhouse: A Memoir* (London, 1905), pp. 105–6; Florence Nightingale to Lord Ripon, 29 June 1883: Ripon Papers, Add. Mss 43546, f. 197, BL; Florence Nightingale, 'Our Indian Stewardship', *NC*, 14 (August, 1883), pp. 329–38; Sir Edward Cook, *The Life of Florence Nightingale*, vol. II (London, 1913), pp. 330–40.

73. Blunt, *Secret History of the English Occupation of Egypt*, p. 77.

74. H. J. S. Cotton, *England and India: An Address delivered at the Positivist School, Chapel Street, London, on June 27, 1883* (London, 1883), pp. 28–9, 35; see also idem, *New India, or India in Transition* (London, 1885).

75. William Digby, 'English Political Organizations and Indian Reform: A Record of What Has Been Attempted', *India*, No. 15 (5 December, 1890), p. 295. See also Howard LeRoy Malchow, *Agitators and Promoters in the Age of Gladstone and Disraeli: A Biographical Dictionary of the Leaders of British*

Pressure Groups Founded between 1865 and 1886 (Garland Reference Library of Social Science, vol. 176, New York and London, 1983), pp. xvii, 62, 241–2.

76. See Mira Matikkala, 'William Digby and the British Radical Debate on India from the 1880s to the 1890s' (unpublished MPhil dissertation, University of Cambridge, 2004).

77. Lord Ripon to William Digby, 31 December 1884: Ripon Papers, Add. Mss 43635, f. 140, BL.

78. William Digby to Herbert Gladstone, 12 December 1884: Viscount Gladstone Papers, Add. Mss 46051, f. 37, BL.

79. William Digby, *India for the Indians – and for England* (London, 1885), passim; the quotation is from ibid., p. xv.

80. Ibid., p. 22.

81. Ibid., pp. 204–5.

82. Ibid., pp. 213–15.

83. Ibid., pp. 224–47.

84. *The Times*, 22 September 1885.

85. William Digby to Herbert Gladstone, 12 December 1884: Viscount Gladstone Papers, Add. Mss 46051, f. 37, BL. Their differences on the matter become clearer in Digby's letter to Herbert Gladstone, 19 April 1885: Viscount Gladstone Papers, Add. Mss 46051, f. 110, BL; see Matikkala, 'William Digby and the British Radical Debate on India', p. 59.

86. Digby, *India for the Indians – and for England*, pp. 199–202.

87. Cotton, *New India, or India in Transition*.

88. Denholm, *Lord Ripon*, pp. 140–1.

89. Annie Besant, *England, India, and Afghanistan* (London, 1878): quoted in Anne Taylor, *Annie Besant: A Biography* (Oxford, 1992), p. 134.

90. Briton Martin, *New India, 1885: British Official Policy and the Emergence of the Indian National Congress* (Berkeley, 1969), pp. 194–5; Sir William Wedderburn, *Allan Octavian Hume: Father of the Indian National Congress, 1829–1912* (Oxford, 2002 [1913]), p. 47.

91. S. R. Mehrotra, *A History of the Indian National Congress, Vol. I, 1885–1918* (New Delhi, 1995), pp. 22–30.

92. See for instance 'The Congress Programme', *India*, No. 1 (February, 1890), p. 15.

93. Dadabhai Naoroji at the Indian National Congress in Bombay, 29 December 1885: quoted in Mehrotra, *A History of the Indian National Congress*, p. 25.

94. Henry Fawcett had demanded simultaneous examinations to be held in Calcutta, Madras, Bombay, and London already in 1868: John Wood, 'Henry Fawcett and the British Empire', *The Indian Economic and Social History Review*, 16 (1979), p. 409.

95. N. N. Sen at the Indian National Congress in Bombay, 28 December 1885: quoted in Mehrotra, *A History of the Indian National Congress*, pp. 22–3.

96. The second day resolution of the Indian National Congress in Bombay, 29 December 1885: quoted in ibid., p. 23.

97. Lord Ripon to William Gladstone, 6 October 1882: quoted in Gopal, *The Viceroyalty of Lord Ripon*, p. 99.

98. The second day resolution of the Indian National Congress in Bombay, 29 December 1885: quoted in Mehrotra, *A History of the Indian National Congress*, p. 23.

99. Cotton, *New India, or India in Transition*, p. 94.

100. R. P. Masani, *Dadabhai Naoroji: The Grand Old Man of India* (London, 1939), p. 96.

101. Naoroji's notes, 19 April 1886, quoted in ibid., p. 233.

102. Naoroji's notes, 29 April 1886, quoted in ibid., p. 234.

103. A memo 'Madras Government – Attacks On': Sir Mountstuart Grant Duff Collection, Mss Eur. F234/96, pp. 1–20, OIOC.

104. The quotation is from Sir George Birdwood's writing in the *Overland Mail* (November, 1885): quoted with approval in the memo 'Madras Government – Attacks On': Sir Mountstuart Grant Duff Collection, Mss Eur. F234/96, p. 12, OIOC.

105. *India*, No. 1 (February, 1890), p. 16.

106. William Digby to Pherozeshah Mehta, 24 April 1888: quoted in Margot Duley Morrow, 'The Origins and Early Years of the British Committee of the Indian National Congress, 1885–1907' (unpublished PhD thesis, University of London, 1977), p. 30. An annual fee of £250 would have been equivalent to an average pay for a professional party agent: see Kathryn Rix, 'The party agent and English electoral culture, 1880–1906' (unpublished PhD thesis, University of Cambridge, 2002), p. 170.

107. *India*, No. 15 (5 December, 1890), p. 296.

108. William Digby's account of the campaign to Lord Ripon, 10 November 1888: Ripon Papers, Add. Mss 43636, f. 149, BL.

109. Wedderburn, *Allan Octavian Hume*, p. 71; Dadabhai Naoroji to D. E. Wacha, 27 July and 31 August 1888: quoted in Masani, *Dadabhai Naoroji*, p. 306; A. O. Hume to the Indian Nationalists, 10 February 1889: quoted in Wedderburn, *Allan Octavian Hume*, p. 70; D. E. Wacha to Dadabhai Naoroji, 22 February 1889: quoted in Dadabhai Naoroji, *Correspondence, Vol. II: Part I. Correspondence with D. E. Wacha, 4.11.1884 to 23.3.1895,* edited with an introduction and notes by R. P. Patwardhan (Bombay, 1977), p. 148.

110. Lord Ripon to Sir William Wedderburn, 7 March 1889: Ripon Papers, Add. Mss 43618, f. 3, BL.

111. A. O. Hume to Dadabhai Naoroji, 12 December 1887: quoted in Mehrotra, *A History of the Indian National Congress*, p. 117.

112. A. O. Hume to the editor of the Allahabad *Morning Post*, 17 May 1888 (reproduced in the *Indian Mirror*, 23 May 1888): quoted in ibid.

113. Naoroji's notes, 15 April 1886: quoted in Masani, *Dadabhai Naoroji*, p. 229.

114. Herbert Spencer to Behramji M. Malabari, 20 July 1890: quoted in David Duncan, *The Life and Letters of Herbert Spencer*: reprinted in *Herbert Spencer: Collected Writings*, vol. II (London, 1996 [1908]), p. 296.

115. Herbert Spencer to Kentaro Kaneko, 26 August 1892: quoted in ibid. p. 321.

116. Anil Seal, *The Emergence of Indian Nationalism: Competition and Collaboration in the Later Nineteenth Century* (Cambridge, 1968), p. 346.

117. Wedderburn, *Allan Octavian Hume*, pp. 63–4.

118. Edward Moulton, 'William Wedderburn and Early Indian Nationalism, 1870–1917', in Ballhatchet and Taylor (eds), *Changing South Asia*, p. 37.

119. On the Committee's moderate lines, see Margot Duley Morrow, 'The British Committee of the Indian National Congress as an Issue in and an Influence upon Nationalist Politics, 1889–1901', in Ballhatchet and Taylor (eds), *Changing South Asia*, pp. 55–66; Morrow, 'The Origins and Early Years of the British Committee of the Indian National Congress'.

120. See the discussion on this in Matikkala, 'Anti-imperialism, Englishness and empire in late-Victorian Britain', pp. 247–52.

121. Samuel Smith, *My Life-Work*, (London, 1902), p. 225n.

122. Charles Bradlaugh's speech at Northampton, 27 April 1890: quoted in Morrow, 'The Origins and Early Years of the British Committee of the Indian National Congress', p. 62.

123. Dadabhai Naoroji to D. E. Wacha, 29 August 1890: quoted in Masani, *Dadabhai Naoroji*, p. 311.

124. William Digby to *The Hindu*, 27 December 1889: quoted in William Digby, *Indian Politics in England: The Story of an Indian Reform Bill in Parliament Told Week by Week; with Other Matters of Interest to Indian Reformers* (Lucknow, 1890), p. 72.

125. Sir Richard Garth, *A Few Plain Truths about India* (London, 1888), pp. 10, 12.

126. Richard Cobden quoted in John Morley, *The Life of Richard Cobden*, vol. II (Jubilee edn, London, 1896 [1879]), p. 207; see also ibid., pp. 205–17, 360–1.

127. S. K. Ratcliffe, *Sir William Wedderburn and the Indian Reform Movement* (London, 1923), p. 11. Italics added.

Chapter 9   India, Africa, and Imperialism in British Party Politics

1. Sir George Campbell spoke in Wedderburn's support, but with strong reservations. The debate in the House of Commons, 13 February 1880: *Hansard's Parliamentary Debates*, 3rd ser., vol. CCL, pp. 593–604.

2. Martin Pugh, 'Lancashire, Cotton, and Indian Reform: Conservative Controversies in the 1930s', *Twentieth Century British History*, 15 (2004), p. 144.

3. Briton Martin, *New India, 1885: British Official Policy and the Emergence of the Indian National Congress* (Berkeley, 1969), p. 215.

4. Sir William Wilson Hunter, 'The Present Problem in India', *CR*, 54 (September, 1888), p. 323.

5. Letter to Florence Nightingale, 4 January 1885: quoted in Sir Edward Cook, *The Life of Florence Nightingale*, vol. II (London, 1913), p. 345. See also Sarvepalli Gopal, 'Gladstone and India', in Donovan Williams and E. Daniel Potts (eds), *Essays in Indian History: In Honour of Cuthbert Collin Davies* (London, 1973), pp. 1–16.

6. William Digby, *Indian Problems for English Consideration, a Letter to the Council of the National Liberal Federation* (Birmingham, 1881), pp. 51–3. The pamphlet was published by the National Liberal Federation and 10 000 copies of it were distributed among Liberal associations: William Digby, 'English Political Organizations and Indian Reform: A Record of What Has Been Attempted', *India*, No. 15 (5 December, 1890), p. 293.

7. Ibid., pp. 293, 295.

8. William Digby, *The General Election, 1885: India's Interest in the British Ballot Box* (London, 1885), pp. v–vi.

9. Ibid., p. 3.

10. Ibid., p. 9.

11. W. S. Blunt to Randolph Churchill, 8 June 1885: Blunt Papers, Ms 389–1977, FM.

12. W. S. Blunt's Autograph diaries, 21 May 1885: Blunt Papers, Ms 333–1975, p. 10, FM.

13. Frederic Pincott, 'Why Conservatives Should Support the Indian Congress', *India*, No. 1 (February, 1890), pp. 2–3.

14. He was a Liberal candidate for Kidderminster in 1886 and for Deptford (Lalmohan Ghose's constituency in 1885 and 1886) at a by-election in 1888, receiving 46.3% and 48.4% of the votes against a Conservative competitor: F. W. S. Craig (ed.), *British Parliamentary Election Results 1885–1918* (London, 1974), pp. 8, 12, 126.

15. W. S. Blunt to the electors of North Camberwell, 7 August 1885: an enclosure in Blunt's 'Indian memoirs' IV: Blunt Papers, Ms 28–1975, p. 148, FM.

16. Craig (ed.), *British Parliamentary Election Results 1885–1918*, p. 12.

17. S. R. Mehrotra, *A History of the Indian National Congress, Vol. I, 1885–1918* (New Delhi, 1995), p. 13.

18. Martin, *New India, 1885*, p. 215.

19. 'An Appeal from the People of India to the Electors of Great Britain and Ireland': see ibid., pp. 228–9.

20. See ibid., pp. 223–5.

21. Ibid., pp. 230–9; R. F. Foster, *Lord Randolph Churchill: A Political Life* (Oxford, 1981), pp. 202–3.

22. Mehrotra, *A History of the Indian National Congress*, p. 13; Martin, *New India, 1885*, pp. 260–3. Digby secured 1,797 votes (42.0 %) in North Paddington against his Conservative competitor's 2,482 votes (58.0 %): Craig (ed.), *British Parliamentary Election Results 1885–1918*, p. 38.

23. Mehrotra, *A History of the Indian National Congress*, p. 27.

24. Martin, *New India, 1885*, p. 265.

25. Randolph Churchill to Lord Dufferin, 27 November 1885: quoted in Martin, *New India, 1885*, pp. 271–2; see also Foster, *Lord Randolph Churchill*, pp. 204–5.

26. Florence Nightingale to Sir William Wedderburn, 27 November 1885: Florence Nightingale Collection, Mss Eur. B151, OIOC.

27. F. Hugh O'Donnell, *A History of the Irish Parliamentary Party*, vol. II (Kennikat Series in Irish History and Culture, New York and London, 1970 [1910]), p. 428.

28. Ibid., p. 428; see also R. P. Masani, *Dadabhai Naoroji: The Grand Old Man of India* (London, 1939), pp. 240–7.

29. Naoroji's notes, 15 April, 1886: quoted in ibid., p. 230.

30. Sir George Birdwood to Dadabhai Naoroji, undated (June 1886): quoted in ibid., p. 240.

31. Evans Bell to Dadabhai Naoroji, 21 and 23 June 1886: Naoroji Papers, Microfilm Acc. No. 404, B–81 (8–9), NAI; John Slagg to Dadabhai Naoroji, 16 April 1886: Naoroji Papers, Microfilm Acc. No. 443, S–166, NAI; Wilfrid Scawen Blunt's Autograph diaries, 24 June 1886: Blunt Papers, Ms 335–1975, pp. 127–8, FM; James L. Sturgis, *John Bright and the Empire* (University of London Historical Studies XXVI, London, 1969), pp. 76–7.

32. W. T. Stead to Dadabhai Naoroji, 21 June 1886: Naoroji Papers, Microfilm Acc. No. 443, S–263, NAI.

33. Herbert J. Gladstone, 'A First Visit to India', *NC*, 22 (July, 1887), pp. 133, 140.

34. 'Mr. William Digby's interview with Right Hon. W. E. Gladstone', 8 April 1889, in [William Digby (ed.)], *India in England, Volume II: Being a collection of Speeches Delivered and Articles Written on the Indian National Congress, in England in 1889*, with an introductory essay by Pandit Bishen Narayan Dar (Lucknow, 1889), p. 61.

35. Ibid., p. 66.

36. Frederic Harrison's speech 'Toast of the Empire' at the National Liberal Club Dinner, 21 January 1889: Harrison Collection, 2/8, BLPES; Martha S. Vogeler, *Frederic Harrison: The Vocations of a Positivist* (New York and Oxford, 1984), p. 232. The banquet was chaired by Lord Ripon: see 'Dinner to Mr. Dadabhai Naoroji', in *The Times*, 22 January 1889.

37. Letters and telegrams from Charles Bradlaugh to William Digby, December 1889 – January 1891: William Digby Collection, Mss Eur D767/7, OIOC. On Bradlaugh and India, see John M. Robertson, 'Charles Bradlaugh: An Account of His Parliamentary Struggle, Politics and Teachings', in Hypatia Bradlaugh Bonner, *Charles Bradlaugh: A Record of His Life and Work*, vol. II (London, 1895), p. 198–200, 409–12, 416; and Bradlaugh's India Councils Bill, Sankar Ghose, *The Western Impact on Indian Politics (1885–1919)* (Bombay, 1967), pp. 29–35.

38. For the preparations for the bill, see letters and telegrams from Charles Bradlaugh to William Digby, December 1889–January 1891 in William Digby Collection, Mss Eur D767/7, OIOC; for details of the bill and its supporters, see *India*, No. 1 (February, 1890), p. 10.

39. Lord Cross presented the bill in the House of Lords on 21 February 1890: *Hansard's Parliamentary Debates*, 3rd ser., vol. CCCXLI, pp. 862–70. On the preparations and background of the bill, see R. J. Moore, 'The Twilight of the Whigs and the Reform of the Indian Councils, 1886–1892', *The Historical Journal*, 10 (1967), pp. 400–14.

40. *Hansard's Parliamentary Debates*, 3rd ser., vol. CCCXLII, pp. 61–103; *India*, No. 3 (18 March, 1890), pp. 45–56.

41. William Digby, *Indian Politics in England: The Story of an Indian Reform Bill in Parliament Told Week by Week; with Other Matters of Interest to Indian Reformers* (Lucknow, 1890), pp. 56–7, 137; *India*, No. 10 (4 July, 1890), pp. 201–3; *India*, No. 11 (25 July, 1890), p. 223; *India*, No. 12 (29 August, 1890), p. 231.

42. William Digby's notes of an interview with Lord Ripon, 10 November 1888: Ripon Papers, Add. Mss 43636, f. 156, BL. The delegates were A. O. Hume, Surendranath Banerjea, Pherozeshah Mehta, M. Ghose, W. C. Bonnerjee, Mr Sharifuddin, Eardley Norton, and R. N. Mudholkar: Surendranath Banerjea, *A Nation in Making: Being the Reminiscences of Fifty Years of Public Life* (London, 1925), p. 103.

43. *India*, No. 4 (11 April, 1890).

44. Charles Bradlaugh to William Digby, 8 February 1890: William Digby Collection, Mss Eur D767/7, OIOC; *India*, No. 5 (25 April, 1890), pp. 87–93.

45. Banerjea, *A Nation in Making*, pp. 105–8; *India*, Nos 6–8 (6 and 23 May, 6 June, 1890); Masani, *Dadabhai Naoroji*, pp. 310–11.

46. *India*, No. 9 (21 June, 1890), p. 175.

47. Lord Ripon to John Morley, 1 January 1889: Ripon Papers, Add. Mss 43541, f. 52, BL; also John Morley to Lord Ripon, 30 December 1888: Ripon Papers, Add. Mss 43541, f. 49, BL.

48. S. Maccoby, *English Radicalism 1886–1914* (London, 1953), pp. 425–6; *India*, No. 28 (11 March, 1892); *India*, No. 29 (15 April, 1892).

49. Telegram from Dadabhai Naoroji to William Digby, 6 June 1891: Naoroji Papers, Microfilm Acc. No. 432, N–1 (1841), NAI.

50. Letters and telegrams from Dadabhai Naoroji to William Digby, Naoroji's notes, newspaper cuttings, and other related material from 1889 to 1892: William Digby Collection, Mss Eur D767/1, 767/2–6, OIOC; William Digby's letters to Dadabhai Naoroji: Naoroji Papers, Microfilm Acc. No. 410, D–118, NAI. Naoroji's campaign was far from smooth: see Dadabhai Naoroji, *Mr. D. Naoroji and Mr. Schnadhorst* [An explanation by the former concerning his candidature for Central Finsbury] (London, 1892); idem, *The First Indian Member of the Imperial Parliament, Being a Collection of the Main Incidents Relating to the Election of Mr. Dadabhai Naoroji to Parliament* (Madras, 1892); Masani, *Dadabhai Naoroji*, pp. 270–5.

51. On his campaign and programme, see William Digby, *The General Election of 1892, South Islington: I. Address of the Liberal Candidate, Wm Digby, C.I.E. II. Mr. Digby's 'Record'* (London, 1892). He achieved 2873 votes (47.4 per cent) in South Islington, against his Conservative competitor's 3194 votes (52.6 per cent): Craig (ed.), *British Parliamentary Election Results 1885–1918*, p. 25. Naoroji achieved only five votes more than his Conservative competitor in Central Finsbury: ibid., p. 13.

52. Sir William Wedderburn, *Allan Octavian Hume: Father of the Indian National Congress, 1829–1912* (Oxford, 2002 [1913]), pp. 76–7; S. K. Ratcliffe, *Sir William Wedderburn and the Indian Reform Movement* (London, 1923), p. 75.

53. Margot Duley Morrow, 'The Origins and Early Years of the British Committee of the Indian National Congress, 1885–1907'(unpublished PhD thesis, University of London, 1977), pp. 34, 136–59.

54. Ratcliffe, *Sir William Wedderburn and the Indian Reform Movement*, p. 103.

55. Smith had turned to Naoroji for advice especially at the time of Indian budget debates: Samuel Smith to Dadabhai Naoroji, 12 and 23 June 1886: Naoroji Papers, Microfilm Acc. No. 443, S–182 and S–182 (1), NAI; Masani, *Dadabhai Naoroji*, pp. 288–9.

56. Sir Charles Wentworth Dilke, *Problems of Greater Britain*, vol. II (London, 1890), pp. 102–3.

57. Morrow, 'The Origins and Early Years of the British Committee of the Indian National Congress', pp. 130–3.

58. Lord Kimberley to Lord Lansdowne, 9 June 1893: quoted in ibid., p. 133.

59. Arnold P. Kaminsky, *The India Office, 1880–1910* (Contributions in Comparative Colonial Studies No 20, New York, 1986), p. 160; on the India Office and the pressure groups, see ibid., ch. 6.

60. The debate in the House of Commons, 2, 5, 8, 15, and 22 June 1893: *Hansard's Parliamentary Debates*, 4th ser., vol. XIII, pp. 102–40, 203–5, 535–6, 1076–7, 1678; and in the House of Lords, 13 June 1893, ibid., pp. 871–9.

61. Dadabhai Naoroji's fourth note to the Royal Commission on Indian Expenditure, 15 February 1896: quoted in Masani, *Dadabhai Naoroji*, p. 382.

62. Dadabhai Naoroji's evidence for the Royal Commission on Indian Expenditure, n.d.: quoted in ibid., p. 387.

63. On the Commission, see Romesh Chunder Dutt, *The Economic History of India in the Victorian Age: From the Accession of Queen Victoria in 1837 to the Commencement of the Twentieth Century* (Trübner's Oriental Series vol. 6, London, 2000 [reprint of the 7th edn 1950; 1st edn 1903]), pp. 555–77; Masani, *Dadabhai Naoroji*, pp. 375–91; B. R. Nanda, *Gokhale: The Indian Moderates and the British Raj* (Princeton, 1977), pp. 93–101, 157.

64. On his views on the matter in the late 1870s, see L. T. Hobhouse and J. L. Hammond, *Lord Hobhouse: A Memoir* (London, 1905), pp. 81–6.

65. Sir Arthur Hobhouse Shortly After His Return from India in 1877: quoted in ibid., pp. 82, 84–5.

66. The First South African War had also caused some minor divisions inside the party in 1877–81, when Leonard Courtney, G. W. E. Russell, Frederic Harrison, and Sir Wilfrid Lawson campaigned actively in favour of British withdrawal from Transvaal: Arthur Davey, *The British Pro-Boers 1877–1902* (Cape Town, 1978), ch. 2.

67. John Bright's diary, 19 May 1882: *The Diaries of John Bright*, edited by R. A. J. Walling (London, 1930), 8 July 1882, p. 485.

68. Ibid., 13 and 24 July 1882, pp. 487, 489.

69. Ibid., 14 July 1882, pp. 487–8.

70. See letters from John Bright to Richard Congreve, 1858–84: Positivist Papers, Add. Mss 45241, ff. 13–29, BL; especially John Bright to Richard Congreve, 31 October 1873: Positivist Papers, Add. Mss 45241, ff. 25–6, BL; John Bright to Richard Congreve, 26 September 1876: Positivist Papers, Add. Mss 45241, f. 27, BL.

71. John Bright to Richard Congreve, 5 March 1884: Positivist Papers, Add. Mss 45241, ff. 28–9, BL.

72. Wilfrid Scawen Blunt, *Gordon at Khartoum: Being a Personal Narrative of Events, in Continuation of 'A Secret History of the English Occupation of Egypt'* (London, 1911), p. 28. On Lawson's account of the Egyptian question in 1882, see Sir Wilfrid Lawson, *A Memoir*, edited by George W. E. Russell (London, 1909), pp. 165–7.

73. W. S. Blunt to Randolph Churchill, 8 June 1885: Blunt Papers, Ms 389–1977, FM. Some correspondence between Blunt and Churchill in 1882–5 has been printed in Blunt, *Gordon at Khartoum*, appendix D on pp. 608–17; Blunt's correspondence with Downing Street in 1882–5 is printed in ibid., appendix C on pp. 568–607.

74. Foster, *Lord Randolph Churchill*, pp. 111, 120.

75. R. J. Hind, *Henry Labouchere and the Empire 1880–1905* (University of London Historical Studies **XXXI**, London, 1972), p. 3.

76. Until the autumn of 1882, Labouchere supported the intervention. On Labouchere and Gladstone's Egyptian policy at large, see Algar Labouchere Thorold, *The Life of Henry Labouchere* (London, 1913), ch. 9; Hind, *Henry Labouchere and the Empire*, ch. 5.

77. W. S. Blunt's diary, 4 April 1884: quoted in Blunt, *Gordon at Khartoum*, p. 213.

78. W. S. Blunt's diary, 4 June 1884: quoted in ibid., pp. 251–2.

79. Henry Labouchere in the House of Commons, in the context of the debate on annexations in Zululand, 19 May 1887: *Hansard's Parliamentary Debates*, 3rd ser., vol. CCCXV, p. 529.

80. G. P. Gooch, *Life of Lord Courtney* (London, 1920), p. 220.

81. D. A. Hamer, *John Morley: Liberal Intellectual in Politics* (Oxford, 1968), pp. 143–4.

82. John Morley to Joseph Chamberlain, 14 February 1885: quoted in ibid., p. 143.

83. The Journal of Kate Courtney, February 1885: quoted in Gooch, *Life of Lord Courtney*, p. 222.

84. W. S. Blunt's diary, 21 February 1885: quoted in Blunt, *Gordon at Khartoum*, pp. 382–3.

85. W. S. Blunt's diary, 12 March 1885: quoted in ibid., p. 399; see also his diary on 23 March 1885: quoted in ibid., p. 402.

86. Sir Wilfrid Lawson to Leonard Courtney, 15 February 1885: quoted in Gooch, *Life of Lord Courtney*, p. 223.

87. Frederic Harrison to Leonard Courtney, 14 February 1885: quoted in ibid.

88. Frederic Harrison to John Morley, 13 February 1885: Harrison Collection, 1/65, BLPES. He gave slightly different numbers to Courtney, calculating that there would easily be 'above thirty to forty English M.P.'s enabling you to be independent of W. Lawson, Labby [Labouchere] and Irish': Frederic

Harrison to Leonard Courtney, 14 February 1885: quoted in Gooch, *Life of Lord Courtney*, p. 223.

89. Frederic Harrison to Leonard Courtney, 14 February 1885: quoted in ibid.

90. Sir William Harcourt to W. S. Blunt, 16 December 1891: Blunt Papers, Ms 52–1975, FM.

91. W. S. Blunt to Sir William Harcourt, 31 July 1892: Blunt Papers, Ms 963–1977, FM.

92. He wrote mainly to Henry Labouchere, Sir William Harcourt, Lord Randolph Churchill, and William Gladstone: the letters are copied in his Autograph diaries, December 1892 – May 1893: Blunt Papers, Ms 302–1976 and 309–1976, FM.

93. Joseph Chamberlain to Sir Charles Dilke, 18 January 1892: quoted in M. E. Chamberlain, 'Sir Charles Dilke and the British intervention in Egypt, 1882: decision making in a nineteenth-century cabinet', *British Journal of International Studies*, 2 (1976), p. 243.

94. H. C. G. Matthew, *The Liberal Imperialists: The Ideas and Politics of a Post-Gladstonian Élite* (Oxford Historical Monographs, London, 1973), p. 133.

95. Edward Spencer Beesly, 'Wei-Hai-Wei', *PR*, 6 (May, 1898), p. 86.

96. Ibid., p. 88.

97. Frederic Harrison to John Morley, 31 August 1899: Harrison Collection, 1/74, BLPES.

98. Francis Hirst's diary, 8 September 1899: quoted in Francis W. Hirst, *In the Golden Days* (London, 1947), p. 179.

99. The meeting was organised by C. P. Scott and L. T. Hobhouse. See John Viscount Morley, *Recollections*, vol. II (London, 1917), pp. 85–7; Gooch, *Life of Lord Courtney*, pp. 369–70.

100. *Manchester Guardian* quoted in ibid., p. 372.

101. Morley, *Recollections*, II, p. 86.

102. Sir William Harcourt to John Morley, 22 September 1899: quoted in ibid., p. 87.

103. Sir William Harcourt to Mrs Morley, 19 October 1899: quoted in ibid.

104. Herbert Spencer to Leonard Courtney, 13 September 1899: quoted in Gooch, *Life of Lord Courtney*, pp. 372–3. See also ibid., pp. 378, 380, and Herbert Spencer to John Morley, 10 November 1901: quoted in David Duncan, *The Life and Letters of Herbert Spencer*: reprinted in *Herbert Spencer: Collected Writings*, vol. II (London, 1996 [1908]), p. 451.

105. *The Annual Register: A Review of Public Events at Home and Abroad for the Year 1899* (London, 1900), p. 7.

106. Sir Henry Campbell-Bannerman to Richard Burdon Haldane, 29 December 1898: quoted in Peter Stansky, *Ambitions and Strategies: The Struggle for the Leadership of the Liberal Party in the 1890s* (Oxford, 1964), p. 285.

107. Matthew, *The Liberal Imperialists*, pp. 34–5.

108. J. Guinness Rogers, 'Liberal Imperialism and the Transvaal War', *CR*, 76 (December, 1899), p. 900.

109. Idem, 'Shall Uganda Be Retained?', *NC*, 33 (February, 1893), pp. 219–34.

110. Rogers, 'Liberal Imperialism and the Transvaal War', p. 903.

111. Ibid., p. 908. He referred to John Morley's speech at Manchester and to the new edition of James Bryce, *Impressions of South Africa* (3rd rev. edn, London, 1899 [1897]).

112. [Anon.], 'A Lead for Liberalism', *FR*, 68 (September, 1900), p. 457.

113. Ibid., p. 461.

114. Ibid., pp. 464–5, 467.

115. Ibid., p. 469.

116. A Liberal without Adjectives, 'The Future of the Liberal Party', *FR*, 68 (December, 1900), p. 934.

117. John Morley to Leonard Courtney, 8 March 1900: quoted in Gooch, *Life of Lord Courtney*, pp. 403–4.

118. John Morley to Leonard Courtney, 5 April 1900: quoted in ibid., p. 404.

119. John Morley, *Liberal Principles and Imperialism: A Speech by the Right Hon. John Morley, M.P., at Oxford, June 9, 1900* (National Reform Union Pamphlets, Manchester, 1900), p. 10.

120. See Lawson's account of the parliamentary session of 1900 in Lawson, *A Memoir*, pp. 252–3.

121. Ibid., p. 253.

122. See Paul Readman, 'The Conservative Party, Patriotism, and British Politics: The Case of the General Election of 1900', *Journal of British Studies*, 40 (2001), pp. 107–45; Matthew, *The Liberal Imperialists*, p. 133; also John W. Auld, 'The Liberal Pro-Boers', *Journal of British Studies*, 14 (1975), pp. 78–99.

123. *Daily Mail*, 6 October 1900: quoted in Readman, 'The Conservative Party, Patriotism, and British Politics', p. 140.

124. Anonymous postcard to Leonard Courtney, stamped in London, 21 March 1900: Courtney Collection, vol. VII, f. 164, BLPES. W. T. Stead, to whom the writer referred alongside Courtney, led the Stop-the-War-Committee.

125. Stefan Collini, *Liberalism and Sociology: L. T. Hobhouse and Political Argument in England 1880–1914* (Cambridge, 1979), p. 85. Hobhouse was, with C. P. Scott, somewhat disappointed in John Morley: ibid., p. 86.

126. William Clarke, 'The Rt. Hon. Leonard Courtney: A Character Sketch', *The Young Man* (August, 1900): reprinted in Herbert Burrows and John A. Hobson (eds), *William Clarke: A Collection of His Writings, with a Biographical Sketch* (London, 1908), p. 269.

127. Ibid., pp. 270–1, 273.
128. William Clarke, 'An English Imperialist Bubble', *North American Review* (July, 1885): reprinted in Burrows and Hobson (eds), *William Clarke*, p. 82.
129. See for instance Frederic Harrison, 'Empire and Humanity', *FR*, 27 (February, 1880), p. 299. Harrison was, nevertheless, a prominent figure in Liberal circles and stood unsuccessfully as a Liberal Irish home-ruler candidate for London University in 1886.
130. Harrison, 'Empire and Humanity', pp. 295–6.

Conclusions

1. Frederic Harrison, 'Empire and Humanity', *FR*, 27 (February, 1880), p. 294.

BIBLIOGRAPHY

I Manuscript Sources

THE BRITISH LIBRARY, London

Additional Manuscripts

John Bright Papers
Viscount Gladstone Papers
Positivist Papers
Lord Ripon Papers

Oriental and India Office Collections

Lord Curzon Collection
William Digby Collection
Sir Mountstuart Grant Duff Collection
Florence Nightingale Collection

THE BRITISH LIBRARY OF POLITICAL AND ECONOMIC SCIENCE, London

Leonard Courtney Collection
Frederic Harrison Collection

FITZWILLIAM MUSEUM, Cambridge

Wilfrid Scawen Blunt Papers

THE NATIONAL ARCHIVES OF INDIA, New Delhi

Dadabhai Naoroji Papers (on microfilms)

SENATE HOUSE LIBRARY, University of London

Herbert Spencer Papers

II   Printed Primary Sources

Aitchison, Sir C., *Lord Lawrence* (Rulers of India Series, Oxford, 1892)

The Annual Register: A Review of Public Events at Home and Abroad for the Year 1899 (London, 1900)

Banerjea, Surendranath, *A Nation in Making: Being the Reminiscences of Fifty Years of Public Life* (London, 1925)

Bartlett, E. Ashmead, *Shall England Keep India?* (London, 1886)

Bell, Evans, *The Annexation of the Punjaub, and the Maharajah Duleep Singh* (London, 1882)

Bell, Evans, *A Letter to H. M. Durand, Esq., C.S.I., of the Bengal Civil Service, Barrister-at-Law* (London, 1884)

Besant, Annie, *The Story of Afghanistan; Or, Why the Tory Government Gags the Indian Press: A Plea for the Weak against the Strong* (London, 1879)

Besant, Annie, *The Transvaal* (London, 1881)

Besant, Annie, *Egypt* (London, 1882)

Blunt, Wilfrid Scawen, *Ideas about India* (London, 1885)

Blunt, Wilfrid Scawen, *The Shame of the Nineteenth Century, a Letter Addressed to the 'Times'* (n.p., 1900)

Blunt, Wilfrid Scawen, *Secret History of the English Occupation of Egypt: Being a Personal Narrative of Events* (London, 1907)

Blunt, Wilfrid Scawen, *India Under Ripon: A Private Diary* (London, 1909)

Blunt, Wilfrid Scawen, *Gordon at Khartoum: Being a Personal Narrative of Events, in Continuation of 'A Secret History of the English Occupation of Egypt'* (London, 1911)

Blunt, Wilfrid Scawen, *The Land War in Ireland: Being a Personal Narrative of Events, in Continuation of "A Secret History of the English Occupation of Egypt"* (London, 1912)

Blunt, Wilfrid Scawen, *The Poetical Works of Wilfrid Scawen Blunt: A Complete Edition*, vol. II (London, 1914)

Blunt, Wilfrid Scawen, *My Diaries: Being a Personal Narrative of Events 1888–1914* (2 vols, London, 1919)

Bourne, H. R. Fox, *The Aborigines Protection Society: Chapters in History* (London, 1899)

Bright, John, *The Public Letters of the Right Hon. John Bright*, edited by H. J. Leech (2nd edn, London, 1895 [1885])

Bright, John, *The Diaries of John Bright*, edited by R. A. J. Walling (London, 1930)

Broadley, A. M., *How We Defended Arábi and His Friends: A Story of Egypt and the Egyptians* (London, 1884)

Bryce, James, *Impressions of South Africa* (3rd rev. edn, London, 1899 [1897])

Campbell, Sir George, *The British Empire* (London, 1887)

Chesney, Sir George, *Indian Polity: A View of the System of Administration in India* (3rd edn, London, 1894 [1868])

Clarke, William, *William Clarke: A Collection of His Writings, with a Biographical Sketch*, edited by Herbert Burrows and John A. Hobson (London, 1908)

Cobden, Richard, *The Political Writings of Richard Cobden*, vol. II (London and New York, 1867)

Comte, Auguste, *Cours de philosophie positive* (6 vols, Paris, 1830–42)

Comte, Auguste, *Système de politique positive* (4 vols, Paris, 1851–4)

Comte, Auguste, *Catéchisme positiviste* (Paris, 1852)

Congreve, Richard, *Essays: Political, Social, and Religious (and Historical Lectures)* (3 vols, London, 1874, 1892, 1900)

Congreve, Richard, et al., *International Policy: Essays on the Foreign Relations of England* (2nd edn, London 1884 [1866])

Cotton, H. J. S., *England and India: An Address Delivered at the Positivist School, Chapel Street, London, on June 27, 1883* (London, 1883)

Cotton, H. J. S., *New India, or India in Transition* (London, 1885)

Dicey, A. V., *Lectures Introductory to the Study of the Law of the Constitution* (London, 1885)

Digby, William, *The Famine Campaign in Southern India (Madras and Bombay Presidencies and Province of Mysore) 1876–1878* (2 vols, London, 1878)

Digby, William, *Indian Problems for English Consideration, a Letter to the Council of the National Liberal Federation* (Birmingham, 1881)

Digby, William, *India for the Indians – and for England* (London, 1885)

Digby, William, *The General Election, 1885: India's Interest in the British Ballot Box* (London, 1885)

[Digby, William (ed.)], *India in England, Volume II: Being a Collection of Speeches Delivered and Articles Written on the Indian National Congress, in England in 1889*, with an introductory essay by Pandit Bishen Narayan Dar (Lucknow, 1889)

Digby, William, *Indian Politics in England: The Story of an Indian Reform Bill in Parliament Told Week by Week; with Other Matters of Interest to Indian Reformers* (Lucknow, 1890)

Digby, William, *British Rule in India: Has It Been, Is It Still, a Good Rule for the Indian People?* (London, 1891)

Digby, William, *The General Election of 1892, South Islington: I. Address of the Liberal Candidate, Wm Digby, C.I.E. II. Mr. Digby's 'Record'* (London, 1892)

Digby, William, *'Prosperous' British India: A Revelation from Official Records* (London, 1901)

Dilke, Sir Charles Wentworth, *Problems of Greater Britain*, vol. II (London, 1890)

Dutt, Romesh, *Open Letters to Lord Curzon on Famines and Land Assessments in India* (London, 1900)

Dutt, Romesh, *Indian Famines: Their Causes and Prevention* (London, 1901)

Dutt, Romesh Chunder, *The Economic History of India in the Victorian Age: From the Accession of Queen Victoria in 1837 to the Commencement of the Twentieth Century* (Trübner's Oriental Series vol. 6, London, 2000 [reprint of the 7th edn 1950; 1st edn 1903])

Fawcett, Henry, *Free Trade and Protection* (London, 1878)

Fawcett, Henry, *Indian Finance: Three essays, Republished from the 'Nineteenth Century'* (London, 1880)

Free Briton, Mr. *Chamberlain against England: A Record of His Proceedings* (London, n.d.)

Freeden, Michael (ed.), *Minutes of the Rainbow Circle, 1894–1924* (Camden Fourth Series vol. 38, London, 1989)

Freeman, Edward A., *Greater Greece and Greater Britain, and, George Washington the Expander of England: Two Lectures* (London, 1886)

Garth, Sir Richard, *A Few Plain Truths about India* (London, 1888)

Geddes, James, *The Logic of Indian Deficit* (London, 1871; 2nd edn, London, 1872)

Gladstone, W. E., *Political Speeches in Scotland, November and December 1879, by the Right Hon. W. E. Gladstone, M.P.* (London, 1879) [reprinted with an introduction as *Midlothian Speeches 1879* (The Victorian Library, Leicester, 1971)]

The Government of India, *Statement Exhibiting the Moral and Material Progress and Condition of India* (published regularly since 1859)

Hamilton, Lord George, *Parliamentary Reminiscences and Reflections, 1868 to 1885* (London, 1917)

Hamilton, Lord George, *Parliamentary Reminiscences and Reflections, 1886–1906* (London, 1922)

Hansard's Parliamentary Debates, 3rd ser., vols CCL (1880), CCCIX (1886), CCCXV (1887), CCCXLI, CCCXLII (1890)

Hansard's Parliamentary Debates, 4th ser., vols XIII (1893), LXXIX, LXXXI, LXXXVI (1900)

Harrison, Frederic, *Martial Law in Kabul (Reprinted from the* Fortnightly Review, *with additions)* (London, 1880)

Harrison, Frederic, *National & Social Problems* (London, 1908)

Harrison, Frederic, *Autobiographic Memoirs* (2 vols, London, 1911)

Hirst, Francis W., *In the Golden Days* (London, 1947)

Hirst, Francis W., Murray, Gilbert, and Hammond, John L., *Liberalism and the Empire: Three Essays*: reprinted in Peter Cain (ed.), *The Empire and Its Critics, 1899–1939: Classics of Imperialism*, vol. II (London, 1998 [1900])

Hobhouse, L. T., *Democracy and Reaction*, edited with an introduction and notes by P. F. Clarke (Society & the Victorians, Brighton, 1972 [1904])

Hobson, J. A., *The War in South Africa: Its Causes and Effects* (2nd edn, London, 1900)

Hobson, J. A., *The Psychology of Jingoism* (London, 1901)

Hyndman, H. M., *The Indian Famine and the Crisis in India* (London, 1877)

Hyndman, H. M., *The Transvaal War and the Degradation of England* (Reprinted from *Justice*, London, 1899)

The Ilbert Bill: A Collection of Letters, Speeches, Memorials, Articles, etc. Stating the Objections to the Bill (London, 1883)

Increased Armaments Protest Committee, *Empire, Trade, and Armaments: An Exposure* (London, 1896)

Keay, J. Seymour, *Spoiling the Egyptians: A Tale of Shame, Told from the Blue Books* (3rd edn, revised and enlarged, London, 1882)

Kidd, Benjamin, *Social Evolution: With Appendix Containing Reply to Criticisms* (3rd edn, London, 1898 [1894])

Kidd, Benjamin, *The Control of the Tropics* (New York and London, 1898)

Lawson, Sir Wilfrid, *A Memoir*, edited by George W. E. Russell (London, 1909)

Lawson, Sir Wilfrid, and Gould, F. Carruthers, *Cartoons in Rhyme and Line* (London, 1905)

Le Bon, Gustave, *Les Lois psychologiques de l'evolution des peuples* (Paris, 1894)

Le Bon, Gustave, *La psychologie des foules* (Paris, 1895)

Lecky, W. E. H., *The History of the Rise and Influence of the Spirit of Rationalism in Europe* (2 vols, London, 1865)

Lecky, W. E. H., *The Empire, Its Value and Its Growth: An Inaugural Address Delivered at the Imperial Institute, Nov. 20, 1893, under the Presidency of H.R.H. the Prince of Wales* (London, 1893)

Little, James Stanley, *A World Empire: Being an Essay upon Imperial Federation* (London, 1879)

Lord Ripon and the People of India: Proceedings of the Public Meeting Held in Willis's Rooms, London, on Wednesday, August 1st, 1883 (London, 1883)

Macfie, R. A., *A Glance at the Position & Prospects of the Empire: An Address Delivered by request of the Musselburgh Young Men's Association, on 19th January, 1872* (London, 1872)

Marvin, Charles, *Russia's Power of Attracting India* (London, 1885)

Masterman, Charles F. G. et al., *The Heart of the Empire: Discussions of Problems of Modern City Life in England, with an Essay on Imperialism* (London, 1901)

Morley, John, *Edmund Burke: A Historical Study* (London, 1867)

Morley, John, *Critical Miscellanies*, vol. III (London, 1886)

Morley, John, *The Life of Richard Cobden*, vol. II (Jubilee edn, London, 1896 [1879])

Morley, John, *Liberal Principles and Imperialism: A Speech by the Right Hon. John Morley, M.P., at Oxford, June 9, 1900* (National Reform Union Pamphlets, Manchester, 1900)

Morley, John Viscount, *Recollections*, vol. II (London, 1917)

Naoroji, Dadabhai, *Poverty of India* (London, 1878)

Naoroji, Dadabhai, *Mr. D. Naoroji and Mr. Schnadhorst* [An explanation by the former concerning his candidature for Central Finsbury] (London, 1892)

Naoroji, Dadabhai, *The First Indian Member of the Imperial Parliament, Being a Collection of the Main Incidents Relating to the Election of Mr. Dadabhai Naoroji to Parliament* (Madras, 1892)

Naoroji, Dadabhai, *Poverty and Un-British Rule in India* (London, 1901)

Naoroji, Dadabhai, *Correspondence, Vol. II: Part I. Correspondence with D. E. Wacha, 4.11.1884 to 23.3.1895,* edited with an introduction and notes by R. P. Patwardhan (Bombay, 1977)

O'Donnell, F. Hugh, *A History of the Irish Parliamentary Party*, vol. II (Kennikat Series in Irish History and Culture, New York and London, 1970 [1910])

Peter the Hermit, *The Brigands in Egypt: Solution of the International Crisis: Letters to an Englishman, by Peter the Hermit* (Translated from the French, London, 1882)

Pollard, Thomas Inwood, *The Indian Tribute and the Loss by Exchange; an Essay on the Depreciation of Indian Commodities in England* (Calcutta, 1884)

Redmond, John E., *Historical and Political Addresses 1883–97* (Dublin, 1898)

Reitz, F. W., *A Century of Wrong*, with preface by W. T. Stead (London, 1900)

Robertson, John M., *The Fallacy of Saving: A Study in Economics* (London, 1892)

Robertson, John M., 'Charles Bradlaugh: An Account of His Parliamentary Struggle, Politics and Teachings', in Hypatia Bradlaugh Bonner, *Charles Bradlaugh: A Record of His Life and Work*, vol. II (London, 1895), pp. 115–421.

Robertson, John M., *Patriotism and Empire*: reprinted in Peter Cain (ed.), *The Empire and Its Critics, 1899–1939: Classics of Imperialism*, vol. I (London, 1998 [1899])

Robertson, J. M., *Wrecking the Empire* (London, 1901)

Sedgwick, W., *India for Sale: Kashmir Sold* (Calcutta, 1886)

Seeley, J. R., *The Expansion of England: Two Courses of Lectures* (London, 1883)

Seeley, John Robert, *A Short History of Napoleon the First* (London, 1886)

Seeley, Sir J. R., *Introduction to Political Science: Two Series of Lectures* (London, 1896)

Shaw, Bernard (ed.), *Fabianism and the Empire: A Manifesto by the Fabian Society* (London, 1900)

Smith, Adam, *An Inquiry into the Nature and Causes of the Wealth of Nations* (2 vols, London, 1776)

Smith, Goldwin, *The Empire: A Series of Letters, Published in 'The Daily News', 1862, 1863* (Oxford and London, 1863)

Smith, Goldwin, *Essays on Questions of the Day: Political and Social* (2nd edn, London, 1894 [1893])

Smith, Goldwin, *A Selection from Goldwin Smith's Correspondence: Comprising Letters Chiefly to and from his English Friends, Written between the Years 1846 and 1910,* collected by Arnold Haultain (London, 1913)

Smith, Samuel, *India Revisited: Its Social and Political Problems* (London, 1886)

Smith, Samuel, *My Life-Work* (London, 1902)

Spencer, Herbert, *Social Statics: Or, the Conditions Essential to Human Happiness Specified, and the First of Them Developed*: reprinted in *Herbert Spencer: Collected Writings*, vol. III (London, 1996 [1851])

Spencer, Herbert, *The Principles of Biology* (2 vols, London, 1864, 1867)

Spencer, Herbert, *The Study of Sociology*: reprinted in *Herbert Spencer: Collected Writings*, vol. VI (London, 1996 [1873])

Spencer, Herbert, *Political Institutions: Being Part V of the Principles of Sociology (The Concluding Portion of Vol. II)*: reprinted in *Herbert Spencer: Collected Writings*, vol. VIII (London, 1996 [1882])

Spencer, Herbert, *The Man versus the State* (London, 1884)

Spencer, Herbert, *Essays: Scientific, Political, & Speculative*, vol. III (London, 1891)

Spencer, Herbert, *Facts and Comments* (London, 1902)

Spencer, Herbert, *An Autobiography*, vol. II (London, 1904)

Stanley, Henry M., *In darkest Africa or, the quest, rescue, and retreat of Emin, Governor of Equatoria* (2 vols, London, 1890)

Stead, W. T., *How Not to Make Peace: Evidence as to Homestead Burning Collected and Examined* (Stop-the-War Committee, London, 1900)

Stephen, James Fitzjames, *Liberty, Equality, Fraternity* (London, 1873)

Stephen, Sir James Fitzjames, *Letters on the Ilbert Bill: Reprinted from the 'Times'* (London, 1883)

Strachey, Sir John, and Strachey, Richard, *The Finances and Public Works of India from 1869 to 1881* (London, 1882)

Strachey, John St. Loe, *The Adventure of Living: A Subjective Autobiography* (London, 1922)

Temple, Sir Richard, *India in 1880* (London, 1880)

Thomson, H. C., *The Supreme Problem in South Africa: Capital and Labour, With Suggestions for the Basis of an Enduring Peace* (Reprinted from the *Investors' Review*, London, n.d.)

Webb, Beatrice, *Our Partnership* (London, 1948)

Wedderburn, Sir David, *British Colonial Policy* (London, 1881)

III   Newspapers and Periodical Reviews

American Journal of Sociology (1895)

Calcutta Review (1872–3)

Contemporary Review (1882–8, 1891, 1898–1900)

Fortnightly Review (1875, 1878–82, 1888–90, 1893, 1899–1900)

Greater Britain (1891)

(The Imperial and) Asiatic Quarterly Review (1890, 1893)

India (1890–1)

Macmillan's Magazine (1885)

Nineteenth Century (1877–80, 1882–7, 1890, 1893–8)

Pall Mall Gazette (1882)
The Positivist Review (1894, 1898–1900)
Progressive Review (1897)
Review of Reviews (1893)
South Place Magazine (1904)
The Times (1882–3, 1885, 1887, 1889, 1896–7)
War Against War in South Africa (1899–1900)

IV   Printed Secondary Works

Alexander, Michael and Anand, Sushila, *Queen Victoria's Maharajah: Duleep Singh 1838–93* (London, 2001 [1980])

Ambirajan, S., 'Dadabhai Naoroji: the First Economist of Modern India', *Research in the History of Economic Thought and Methodology*, 16 (1998), pp. 155–78.

Anderson, Nancy Fix, 'Bridging Cross-Cultural Feminisms: Annie Besant and Women's Rights in England and India, 1874–1933', *Women's History Review*, 3 (1994), pp. 563–80.

Anderson, Nancy Fix, ' "Mother Besant" and Indian National Politics', *The Journal of Imperial and Commonwealth History*, 30:3 (2002), pp. 27–54.

Appleton, Lewis, *Memoirs of Henry Richard, the Apostle of Peace* (London, 1889)

Auld, John W., 'The Liberal Pro-Boers', *Journal of British Studies*, 14 (1975), pp. 78–99.

Bandyopadhyay, Premansukumar, *Indian Famine and Agrarian Problems: A Policy Study on the Administration of Lord George Hamilton, Secretary of State for India 1895–1903* (Calcutta, 1987)

Baylen, J. O., 'W. T. Stead as Publisher and Editor of the *Review of Reviews*', *Victorian Periodicals Review*, 12 (1979), pp. 70–84.

Bayly, C. A., *Imperial Meridian: The British Empire and the World 1780–1830* (London, 1989)

Bebbington, D. W., *The Nonconformist Conscience: Chapel and Politics, 1870–1914* (London, 1982)

Bevir, Mark, 'In Opposition to the Raj: Annie Besant and the Dialectic of Empire', *History of Political Thought*, 19 (1998), pp. 61–77.

Blitz, David, 'Russell and the Boer War: From Imperialist to Anti-Imperialist', *Russell: the Journal of Bertrand Russell Studies*, 19 (2000), pp. 117–42.

Bodelsen, C. A., *Studies in Mid-Victorian Imperialism* (Copenhagen, 1924)

Bose, Nemai Sadhan, *Racism, Struggle for Equality and Indian Nationalism* (Calcutta, 1981)

Brasted, Howard, 'Indian Nationalist Development and the Influence of Irish Home Rule, 1870–1886', *Modern Asian Studies*, 1 (1980), pp. 37–63.

Brasted, H. V., 'The Irish Connection: The Irish Outlook on Indian Nationalism 1870–1906', in Kenneth Ballhatchet and David Taylor (eds), *Changing South Asia: Politics and Government* (London, 1984), pp. 67–78.

Brown, R. Craig, 'Goldwin Smith and Anti-imperialism', *Canadian Historical Review*, 43 (1962), pp. 93–105.

Burgess, M. D., 'Imperial Federation: Edward Freeman and the Intellectual Debate on the Consolidation of the British Empire in the Late Nineteenth Century', *Trivium*, 13 (1978), pp. 77–94.

Burrows, Herbert, 'Biographical Sketch: His Later Years', in Herbert Burrows and John A. Hobson (eds), *William Clarke: A Collection of His Writings, with a Biographical Sketch* (London, 1908), pp. xi–xxix.

Cain, Peter J., 'British Radicalism, the South African Crisis, and the Origins of the Theory of Financial Imperialism', in David Omissi and Andrew S. Thompson (eds), *The Impact of the South African War* (Basingstoke and New York, 2002), pp. 173–93.

Cain, P. J., *Hobson and Imperialism: Radicalism, New Liberalism, and Finance 1887–1938* (Oxford, 2002)

Cain, Peter J., and Harrison, Mark (eds), *Imperialism: Critical Concepts in Historical Studies* (3 vols, London and New York, 2001)

Cain, P. J. and Hopkins, A. G., 'Afterword: The Theory and Practice of British Imperialism', in Raymond E. Dumett (ed.), *Gentlemanly Capitalism and British Imperialism: The New Debate on Empire* (London and New York, 1999), pp. 196–220.

Cain, P. J. and Hopkins, A. G., *British Imperialism, 1688–2000* (2nd edn, Harlow, 2002)

Call, Steven C., 'Protesting against Modern War: A Comparison of Issues Raised by Anti-Imperialists and Pro-Boers', *War in History*, 3 (1996), pp. 66–84.

Cell, John, 'The Imperial Conscience', in Peter Marsh (ed.), *The Conscience of the Victorian State* (New York, 1979), pp. 173–213.

Chamberlain, M. E., 'Sir Charles Dilke and the British Intervention in Egypt, 1882: Decision Making in a Nineteenth-Century Cabinet', *British Journal of International Studies*, 2 (1976), pp. 231–45.

Chamberlain, M. E., 'British Public Opinion and the Invasion of Egypt, 1882', *Trivium*, 16 (1981), pp. 5–28.

Chandra, Bipan, *The Rise and Growth of Economic Nationalism in India: Economic Policies of Indian National Leadership, 1880–1905* (New Delhi, 1966)

Charlesworth, Neil, *British Rule and the Indian Economy 1800–1914* (Studies in Economic and Social History, London and Basingstoke, 1982)

Clarke, P. F., *Lancashire and the New Liberalism* (Cambridge, 1971)

Clarke, Peter, *Liberals and Social Democrats* (Modern Revivals in History, Aldershot, 1993 [1978])

Cocks, Paul, 'The Rhetoric of Science and the Critique of Imperialism in British Social Anthropology, c. 1870–1940', *History and Anthropology*, 9 (1995), pp. 93–119.

Colley, Linda, *Britons: Forging the Nation, 1707–1837* (London, 2003)

Collini, Stefan, *Liberalism and Sociology: L. T. Hobhouse and Political Argument in England 1880–1914* (Cambridge, 1979)

Collini, Stefan, *Public Moralists: Political Thought and Intellectual Life in Britain 1850–1930* (Oxford, 1991)

Colls, Robert, 'Englishness and the Political Culture', in Robert Colls and Philip Dodd (eds), *Englishness: Politics and Culture 1880–1920* (London, 1986), pp. 29–61.

Cook, Sir Edward, *The Life of Florence Nightingale*, vol. II (London, 1913)

Craig, F. W. S. (ed.), *British Parliamentary Election Results 1885–1918* (London, 1974)

Crook, D. P., *Benjamin Kidd: Portrait of a Social Darwinist* (Cambridge, 1984)

Cunningham, Hugh, 'Jingoism in 1877–78', *Victorian Studies*, 14 (1971), pp. 429–53.

Cunningham, Hugh, 'The Conservative Party and Patriotism', in Robert Colls and Philip Dodd (eds), *Englishness: Politics and Culture 1880–1920* (London, 1986), pp. 283–307.

Cuthbertson, Greg, 'Preaching Imperialism: Wesleyan Methodism and the War', in David Omissi and Andrew S. Thompson (eds), *The Impact of the South African War* (Basingstoke and New York, 2002), pp. 157–72.

Davey, Arthur, *The British Pro-Boers 1877–1902* (Cape Town, 1978)

Davis, Lance E. and Huttenback, Robert A., *Mammon and the Pursuit of Empire: The Political Economy of British Imperialism, 1860–1912* (Interdisciplinary perspectives on modern history, Cambridge, 1986)

Deane, Phyllis, 'Henry Fawcett: The Plain Man's Political Economist', in Lawrence Goldman (ed.), *The Blind Victorian: Henry Fawcett and British Liberalism* (Cambridge, 1989), pp. 93–110.

Denholm, Anthony, *Lord Ripon 1827–1909: A Political Biography* (London, 1982)

Dewey, Clive, 'The End of the Imperialism of Free Trade: the Eclipse of the Lancashire Lobby and the Concession of Fiscal Autonomy to India', in Clive Dewey and A. G. Hopkins (eds), *The Imperial Impact: Studies in the Economic History of Africa and India* (Commonwealth Papers 21, University of London, Institute of Commonwealth Studies, London, 1978), pp. 35–67.

Dumett, Raymond E. (ed.), *Gentlemanly Capitalism and British Imperialism: The New Debate on Empire* (London and New York, 1999)

Duncan, David, *The Life and Letters of Herbert Spencer*: reprinted in *Herbert Spencer: Collected Writings*, vol. II (London, 1996 [1908])

Durrans, P. J., 'A Two-Edged Sword: The Liberal Attack on Disraelian Imperialism', *Journal of Imperial and Commonwealth History*, 10:3 (1982), pp. 262–84.

Durrans, P. J., 'Beaconsfieldism', in C. C. Eldridge (ed.), *Empire, Politics and Popular Culture: Essays in Eighteenth and Nineteenth Century British History* (Lampeter, 1989 [*Trivium*, vol. 24]), pp. 58–75.

Edelstein, Michael, *Overseas Investment in the Age of High Imperialism: The United Kingdom, 1850–1914* (London, 1982)

Eisen, Sydney, 'Frederic Harrison and Herbert Spencer: Embattled Unbelievers', *Victorian Studies*, 12 (1968), pp. 33–56.

Eldridge, C. C., *England's Mission: The Imperial Idea in the Age of Gladstone and Disraeli 1868–1880* (London, 1973)

Eldridge, C. C., 'Mid-Victorian Imperialism Reconsidered', *Trivium*, 15 (1980), pp. 63–72.

Eldridge, C. C., *Disraeli and the Rise of a New Imperialism* (The Past in Perspective, Cardiff, 1996)

Emy, H. V., *Liberals, Radicals and Social Politics 1892–1914* (Cambridge, 1973)

Evans, Howard, *Sir Randal Cremer: His Life and Work* (London, 1909)

Forbes, Geraldine Hancock, 'The English Positivists and India', *Bengal Past and Present*, 93 (1974), pp. 74–83, 173–80.

Foster, R. F., *Lord Randolph Churchill: A Political Life* (Oxford, 1981)

Freeden, Michael, 'Hobson's Evolving Conceptions of Human Nature', in idem (ed.), *Reappraising J. A. Hobson: Humanism and Welfare* (London, 1990), pp. 54–73.

Ganguli, B. N., *Dadabhai Naoroji and the Drain Theory* (London, 1965)

Gardiner, A. G., *The Life of Sir William Harcourt* (2 vols, London, 1923)

Ghose, Sankar, *The Western Impact on Indian Politics (1885–1919)* (Bombay, 1967)

Gilbert, Martin, 'Famine in India: Sir Antony MacDonnell and a Policy Revolution in 1902', in Donovan Williams and E. Daniel Potts (eds), *Essays in Indian History: In Honour of Cuthbert Collin Davies* (London, 1973), pp. 152–71.

Goldman, Lawrence, 'Introduction: "An Advanced Liberal": Henry Fawcett, 1833–1884', in idem (ed.), *The Blind Victorian: Henry Fawcett and British Liberalism* (Cambridge, 1989), pp. 1–38.

Gooch, G. P., *Life of Lord Courtney* (London, 1920)

Gopal, S. *The Viceroyalty of Lord Ripon 1880–1884* (Oxford Historical Series: British Series, London, 1953)

Gopal, Sarvepalli, 'Gladstone and India', in Donovan Williams and E. Daniel Potts (eds), *Essays in Indian History: In Honour of Cuthbert Collin Davies* (London, 1973), pp. 1–16.

Gray, Tim, 'Herbert Spencer's Liberalism – From Social Statics to Social Dynamics', in Richard Bellamy (ed.), *Victorian Liberalism: Nineteenth-Century Political Thought and Practice* (London and New York, 1990), pp. 110–30.

Green, E. H. H., *The Crisis of Conservatism: The Politics, Economics and Ideology of the British Conservative Party, 1880–1914* (London and New York, 1995)

Green, E. H. H., 'Gentlemanly Capitalism and British Economic Policy, 1880–1914: The Debate Over Bimetallism and Protectionism', in Raymond E. Dumett (ed.), *Gentlemanly Capitalism and British Imperialism: The New Debate on Empire* (London and New York, 1999), pp. 44–67.

Gupta, J. N., *Life and Work of Romesh Chunder Dutt C.I.E.* (London, 1911)

Hamer, D. A., *John Morley: Liberal Intellectual in Politics* (Oxford, 1968)

Hammond, J. L., *Gladstone and the Irish Nation* (London, 1964 [1938])

Harnetty, P., 'The Indian Cotton Duties Controversy, 1894–1896', *English Historical Review*, 77 (1962), pp. 684–702.

Harnetty, Peter, *Imperialism and Free Trade: Lancashire and India in the Mid-Nineteenth Century* (Manchester, 1972)

Herrick, Jim, 'The Politician', in G. A. Wells (ed.), *J. M. Robertson (1856–1933), Liberal, Rationalist, and Scholar: An Assessment by Several Hands* (London, 1987), pp. 31–57.

Hind, R. J., *Henry Labouchere and the Empire 1880–1905* (University of London Historical Studies XXXI, London, 1972)

Hinden, Rita, *Empire and after* (London, 1949)

Hirschmann, Edwin, *'White Mutiny': The Ilbert Bill Crisis in India and Genesis of the Indian National Congress* (New Delhi, 1980)

Hirst, F. W., *Early Life & Letters of John Morley* (2 vols, London, 1927)

Hobhouse, L. T. and Hammond, J. L., *Lord Hobhouse: A Memoir* (London, 1905)

Hopkins, A. G., 'The Victorians and Africa: A Reconsideration of the Occupation of Egypt, 1882', *Journal of African History*, 27 (1986), pp. 363–91.

Howe, Anthony, *Free Trade and Liberal England 1846–1946* (Oxford, 1997)

Irschick, Eugene F., *Dialogue and History: Constructing South India, 1795–1895* (Berkeley, 1994)

James, Robert Rhodes, *Rosebery: A Biography of Archibald Philip, Fifth Earl of Rosebery* (London, 1963)

Janin, Hunt, *The India–China Opium Trade in the Nineteenth Century* (Jefferson and London, 1999)

Kaminsky, Arnold P., *The India Office, 1880–1910* (Contributions in Comparative Colonial Studies No 20, New York, 1986)

Kaul, Chandrika, 'England and India: The Ilbert Bill, 1883: A Case Study of the Metropolitan Press', *Indian Economic and Social History Review*, 30 (1993), pp. 413–36.

Kennedy, Paul, 'Debate: The Costs and Benefits of British Imperialism 1846–1914', *Past and Present*, No. 125 (1989), pp. 186–92.

Kent, Christopher, *Brains and numbers: Elitism, Comtism, and Democracy in Mid-Victorian England* (Toronto, 1978)

Kent, Susan Kingsley, *Sex and Suffrage in Britain, 1860–1914* (Princeton, 1987)

Klein, Ira, 'English Free Traders and Indian Tariffs, 1874–96', *Modern Asian Studies*, 5 (1971), pp. 251–71.

Knox, B. A., 'Reconsidering Mid-Victorian Imperialism', *The Journal of Imperial and Commonwealth History*, 1 (1973), pp. 155–72.

Koebner, Richard and Schmidt, Helmut Dan, *Imperialism: The Story and Significance of a Political Word, 1840–1960* (Cambridge, 1965)

Koss, Stephen (ed.), *The Pro-Boers: The Anatomy of an Antiwar Movement* (Studies in Imperialism, Chicago and London, 1973)

Kubicek, Robert, 'British Expansion, Empire, and Technological Change', in Andrew Porter (ed.), *The Oxford History of the British Empire, vol. III: The Nineteenth Century* (Oxford, 1999), pp. 247–69.

Laity, Paul, *The British Peace Movement 1870–1914* (Oxford Historical Monographs, Oxford, 2001)

Laity, Paul, 'The British Peace Movement and the War', in David Omissi and Andrew S. Thompson (eds), *The Impact of the South African War* (Basingstoke and New York, 2002), pp. 138–56.

Liveing, Susan, *A Nineteenth-Century Teacher: John Henry Bridges, M.B., F.R.C.P.* (London, 1926)

Long, David, *Towards a New Liberal Internationalism: The International theory of J. A. Hobson* (LSE Monographs in International Studies, Cambridge, 1996)

Longford, Elizabeth, *A Pilgrimage of Passion: The Life of Wilfrid Scawen Blunt* (London, 1979)

Louis, Wm. Roger (ed.), *Imperialism: The Robinson and Gallagher Controversy* (New Viewpoints, New York and London, 1976)

Maccoby, S., *English Radicalism 1886–1914* (London, 1953)

MacDonagh, Oliver, 'The Anti-Imperialism of Free Trade', *Economic History Review*, 2nd series, 14 (1962), pp. 489–501.

McGee, John Edwin, *A Crusade for Humanity: The History of Organised Positivism in England* (London, 1931)

MacKenzie, John M., *Propaganda and Empire: The Manipulation of British Public Opinion, 1880–1960* (Manchester, 1984)

MacKenzie, John M. (ed.), *Imperialism and Popular Culture* (Manchester, 1986)

MacKenzie, John M., 'Empire and Metropolitan Cultures', in Andrew Porter (ed.), *The Oxford History of the British Empire, vol. III: The Nineteenth Century* (Oxford, 1999), pp. 270–93.

MacKillop, I. D., *The British Ethical Societies* (Cambridge, 1986)

Mahajan, Sneh, *British Foreign Policy 1874–1914: The Role of India* (Routledge Studies in Modern European History, London and New York, 2002)

Malchow, Howard LeRoy, *Agitators and Promoters in the Age of Gladstone and Disraeli: A Biographical Dictionary of the Leaders of British Pressure Groups Founded between 1865 and 1886* (Garland Reference Library of Social Science, vol. 176, New York and London, 1983)

Markowitz, Gerald E. (ed.), *American Anti-imperialism 1895–1901* (The Garland Library of War and Peace, New York and London, 1976)

Marshall, P. J., 'Imperial Britain', *The Journal of Imperial and Commonwealth History*, 23:3 (1995), pp. 379–94.

Martin, Briton, *New India, 1885: British Official Policy and the Emergence of the Indian National Congress* (Berkeley, 1969)

Martin, Ged, '"Anti-Imperialism" in the Mid-Nineteenth Century and the Nature of the British Empire, 1820–70', in Ronald Hyam and Ged Martin, *Reappraisals in British Imperial History* (Cambridge Commonwealth Series, London, 1975), pp. 88–120.

Masani, R. P., *Dadabhai Naoroji: The Grand Old Man of India* (London, 1939)

Matikkala, Mira, 'William Digby and the Indian Question', *Journal of Liberal History*, issue 58 (2008), pp. 12–20.

Matthew, H. C. G., *The Liberal Imperialists: The Ideas and Politics of a Post-Gladstonian Élite* (Oxford Historical Monographs, London, 1973)

Mehrotra, S. R., 'Imperial Federation and India, 1868–1917', *Journal of Commonwealth Political Studies*, 1 (1961), pp. 29–40.

Mehrotra, S. R., *A History of the Indian National Congress, Vol. I, 1885–1918* (New Delhi, 1995)

Mehta, Uday Singh, *Liberalism and Empire: A Study in Nineteenth-Century British Liberal Thought* (Chicago and London, 1999)

Metcalf, Thomas R., *Ideologies of the Raj* (The New Cambridge History of India III:4, Cambridge, 2003 [1995])

Miall, Charles S., *Henry Richard, M.P.: A Biography* (London, 1889)

Moore, R. J., 'The Twilight of the Whigs and the Reform of the Indian Councils, 1886–1892', *The Historical Journal*, 10 (1967), pp. 400–14.

Morley, John, *The Life of Richard Cobden*, vol. II (Jubilee edn, London, 1896 [1879])

Morrow, Margot Duley, 'The British Committee of the Indian National Congress as an Issue in and an Influence upon Nationalist Politics, 1889–1901', in Kenneth Ballhatchet and David Taylor (eds), *Changing South Asia: Politics and Government* (London, 1984), pp. 55–66.

Moulton, Edward, 'William Wedderburn and Early Indian Nationalism, 1870–1917', in Kenneth Ballhatchet and David Taylor (eds), *Changing South Asia: Politics and Government* (London, 1984), pp. 37–54.

Moulton, Edward C., 'William Digby', in Joseph O. Baylen and Norbert J. Gossman (eds), *Biographical Dictionary of Modern British Radicals*, vol. 3: 1870–1914 (New York and London, 1988), pp. 269–73.

Nanda, B. R., *Gokhale: The Indian Moderates and the British Raj* (Princeton, 1977)

Niyogi, Sumanta, 'The Defence of Colony's Interests in Parliament: Henry Fawcett and the Indian Cotton Duties', *Quarterly Review of Historical Studies*, 18 (1979), pp. 230–4.

O'Brien, Patrick K., 'The Costs and Benefits of British Imperialism 1846–1914', *Past and Present*, No. 120 (1988), pp. 163–200.

Offer, Avner, 'Costs and Benefits, Prosperity and Security, 1870–1914', in Andrew Porter (ed.), *The Oxford History of the British Empire, vol. III: The Nineteenth Century* (Oxford, 1999), pp. 690–711.

Owen, Nicholas, 'Critics of Empire in Britain', in Judith M. Brown and Wm. Roger Louis (eds), *The Oxford History of the British Empire, vol. IV: The Twentieth Century* (Oxford, 1999), pp. 188–211.

Parry, J. P., 'Disraeli and England', *The Historical Journal*, 43 (2000), pp. 699–728.

Parry, J. P., 'The Impact of Napoleon III on British Politics, 1851–1880', *Transactions of the Royal Historical Society*, 6th series, 11 (2001), pp. 147–75.

Pelling, Henry, *Popular Politics and Society in Late Victorian Britain* (2nd edn, London and Basingstoke, 1979 [1968])

Porter, Andrew, 'Religion, Missionary Enthusiasm, and Empire', in idem (ed.), *The Oxford History of the British Empire, vol. III: The Nineteenth Century* (Oxford, 1999), pp. 222–46.

Porter, Andrew, 'Trusteeship, Anti-Slavery, and Humanitarianism', in idem (ed.), *The Oxford History of the British Empire, vol. III: The Nineteenth Century* (Oxford, 1999), pp. 198–221.

Porter, Bernard, *Critics of Empire: British Radical Attitudes to Colonialism in Africa 1895–1914* (London, 1968) / *Critics of Empire: British Radicals and the Imperial Challenge* (2nd edn., London, 2008)

Porter, Bernard, *The Absent-Minded Imperialists: Empire, Society, and Culture in Britain* (Oxford, 2004)

Price, Richard, *An Imperial War and the British Working Class: Working-Class Attitudes and Reactions to the Boer War 1899–1902* (Studies in Social History, London and Toronto, 1972)

Pugh, Martin, 'Lancashire, Cotton, and Indian Reform: Conservative Controversies in the 1930s', *Twentieth Century British History*, 15 (2004), pp. 143–51.

Ratcliffe, S. K., *Sir William Wedderburn and the Indian Reform Movement* (London, 1923)

Readman, Paul, 'The Conservative Party, Patriotism, and British Politics: The Case of the General Election of 1900', *Journal of British Studies*, 40 (2001), pp. 107–45.

Robertson, John M., 'Charles Bradlaugh: An Account of His Parliamentary Struggle, Politics and Teachings', in Hypatia Bradlaugh Bonner, *Charles Bradlaugh: A Record of His Life and Work*, vol. II (London, 1895), pp. 115–421.

Robinson, Ronald and Gallagher, John, 'The Imperialism of Free Trade', *Economic History Review*, 2nd series, 6 (1953), pp. 1–15.

Robinson, Ronald, Gallagher, John, with Denny, Alice, *Africa and the Victorians: The Official Mind of Imperialism* (2nd edn, London and Basingstoke, 1981 [1961])

Saab, Ann Pottinger, *Reluctant Icon: Gladstone, Bulgaria, and the Working Classes, 1856–1878* (Harvard Historical Studies 109, Cambridge, Mass., 1991)

Schults, Raymond L., *Crusader in Babylon: W. T. Stead and the Pall Mall Gazette* (Lincoln, 1972)

Schuyler, R. L., 'The Climax of Anti-Imperialism in England', *Political Science Quarterly*, 36 (1921), pp. 537–60.

Schuyler, R. L., 'The Rise of Anti-Imperialism in England', *Political Science Quarterly*, 37 (1922), pp. 440–71.

Seal, Anil, *The Emergence of Indian Nationalism: Competition and Collaboration in the Later Nineteenth Century* (Cambridge, 1968)

Searle, G. R., *The Quest for National Efficiency: A Study in British Politics and Political Thought, 1899–1914* (Oxford, 1971)

Semmel, Bernard, *Imperialism and Social Reform: English Social-Imperial Thought 1895–1914* (Studies in Society 5, London, 1960)

Semmel, Bernard, *The Rise of Free Trade Imperialism: Classical Political Economy, the Empire of Free Trade, and Imperialism, 1750–1850* (Cambridge, 1970)

Semmel, Bernard, *The Liberal Ideal and the Demons of Empire: Theories of Imperialism from Adam Smith to Lenin* (Baltimore and London, 1993)

Shannon, R., *Gladstone and the Bulgarian Agitation* (London, 1963)

Smith, Dennis, 'Englishness and the Liberal Inheritance after 1886', in Robert Colls and Philip Dodd (eds), *Englishness: Politics and Culture 1880–1920* (London, 1986), pp. 254–82.

Smith, Iain R., *The Emin Pasha Relief Expedition, 1886–1890* (Oxford, 1972)

Smith, Iain R., *The Origins of the South African War, 1899–1902* (Origins of Modern Wars, London and New York, 1996)

Smith, K. J. M., *James Fitzjames Stephen: Portrait of a Victorian Rationalist* (Cambridge, 1988)

Stansky, Peter, *Ambitions and Strategies: The Struggle for the Leadership of the Liberal Party in the 1890s* (Oxford, 1964)

Stokes, Eric, *The Political Ideas of English Imperialism: An Inaugural Lecture given in the University College of Rhodesia and Nyasaland* (London, 1960)

Sturgis, James L., *John Bright and the Empire* (University of London Historical Studies XXVI, London, 1969)

Taylor, A. J. P., *The Trouble Makers: Dissent over Foreign Policy 1782–1939* (London, 1957)

Taylor, Anne, *Annie Besant: A Biography* (Oxford, 1992)

Taylor, M. W., *Men versus the State: Herbert Spencer and Late Victorian Individualism* (Oxford Historical Monographs, Oxford, 1992)

Taylor, Miles, 'Imperium et Libertas? Rethinking the Radical Critique of Imperialism during the Nineteenth Century', *The Journal of Imperial and Commonwealth History*, 19:1 (1991), pp. 1–23.

Thompson, Andrew S., *Imperial Britain: The Empire in British Politics, c. 1880–1932* (Harlow, 2000)

Thornton, A. P., *The Imperial Idea and its Enemies: A Study in British Power* (London, 1966)

Thorold, Algar Labouchere, *The Life of Henry Labouchere* (London, 1913)

Tiberi, Mario, *The Accounts of the British Empire: Capital Flows from 1799 to 1914*, translated from Italian by Judith Turnbull (Aldershot, 2005)

Tomlinson, B. R., *The Economy of Modern India, 1860–1970* (The New Cambridge History of India III:3, Cambridge, 1993)

Tompkins, Edwin Berkeley, *Anti-imperialism in the United States: the Great Debate, 1890–1920* (Philadelphia, 1970)

Varouxakis, Georgios, ' "Patriotism", "Cosmopolitanism" and "Humanity" in Victorian Political Thought', *European Journal of Political Theory*, 5 (2006), pp. 100–18.

Vogeler, Martha S., *Frederic Harrison: The Vocations of a Positivist* (New York and Oxford, 1984)

Ward, Paul, *Red Flag and Union Jack: Englishness, Patriotism and the British Left, 1881–1924* (Royal Historical Society Studies in History, New Series, Woodbridge, 1998)

Wedderburn, Sir William, *Allan Octavian Hume: Father of the Indian National Congress, 1829–1912* (Oxford, 2002 [1913])

Weiler, Peter, 'William Clarke: The Making and Unmaking of a Fabian Socialist', *The Journal of British Studies*, 14 (1974), pp. 77–108.

Whyte, Frederic, *Life of W. T. Stead* (2 vols, London, 1925)

Williams, Richard, *The Contentious Crown: Public Discussion of the British Monarchy in the Reign of Queen Victoria* (Aldershot, 1997)

Wiltshire, David, *The Social and Political Thought of Herbert Spencer* (Oxford Historical Monographs, Oxford, 1978)

Winch, Donald, *Classical Political Economy and Colonies* (Cambridge, Mass., 1965)

Winter, James, *Robert Lowe* (Toronto, 1976)

Wohl, Anthony S., '"Dizzi-Ben-Dizzi": Disraeli as Alien', *Journal of British Studies*, 34 (1995), pp. 375–411.

Wolf, Lucien, *Life of the First Marquess of Ripon*, vol. II (London, 1921)

Wood, John, 'Henry Fawcett and the British Empire', *The Indian Economic and Social History Review*, 16 (1979), pp. 395–414.

Wormell, Deborah, *Sir John Seeley and the Uses of History* (Cambridge, 1980)

Wright, T. R., *The Religion of Humanity: The Impact of Comtean Positivism on Victorian Britain* (Cambridge, 1986)

Young, G. M., *Portrait of an Age* (2nd edn, London, 1952 [1936])

V   Unpublished Dissertations

Bell, Duncan S. A., 'The Debate about Federation in Empire Political Thought, 1860–1900' (unpublished PhD thesis, University of Cambridge, 2004)

Matikkala, Mira, 'William Digby and the British Radical Debate on India from the 1880s to the 1890s' (unpublished MPhil dissertation, University of Cambridge, 2004)

Matikkala, Mira, 'Anti-Imperialism, Englishness and Empire in Late-Victorian Britain' (unpublished PhD thesis, University of Cambridge, 2006)

Morrow, Margot Duley, 'The Origins and Early Years of the British Committee of the Indian National Congress, 1885–1907' (unpublished PhD thesis, University of London, 1977)

Rix, Kathryn, 'The Party Agent and English Electoral Culture, 1880–1906' (unpublished PhD thesis, University of Cambridge, 2002)

INDEX